W9-CKH-498

Days of Greatness

Days of Greatness

Walter Kempowski

Translated by Leila Vennewitz

Alfred A. Knopf

New York   1981

THIS IS A BORZOI BOOK
PUBLISHED BY ALFRED A. KNOPF, INC.

English-language translation Copyright © 1981
by Alfred A. Knopf, Inc.

All rights reserved under International and Pan-American
Copyright Conventions. Published in the United States by
Alfred A. Knopf, Inc., New York, and simultaneously in
Canada by Random House of Canada Limited, Toronto.
Distributed by Random House, Inc., New York. Orig-
inally published in West Germany as *Aus grosser Zeit*
by Albrecht Knaus Verlag, Hamburg. Copyright © 1978
by Albrecht Knaus Verlag, Hamburg.

Assistance with the translation of this book
was provided by Inter Nationes.

LIBRARY OF CONGRESS CATALOGING IN PUBLICATION DATA
Kempowski, Walter.
Days of greatness.
Translation of Aus grosser Zeit.
I. Title.
PT2671.E43A9413 1981 833'.914 80-27695
ISBN 0-394-50956-0

Manufactured in the United States of America
First American Edition

For Fritz J. Raddatz

And ye shall seek me, and find me,
when ye shall search for me with
all your heart.
                    Jeremiah 29:13

To my husband William, my thanks for all the knowledge, skill, and patience with which he has helped me throughout this translation.

Leila Vennewitz

Days of Greatness

Pictures

Three pictures of Rostock hang over my desk: an engraving, an oleograph, and a photo.

The engraving shows the houses clustered near the churches. The word ROSTOCHIUM appears in the clouds: ROSTOCHIUM URBS VANDALICA ET MEGAPOLITANA. To left and right, winged lions with eagles' beaks: "Anno 1620." The town is beside a river, the Warnow, in which numerous sailing ships lie anchored, fishermen are fishing, and even two swans are floating.

In the foreground, merchants stand about wearing close-fitting trousers, a ruff under each Vandyke beard. The merchants point wordlessly at their city: times are bad. Due to rising prices it has been necessary to pass special laws forbidding buyers from going out into the countryside, for instance, in an attempt to buy up grain from the peasants before it has been harvested. Grain may be offered for sale only in the marketplace, in free competition.

Beside the men who are pointing wordlessly at their city stand their wives in their long, lace-trimmed, conical gowns. They wear high, slashed puff sleeves and stand-up collars: rye dough rolled thin and thrown into simmering fat is filling and cheap in these times of hunger.

Pursued by the frantic barking of a small dog, a body of armed men bearing drums and lances is advancing on the town. Are they homeward-bound defenders? Or is it the advance guard of the unpopular sovereign? Or possibly even those hated Danes? They wear long feathers in their hats, and between their puffy thighs hang leather pouches of inordinate size.

. . .

Rostock: a wall girdles the town like a ribbon, once all the way around; it holds the town together.

The wall is perforated by twenty-three gates, some small and gabled, others large with towers, some dilapidated and others magnificent: it is through these gates that the town breathes.

> Sit intra te concordia
> et publica felicitas.

This wish is carved over Stone Gate, and no doubt it is heartfelt.

Like all the other gates, Stone Gate turns its impressive side toward the town while the side facing away is unadorned. Outer gates lead up to its huge forecourt. Every evening the guards lower the portcullis with a clang. Latecomers must seek shelter at the White Cross Inn or sleep on the ramparts, where they are likely to be scared by owls and roaming dogs.

Numerous towers and turrets protrude from the wall or squat on top of it. They serve a variety of purposes: Lagebusch Tower is used for the incarceration of felons, chains are fastened to the wall. It costs four shillings to be locked up and four shillings to be released when the time comes. Visits are permitted from a father or a wife, who is allowed to bring bread or beer or straw.

The Blue Tower is used to store weapons, halberds of various designs, crossbows and spiked clubs. There are four thousand men capable of bearing arms in the city.

> Rostochienses
> Sunt velut enses
> Semper acuti
> Proelia poscunt
> Ensibus uti.

"The men of Rostock, like their swords, are ever sharp. They know how to fight and how to use their swords." That's how the translation goes.

. . .

One of the towers has a windmill on its flat roof, a hydraulic device for the distribution of water, needed especially by the brewers of this city.

Four large churches appear on the engraving, as well as other, smaller ones. Inside them, candles flicker in front of carved altars. The shadows of these candles play on the gilded martyrs shown with wheels, grills, and saws: the tools of the torture they endured. Men and women kneel before them, praying and moaning: Why me? Why me? And far back in the vaulted space, surrounded by whispering darkness, a gaunt woman: there is still hope, all is not yet lost.

On the left stands St. Peter's, the smallest of the churches, its spire the highest but slightly wind-hunched. It serves as a landmark for sailors out on the Baltic on their return with a cargo of furs from Reval, or of timber from South Carelia.

St. Peter's has gathered hovels and cottages about itself. Women lean on windowsills watching boys scuffling in the street. A dog hops up the steps to the church and pees against the entrance. The people living in the hovels don't even have beds to call their own. Yet they are better off than those living in cellars, with neither light nor heat.

To the right of St. Peter's, slightly set back, is the church of St. Nicholas with its silver Saint Nicholas, the patron saint of fishermen, in the octagon. It is to him they pray when the herring fail to run, or the mackerel. It is he whom they thank when the mast breaks yet the boat still manages to reach home.

The tall spire has collapsed, for the second time; the sexton was killed by the falling bell. The rubble was taken to Warnemünde to build a fortification against the Danes, who continue their harassments.

In the center of my picture stands St. Mary's, a monster of a church with a mighty west face, big enough to carry three towers but hurriedly finished off with a makeshift little helmet: energy to finish the job was lacking, revenue from the sale of indulgences petered out, and so did donations.

The main attraction for visitors is the great statue of the Virgin. Her head is hollow and filled with water, with little fish swimming about in it. As the fish move, water is pressed out of Mary's eyes, and the worshiper believes she is weeping for his sins.

Somewhere in this church there is also the skeleton of a whale: over thirty feet long, the object of equal amazement. And back in the choir an astronomical clock ticks away, with sunrises and sunsets: a wooden man (Julius Caesar, in fact) is pointing to the date with a stick.

> Here at any time you may
> Observe the passing hour of day.

He has been doing this since 1472 and, barring accidents, will go on doing it until the year 2047. Above the three-foot clock face, the twelve apostles march in a circle one behind the other while the carillon plays: "Now Thank We All Our God." They wear blue and red robes bordered with gold. Judas brings up the rear of the jerky procession, and the gates of Paradise are slammed in his face: at midnight, when the pigeons, which otherwise fly up into the vaulted roof, perch on the clock, and at noon, when townspeople stand in front of it showing off their wondrous contraption to relatives from the country.

Farther to the right on my picture appears the elegant and ambitious church of St. James: box pews for the burghers and comfortable standing room for the uncouth students who munch during the sermon or play cards or even throw plums around. St. James's has English ancestors: the twelve pillars are all different. On closer inspection it is obvious that it was intended to be a cathedral, but the priest promoting the plan was beaten to death by a furious mob. They didn't want a bishop in their town.

The town's narrow streets are lined with countless gabled houses, grand ones and not so grand, each with an archway leading to the courtyard where there are sheds for storing nuts, wax, or salt, as well as stables for horses and cattle. These gabled houses are less than thirty feet wide and three, sometimes four, stories high: all pretty much alike. Pigs encrusted with mud wallow on the street in the refuse. At night they have to be shut up, otherwise they will be pinched.

A puppeteer's showcart comes rumbling along. On account of the "bad times" there has been a row. The puppet Punchinello had bared his behind to the figure of Death, so people were saying, and had thus brought misfortune upon the town. Moreover, the young people, it was said, had been committing indecencies in the dark, which was probably the real reason for expelling the puppeteers.

Not only times are bad, youth is too. It is quite unaccountable.
"Boys must not go around in gangs, making a noise and causing a commotion, shouting abuse to people who are pursuing their lawful business, or pelting them with snowballs or ordure." Thus an ordinance dated 1622. "Those defying this regulation are to be placed in the iron collar." They are also warned to desist from "rowdiness" and noisy behavior in church.

The people living in Rostock are shipbuilders, tanners, shoemakers, or brewers. They are called Kröger, Kramer, or Kröpelin. The master of the coopers' guild is called Holtfreter: the barrels have to be made of oak, and it is his job to see that this is done; they must have a capacity of three and a half firkins, no more and, above all, no less.
"Herring! Fresh herring and cod!" cry the fishwives in the market, lifting up their scaly hand-scales like living statues of Justice, but nobody comes to buy because money has become so scarce.

Not far off a madman shrieks in his lunatic's cage. The only reason he has not been cast out beyond the city walls is that he is of good family. And somewhere behind the leaded panes of a bay window sits a solitary merchant—dried cod from Bergen and rye for Visby? The storage lofts above him are empty, and beneath him the house is empty too, empty and silent. Death has robbed him

of eight children and two wives. Everything keeps going wrong
for him.

ROSTOCHIUM URBS VANDALICA . . . At the top of the picture, above
the town, among the clouds, a bird is flying. It comes from the gallows hill, where more birds are to be seen, in irregular wedge for-
mation, gallows birds that have gorged themselves on the hanged.
A gallows with room for three stands on the hill, not far from the
many busy windmills. Two ragged corpses hang there like scare-
crows: brothers who had long withstood the red-hot pincers, the
rack, the screws, and the scourges. It was to save their wives that
they endured: the wives had had nothing to do with it, with steal-
ing timber, the crime punishable by death.

Right beside the gallows, on a high pole, a wheel. A disjointed corpse
hangs over the rim, broken with eleven blows and forced through
the spokes of the wheel: the bones are poking through the flesh.
The felon's blood- and sweat-stained face is lifeless. For many hours
he pleaded for water and for death. The silent townspeople stood
by counting the hours as they struck: How long would it take this
time? they wondered.

Rostock two hundred years later: 1820.

> With widespread peace, a longed-for goal,
> Our town and land remain one whole.

The second view of the city that hangs over my desk is an oleograph. The original hangs in the civic museum, in a heavy gilt frame.

Along the dusty country road a carriage approaches the town,
passing the Red Rag Inn and a flock of sheep, the shepherd leaning
on his staff. Seated in the green carriage is a man who has been
away for a long time, in faraway places. He is protected from the
sun by a canvas top stretched over willow hoops.

How much he has to tell his parents! Berlin, Leipzig, Dresden! In
his trunk is a sketchbook bound in red leather, he's going to show
it to them. Nothing has been lost, only time: that's gone forever.

· · ·

The picture, now darkened with age, has a lot of green in it: old trees, gardens. High above the bastions, where women are strolling about in white dresses, with parasols and tiny dogs, the old familiar copper-clad spires still stand: good fathers, good mothers. St. Peter's, as always, hunched against the wind, St. Nicholas's with its new spire that seems a little too short, and St. James's, alien.

The broad-based bulk of St. Mary's. How great a portion of the earth's surface is pressed down and covered by it! Not a single blade of grass will ever force its way into that crypt.

The apostles still jerk their way around the clock, now thank we all our God, twice daily at twelve. Fifteen minutes later they rattle their way back. A performance that still has a long way to go.

Thirty-nine altars have been ripped out of this church, in addition to the giant Crucifix and the tearful Virgin: chopped up and thrown away.

Instead of the altars that once adorned the sides, the throne of the Grand Duke now stands resplendent at the west end of the nave, complete with red velvet canopy and gilded crown. And above the throne an organ soars up into the vaulting, five thousand seven hundred pipes, surmounted by trumpeting angels and a great golden sun.

For the enlightenment and entertainment of the populace, a theater has been built. *The Hermit by the Warnow* is being performed, also pantomimes and ballet. The ladies knit, seated on chairs that have been placed at an angle so the men can see them all at a glance. It is unwise to come too close to the students with their spurred and polished boots if you don't want to catch your stockings.

"Boys must not ride their toboggans on the slopes of the town. Those defying this regulation will be subject to confiscation of their toboggans, arrest, and due punishment." Thus runs the city ordinance. The younger generation, they're still a bad lot, that's for sure, but times are better.

> The times are ever changing,
> Bloodshed and war forgot.

> Heaven has shown us mercy,
> Let us enjoy our lot.

The Thirty Years' War with its incursions by Imperial and Swedish troops, its murders, atrocities, and devastation: forgotten.

Forgotten too is the Great Fire of 1677 that broke out on August 4, in Fishermen's Lane, at nine in the evening, and devoured its way through the streets. Seven hundred buildings burned to the ground, the magnificent princes' palace, the town hall on Old Market, the gabled and timbered houses, the cottages and hovels with their wailing, shrieking women: When, oh when, will the wind change?

The city has been rebuilt.

> Herring, green herring and cod!

cry the fishwives on New Market, lifting their scales on high as of old. The new addition to the front of City Hall is not very attractive—"puny baroque"—but prosperity continues:

> Pip, Dane, pip!
> Of your prize you now are rid!

The marauding, plundering Danes have been forgotten, and the French have disappeared, those of 1812. No more wagons to be supplied, no more press gangs to fear. No more fleeing into the forest (where other fugitives are encountered), no more boats at night with dimmed lanterns, no more hiding among the rafters of the towers. The ravaged fields have been replanted, the denuded forest has grown up again.

Just as the Prussian king is no more, the one who looked upon Mecklenburg as a sack of flour that needed only to be beaten to yield flour, so the Corsican, too, is no more.

The Rostock fleet numbers three hundred and forty-seven sailing ships; it is now the largest in the Baltic region. The ships are built of oak. Some sink on their maiden voyage, and some last for fifty or eighty years: fast, full-rigged ships and broad, heavy barks, to be met with in all waters. "You fellows have strung up William of Orange by his heels," claim the Dutch, because the Rostock flag flies the Dutch colors upside down, and this triggers many a brawl.

Painters reduce the size of large objects and increase that of small ones. They compress the buildings of a city in order to fit them into the composition. With photos this won't work: Rostock 1885— that's the third picture over my desk.

KARL STEENBOCK

Photographer to the Court of the Grand Duke

The buildings are a blurred mass running this way and that, high and low, and in this mass, competing with wooden fences and smoking chimneys, the great solitary old walls, exposed in their nakedness to the stormy wind. How long is it worth maintaining them?

The streets at the riverside are gaping mouths, gasping for air, since the old gates have been demolished, Mill Gate with its outer gates (because a townsman wanted the stones for his house), Bramow Gate, and even Fortress Gate with its adjacent toll booth, of which a photo is still extant. Here everything is in process of dissolution.

Even the massive forecourt adjoining Stone Gate was blown up; engineers of the Prussian Army had to be called in to assist. "At last traffic can move freely . . ." Walls ten feet thick—no easy job.

And even the bastions have been razed, except for two that the local inhabitants refused to part with; just the place for a pleasant stroll, and in winter there's tobogganing down the ramps.

Watch out, down the hill!
If you don't keep straight
You'll have a spill!

They are even skating on the moats, also on the Devil's Dip, though it feels a bit eerie there.

The keeper of the ramparts is Jochen Stut. As he approaches the upper rampart you can hear him call: "Jochen a-comin'!" and all the boys run away, knowing that the ramparts keeper wields a pliant switch.

The illustrated guidebook consists of only a few pages: St. John's Monastery has been pulled down, as has St. Michael's Church, that wondrous edifice with its five transepts. The guide lists the vestiges of past glory and extols the new pseudo-Gothic water tower, Friedrich-Franz railway station, and the tall smokestack of the largest brewery. It also lists good places to eat, such as the Winter Garden and the Hôtel de Russie: "Electric light, central heating; all trains met." It also records that the best trusses are to be obtained at Frahm's Medical Supply House.

FRIEDRICH'S FIRST VACUUM-STEAM
SUGAR AND CANDY FACTORY

The A. Seitz Coffin Factory will attend to all your funeral and burial needs.

There were no movies yet in those days. But at the spring fair there was already a man with a flicker-box. He showed moving pictures, and the inhabitants of Rostock were "bowled over."

The people living in Rostock, factory owners, craftsmen, or laborers, are still called Kröger, Kramer, or Kröpelin. Recently they have even been called Kempowski . . .

Part One

The merchant class was respected; it still contained something of the spirit of the old Hanseatic League; hats off to them, one felt. Fine gentlemen, those men, who not only knew how to make money but were also aware of their responsibility toward the city.   P. S.

In those days, of course, everyone spoke Low German dialect, no matter whether he was a dock worker or a captain or the shipowner himself. In Rostock everyone spoke Low German, nobody felt it was beneath him.   L. N.

At the corner of our street lived Consul Brüdigam. When he left his house in the morning he would first look right and left, as if sniffing the air, then make off in the direction of City Hall.
                                        A. Sch.

Merchants? They were pretty down-to-earth people who thought more or less in terms of profits. One took care not to get on the wrong side of them as that might have unpleasant consequences.   V. Z.

My father owned a fairly large brickworks, and at school—something that embarrassed me—there was no denying that the teacher's attitude toward us was obsequious.

The upper-class families had their own pastor,

too. Children of our sort were confirmed by
Pastor Magen.

"Is Pastor Magen doing it for you too?"
Something like that.

In other respects the church didn't have much
say.   P. G.

St. Mary's Church contained the Grand Duke's
throne. He is even supposed to have sat on it
now and again. I wouldn't know about that. All
I remember is that he was said to be quite a
jolly character.   L. O.

When the Grand Duke visited the city we had
to scatter flowers. He asked me: "What do you
want to be when you grow up?" and I said:
"Empress." My brother said: "A coachman"; he
had been more impressed by the liveried coach-
man than by the Grand Duke.   G. F.

My cousins had albums full of picture postcards
of royalty. We used to swap pictures in school.
The Crown Prince, always shown as a very
dashing figure, would be swapped for a picture
of the majestic Empress.   G. F.

Our parents had nothing against the Grand
Duke because they had heard nothing bad
about him. People like us felt they were living
within a state that was absolutely secure. The
seafaring population, I realized at the time, were
frequently of a different opinion.   K. F.

We often used to walk around the Grand Duke's
summer palace. It was an afternoon excursion.
"Are they in residence?" we would wonder.
                                                        P. SCH.

1

Robert William Kempowski: he is driven every morning to the office in a horse-drawn cab, slowly, bowing repeatedly to left and right. He drives along Stephan-Strasse—lovely warm air—past Consul Viebrock's house. Privy Counselor Öhlschläger has built himself a regular palace at the corner of Graf-Schack-Strasse, with a tower and a galvanized iron horseman on the roof.

Robert William Kempowski continues on his way, past the Reichsbank, where he is highly regarded, and past the brand-new Civic Theater, where he has taken a stage box for his wife Anna,

A baro- and a thermo-
Journey to Palermo.

As the carriage passes through Stone Gate, the coachman has to dismount and tap the barometer—"Falling!"—then drives on across New Market and past City Hall with its masked Gothic façade. Mr. Kempowski knows nothing whatever about masked Gothic façades, and whether this one is surmounted by seven turrets or eight is a matter of indifference to him. Down there, by the harbor, Monks' Gate and right beside it his office: that's his world, that's where his interests lie.

At the entrance to the spacious building that houses the company's offices there is an iron fountain: the top basin is meant for the pigeons to drink from, the middle one for horses, and the bottom one for dogs, hence not a Roman fountain but a multilevel one, to each his own. Street urchins hold their hands over the water spouts and spray passers-by, but not, of course, while Mr. Kempowski is descending from his carriage: one stern look from him, and the urchins run away.

Robert William's desk is placed to advantage in his private office. On the shelf above the half-paneling stand ships' models and photographs in filigree wire frames.

Through the window, past the fountain, he has a view of the street, where a heavy wagon laden with grain happens to be passing, pulled by massive draft horses with huge hindquarters and tiny, cropped tails, and of the water, where Scandinavian sailing vessels lie at anchor. A fair number of these still sport a figurehead, seminaked and garishly painted, and each ship has a mongrel on board that barks whenever anyone prepares to go ashore.

Mr. Kempowski sits at his neat desk, his hands folded on his stomach, smoking a cigar, "Principe de la Paz," meaning "Prince of Peace." Behind him stands the office safe with its Gothic decoration and two keyholes, one large and one small. On his nose sits a steel-rimmed pince-nez with an "anchor chain" to catch it when it falls. By profession he is a ship's broker and the owner of two steamers: the days are long past when he had to row himself out to approaching Finnish and Swedish sailing ships so as to get ahead of his competitors. Now he has two young men to do this job. Moreover, an old retired sea captain sits on the west mole in Warnemünde with a spyglass. On sighting a ship heading for the mouth of the Warnow, he shouts into the crank-telephone. In Rostock they start preparing the "B/L's," the bills of lading, and look up the captain's name and first name in a notebook so that he can be greeted personally. The book is bound in wax cloth and contains notes on the captain's favorite drink and whether he is married and to whom.

In one direction Robert William Kempowski looks through the window to the outdoors and in the other through the glass door toward the interior, where the employees are writing at their high desks, one behind the other, perched on their high stools with bowed backs, *his* employees. Gladow, the old bookkeeper; Sodemann, the fat head clerk; and the young men in their Sunday best.

The apprentices are having fun with Gladow, the seventy-year-old bookkeeper, whose full beard makes him look as if *he* were the boss. They lift up his jacket and pretend to smack his behind.

When old Mr. Kempowski, who isn't all that old, sees this, or when he notices Gladow nodding off once again, he throws his pen against the glass door panel and makes a money-counting gesture with thumb and forefinger: it is *his* money being idled away, and he *too* had had to hustle, back in the Königsberg days when his father lost all five sailing ships, all in one year . . . *He'd* had to work for everything, *he'd* had to go without shoes as a child.

Gladow had been with the firm for almost fifty years, from the very first days when the office was still a tavern and the broker sold beer on the side. Padderatz was his name, "Always give a mite" his motto, and it had served him well. It's *his* money, says Robert William Kempowski, and *his* company, that belongs to *him*, and he says it very loud, whereupon Gladow gazes stoically into the distance with his fine blue Warnow eyes. He runs his fingers through his old man's beard, and his motionless lips mutter something, nothing flattering, you can be sure.

In the evening his wife comes for him: "Well, old dear? How many times did you fall in the shit today?"

Fat Mr. Sodemann weighs three hundred pounds, his behind overflows the edge of the stool. When he speaks High German it is the way a speaker of Low German imagines High German to be spoken. "Helsinski," he says, and he never removes the band from his cigar. "Dunno" and "Can't be helped" are the phrases most often heard from him. Sometimes also: "All I'm saying is . . ."

For lunch he goes with Gladow to Alphons Köpcke, of course, fat Sodemann with old Gladow, to join a regular group calling itself "The Jolly Teapot" that meets in the inn's exotically decked-out back room. Let's see who's here today: Captain Saatmann perhaps, from Ribnitz, who has donated an Indonesian dance mask toward the decoration; or Rübesahm, from Emden, who has declared an ordinary chunk of rock to be the petrified arse of a South Sea Islands girl.

Cheers!
Mud in your eye!

Let's see who's here today, and then a little something to warm us up won't do us any harm, will it?

Meanwhile Mr. Kempowski has wound his watch and placed it on the filigree stand before him on the desk. The lunch hour seems to be getting longer every day, he thinks, and he wonders about it. Things had been very different back in the old Königsberg days.

The bottom right-hand drawer of his desk contains a little bottle of Jenever from which he pours himself a drink, and on raising his eyes he sees that the two fellows in there have just returned.

Of course they refrain from looking across, for their boss is pointedly shaking his head and picks up his watch from its filigree stand and gives it a few more turns.

Mr. Kempowski owns two ships. The names of the two steamers, which were built in England and have good British engines, are *Consul* and *Clara*, not, as you might expect, *Robert* or *Anna*. No. He has no desire to name them after himself or his own family: "I know my own name; and my wife's name, I know that too." The *Consul* had been named after Consul Besendiek, and the *Clara* after the Consul's wife because of the handsome cargoes he provides, timber for Lübeck, for example, and almost every week at that. This is one way of putting him under an obligation.

A third vessel, the *Henriette Schüssler*, was owned by the firm for only a short time, a coffin ship held together by little more than her coat of paint. He was able to sell her to Greece just before the classification, and then only by the skin of his teeth.

The proceeds were used to buy the fine house on Stephan-Strasse that had belonged to Gütschow—Gütschow the wine merchant who had just declared bankruptcy.

"Kempowski! Keep out of my way!"

Two years after the sale, the *Henriette Schüssler* went down with all hands on board, just as the five sailing ships sank that had belonged to the Königsberg Kempowski, in 1875, all within a year.

"How quietly they lie, all those dead," says old Mr. Kempowski, who isn't all that old, when the conversation turns to his father's sailing vessels, pictures of which now hang in his office next to the picture of the *Henriette Schüssler* and those of the *Consul* and the *Clara*. At the time of their sinking he moved from Königsberg to Rostock because he couldn't stand the sight of his father doing nothing but read the newspaper all day. He used to row out to meet the ships himself until he met Anna, Anna Martens with her fortune of thirty thousand gold marks, money he employed to buy the firm, *his* firm, as he is fond of saying. His "eternally young bride who has to be wooed every day afresh." And now it's up to his young men to row out to the ships, damn it all.

As a broker, Robert William Kempowski is doing very nicely. All the Rostock coal merchants obtain their coal through him, except for the Black Diamond Company, and he imports natural ice from Norway and wood for papermaking from Finland.

"If a man wants to buy a horse, and you don't have a horse, then you just have to sell him a donkey," he says, and that's the way he operates.

An item for commission paid to Otto Bellmann appears from time to time in the big ledgers, in Gladow's flowing, copperplate hand. But with the best will in the world, no Otto Bellmann can be turned up in any directory, a search would be quite useless, and Gladow will have to be employed by the company till the day he "keels over" for good.

Anna Kempowski, née Martens, drives to town in an elegant closed carriage. She spends the money that Robert William earns, and has every right to do so. She picked him up out of the gutter, she will say in heated moments, without her he would have gone to the dogs! She wears a black tailored suit, trimmed with ermine, very elegant.

Who has the biggest picture book?
The merchant, children, have a look!

She drives to Krüger's, the specialty food store on Blut-Strasse. A stuffed boar's head hangs over the door. The place is long and narrow and smells of pineapple and goose drippings.

As Anna enters the store, old Krüger, in his blood-streaked apron, comes shuffling out from the rear. You can tell just by looking at him that he loves to eat: he has fabulous cheeses and fantastic country sausages.

"*This* one comes from Gross-Viegeln," he says, "and *this* one from Hohen-Sprenz."

Anna tastes the sausages as well as the different types of butter. She also samples the fruit, although she doesn't buy her fruit from Krüger but "up country."

Whatever she selects is delivered to the house, even if it is only a quarter of a pound of salami. (Usually it is more.) The matter of payment is never so much as mentioned, everything is charged, and at New Year the bill is sent to the house, signed: "Your humble servant."

The Kempowskis have two children, and one of the photos shows little Karl with his sister Silbi.

GLOBUS STUDIO 1904
Specializing in Enlargements of All Kinds

Actually her name is Sylvia. She has five pfennigs' worth of mixed candy in her pocket: she always has to have something to nibble on. Dark eyes and pouting lips. In her hair a bow of checked taffeta.

Karl, my son,
Go get me a bun.

In fine weather they sit on the swing, their arms tightly around each other, or Karl sits and Silbi stands up behind him, leaning back to give the swing momentum, completely enveloping him in her white dress. Will the hook up there hold?

Stribold, the black puppy bought at the fair for thirty pfennigs, runs to and fro three steps at a time, in futile pursuit. He doesn't like them swinging back and forth. He wants them to stop and take him along.

In fall, when the leaves flutter down from the pear tree and eddy around outside the cellar door, they sit on the veranda, snipping at cutouts: a village with cows, chickens, and pigs, and deer emerging from the forest.

Rain drums on the tarred roof and splashes against the window-panes, and Karl and Silbi eat liver-sausage sandwiches, one after another, and drink cold milk. The cows and pigs are stuck onto cardboard by means of the folded tabs, and if you lay your head sideways on the table it looks like a real village: big farmhouses and little cottages, stables with horses looking out of them, and shirts and pants flapping on the washing line strung between posts.

That winter the village is carried out to the front of the house and set alight. Everybody looks on.

At night, when the wind howls around the house and tugs at the roof, they crawl into one bed. Later they never tire of telling each other what happened the night the lumberyard outside St. Peter's Gate caught fire, the whole sky red and people blowing trumpets and shouting. Their father had got them out of bed, and shivering with the cold they had stood at the window to watch.

Sheets and quilts are used to make a cave, and picture books are looked at, the kind where you pull tabs to make ducks stick their heads into water. Or folding books: a man sitting on a powder keg smoking a pipe. When you lift the man aside there's a picture underneath of the powder keg exploding.

Indestructible picture books:

> Gilly-gilly
> Piccalilli
> Boo!

And frightening ones: about the Hairy Man carrying a sackful of naughty children.

Little children end this way
When from Truth they dare to stray.

All night long Karl thinks about the Hairy Man, and years later, when he is much older, he still thinks about him. And about the way he used to lie in the bed-cave with Silbi, so soft and snug, while the wind howled outside.

2 The Neighbor

My name is Maria Jesse, my husband was a veterinarian, he died back in 1920 from blood poisoning. As you see, I am almost blind, please come in and sit down over here.

So you want to know something about Rostock and, I presume, about the Kempowskis.

Well, I'd say Rostock wasn't bad at all: up to 1939 Rostock was a nice little town. Before all those Heinkel people arrived from Saxony and Thuringia, all those engineers and mechanics, when we still had it to ourselves, it was a really friendly place. I lived there for sixty years. Not that it had anything special to offer, mind you, but everyone who knew the town was fond of it. A blend of harbor, university, and countryside.

Only the other day, when I was on my way to visit my son in Mannheim, I got talking to a gentleman on the train, a man who had studied at Rostock University. "You're from Rostock?" said this man. "Ah, I spent the best years of my life in Rostock!" and he went on to tell me about his student days there and how they always took the train to Warnemünde and lay on the beach there and all that.

Rostock was a really friendly place. On the one hand the town was small enough for everyone to know each other, but on the other big enough for anyone to live incognito if that's what they wanted. In Rostock people weren't in the habit of broadcasting every scrap of news.

The Kempowski family, well, I'd say they weren't exactly out of the very top drawer. I lived across the street from them and had been there at the time of the whole drama with Gütschow, Gütschow the wine merchant. From the day he built that wonderful house to when he lost everything.

"Just look, Mrs. Jesse, this beautiful alcove," he once said to me. "This is where I'll be sitting and looking across to you . . ."

I was there when his business collapsed and his wife left him. Everything around him went to pieces, poor man. I felt so sorry for him! One night he came knocking on my back door and handed me his Meyer's Encyclopedia and six yards of Chinese silk to save them from the hands of the bailiff.

Kempowski bought the house from him in the bankruptcy sale, for a song. "Did him out of it" is what I should really say. Tricked him out of it. Kempowski had the money, of course, and at the right moment, and he had the gift of the gab, so he brought it off. Gütschow had to be glad to find a buyer at all, and so fast.

I can still see them moving in, the Kempowskis, it must have been around 1900, the linden trees were still quite small, had just been planted, by now some of them have already been cut down again. Gütschow out by the back door, the Kempowskis in by the front, something like that. They arrived with three vanloads of furniture, full of armchairs and sofas and I don't know what all. Thirteen clocks they had, grandfather clocks, wall clocks, and those little pinging things under glass domes. You couldn't help wondering: Isn't one enough? Do they really have to have thirteen clocks? And two grand pianos? And three dogs?

Those dogs were that wild, when they were running loose outside no one could get past. My little boy Berti came in one day and said: "Kempowskis' doggies are outside!" He didn't dare go to school, he was that scared!

And the messes they made everywhere, and Mrs. Kempowski had the nerve to laugh!

I tell you . . .

And when Stribold, one of the three dogs, got sick, they didn't bring him to my husband although we were living just across the street (which added insult to injury) but to Dr. Wagenmast on Lange-Strasse.

. . .

After that, Gütschow used to come and see me quite often, we would stand at the window behind the curtains and look to see what was going on over there. Oh, let me tell you, that was a busy place! From left and right they came, tradesmen and deliverymen with parcels and boxes, with trays of cakes and bouquets of flowers, great huge things. Sometimes even a messenger boy in page's uniform and pillbox hat. We used to wonder what business *he* had there!

And then visitors, every day, morning, noon, and night. Visitors, visitors, visitors. You could tell right away: that's someone for the Kempowskis, it's written all over him!

Mr. Kempowski had a carriage with two fine horses, and his wife had a dog cart, or whatever those things are called, for her own use. Gütschow used often to say: "Pride goeth before a fall." And: "I must have been crazy, that beautiful house." And: "Have you ever seen anything like it?"

Actually Anna Kempowski came from a good family, her maiden name was Martens, she was a daughter of Dr. Martens on Kossfelder-Strasse. He was a nice old gentleman who wore a long gray overcoat and a bowler hat. He used to always poke at the paving with his walking stick looking for a loose stone, and when he found one he would make a note and report it so no one would stumble over it. In this day and age he couldn't have existed, he would have had to make a terrible lot of notes.

Dr. Martens died in 1903, and his wife was moved to the Home of the Holy Spirit, she wasn't quite right in the head, she had a way of undressing in broad daylight, in public. That's where Anna Kempowski probably got her kink from: the fuss she made when she went for a drive! Oh my, what a production! The maids kept running in and out. This, that, and the other thing, then the coachman asking whether everything was all right, I can't begin to describe it. People passing by would actually stop and stare. I s'pose that's what they were meant to do!

I saw everything there was to see from my window. The Kempowskis were real outsiders on our street; left and right, all high-class folk, the Kempowskis were really quite vulgar, I'd say, and gave themselves such airs.

And at night, when they had parties! All that banging of doors, all that whooping and laughing! And always playing the piano with the windows wide open. For Rostock I'd say that was rather unusual. If it's a birthday or an anniversary it's all right to celebrate, I don't mind that, but surely not in the middle of the week! Gütschow used to say to me quite often: "What was all that racket again last night?" What did he imagine it was? They were having a party, one binge after another.

I always said: "It's bound to lead to trouble, it's *bound* to," and I was right.

Mr. Kempowski himself, the old gentleman, well, I'd say there was nothing really wrong with him. Always a cheery "good morning" when he saw me—he did have an eye for the ladies—he would sweep off his hat with a flourish, quite the cavalier and always a bit of a wag. And when it was time for Berti to go to university, in 1921, he lent me the money. Basically, I'd say, he was a simple man, a bit common too, but his heart was in the right place. He arrived in Rostock with hardly a penny in his pocket, a bit of a mystery, I've no idea what his background was.

He was simple, you know, and very straightforward. He once offered me a quid of chewing tobacco, cut off a piece for himself and asked whether I'd like some too!

For years I had a parrot, my dear old Polly (I still have a photo of him), *one* parrot, not *three*. In summer Polly always sat outdoors, on the fence, when the weather was fine, of course, and I sat in the lilac arbor, we would chat and look across the street, and believe me, there was plenty to look at, it could keep a person busy all day.

It was a bit embarrassing, I must say, that, when Mrs. Kempowski showed up across the street, Polly would always shriek "Ohmygoodnessme!" He must have picked it up someplace.

No, the Kempowskis didn't belong to Rostock's old established society. Such people are quiet and modest and simple and not so ostentatious. And there's no mistaking what that led to. I myself stayed on in Rostock till 1972, in my house on Stephan-Strasse, and then left East Germany legally with all my belongings, which God knows wasn't easy. But the Kempowskis? Vanished into thin air.

One time her high-and-mightiness suddenly turned up and presented me with a bunch of white roses, just like that, across the fence and out of a clear blue sky. I was flabbergasted! Comes sailing across the street and presses a bunch of white roses into my hands! What was *that* supposed to mean?

You could never tell with her.

Maybe she had a bad conscience, because of course I could always see what was going on "unofficially," if you get my meaning. Visitors sneaking up and slipping through the door. And soon the light would go out; only in her room it stayed on.

Gone are the days when Karl sits on his father's lap and is allowed to eat the "sugar fish" from his dad's cup of coffee.

> Karl, Karl, suck your thumb,
> Go to school and don't be dumb.

The sugar left at the bottom of the cup, exactly a spoonful, tasting pleasantly of coffee.

Karl now attends Miss Seegen's private school, and he has to walk there, something to do with exercise being good for you. No need to learn how to take the streetcar, you can pick that up later without even trying.

He saunters along Stephan-Strasse, and the horse-drawn streetcar comes rocking along, seats for twelve and standing room for nine, no more and no less. Outside RISSE THE BARBER stands Mr. Risse looking up into the sunshine. He has invented a special kind of moustache sling that he talks every customer into buying. Above his head gleams the symbol of his trade, the polished brass shaving basin, swinging in the wind.

Karl has to cross the Reiferbahn where the gallows used to stand. Now, in the shade of chestnut trees, men with tattooed arms are twisting ropes. They have a bale of hemp tied to their stomachs and pluck threads from it. They walk backward as they twist the threads together.

There is a smell of fresh rope and tar.

Miss Seegen's school is on Friedrich-Franz-Strasse, in a little white house with green trim. The door knocker is in the shape of a sea horse, but it's not to be used because it makes too much noise.

In the dark hallway—there is no electric light here ("You might get a shock from it!")—on the far side of a curving old closet there sometimes stands a boy who has been "impertinent." He has to stand here by the closet and wait until he is allowed to go in again and join in the lesson on windmills, coffee mills, peppermills, paper mills, and powder mills. An old house cat, its paws tucked under, gazes at him fixedly. On the left, beside the white staircase mounting in a curve to the upper floor, is the classroom, the only classroom in this school, which Karl, on his first day, with his brand-new sealskin satchel, refused to enter. All the pushing and pulling in the world didn't help, not even when one of the older girls took him by the hand.

There was pudding with jam sauce in there, he was finally told, and that did the trick.

It is a dark classroom, the tall linden tree in the front yard keeping out the light. Those who don't speak up have to stand under this linden tree and read aloud or recite their poem from there. That is Miss Seegen's method.

Up front stands the movable blackboard, with a rusty weight at the back that slides down when the blackboard is raised.

> Up, down, up,
> A little dot on top!

In the corner stands a brown-stained cupboard, with a glass jar on top containing a floating dead snake. The doors are fastened with a crooked rusty nail; it contains the big "Kühnel" arithmetic tables, a lump of chalk from the island of Rügen, two keys belonging to no one knows what, some old exercise books, and an apothecary's scale whose weights have long since disappeared.

On the wall hangs a picture chart: "In the Poultry Yard," with cock, hen, and chicks picking away at a worm. Above them in the clouds hovers a hawk estimating his chances of snatching the little baby chicks down below; the chickens haven't noticed him yet.

At Miss Seegen's, Karl learns Reading, Writing, and, above all, of course, Arithmetic: first, "one and one is two," and later that seventeen gross of eggs cost so-and-so much: "Therefore how much do two dozen cost?" It is worked out on the slate, with a slate pencil, not with a crayon; soft crayons don't exist yet.

With every slate, which is in a wooden frame and is ruled with squares on one side and lines on the other—it cracks very easily—comes a lacquered sponge box of pressed black cardboard with flowers painted on the lid. The slate pencils, wrapped in paper with a silvery design, lie in a two-tier pencil box, also painted with flowers. This pencil box also contains the pen plus a little box for spare nibs, and the yellow washleather pen wiper that folds up like a tiny fan.

Writing, Arithmetic, Reading. And, of course, Religion.
    "What did Jesus do when He was twelve years old?"
    During Religion you mustn't laugh, even the first-graders know that, even if the laughter is because the cat has jumped onto the windowsill outside and is pawing the windowpane. In Religion you have to be serious: the entry into Jerusalem, with people climbing up into the palm tree to see Jesus and shouting "Hosannah!" and a few days later they would have nothing more to do with Him.
    The expulsion from the temple: little pictures are handed out showing Jesus flailing around among the money changers with a scourge. The pigeon baskets have burst open, and lambs are running around freely. All that money rolling off the tables, it does seem a shame, and: fancy their not defending themselves, those big strong money-changer types with their dark beards, and fancy that mild Jesus getting into such a rage, it makes you wonder.

During Singing the children have to sit *on* their desks, their legs on the bench. Miss Seegen sits down at the piano and, because she has to turn her back on the children while she plays, she first has her sister, also called Miss Seegen, come from the kitchen. One of the older girls must meanwhile stir the pea soup, and the other Miss Seegen sits down by the door with her knitting and solemnly watches the children while they sing.

"Korl, I can see you!"
"I can see you too!"

Before the real Miss Seegen starts playing the songs, she plays an arpeggio to make sure her fingers can still play and that the piano still works. A speck on the keys is removed with a bit of spit: There, now we can start.

> Oh my dear old Augustine, Augustine, Augustine!
> Oh my dear old Augustine, everything's gone!

That's an easy song. But it's also a silly song. Why didn't he take better care of his things? It's annoying. Did he exchange them for liquor? Or did he gamble them away? Inexplicable. And then to be found lying in the dirt?

The next song, the one about the mill, is much more satisfying to sing.

> The clattering mill by the bubbling stream . . .

The kindly prosperous miller, standing there beaming in his doorway, his hands folded across his stomach. Besides, the children are permitted to clap hands, which gives the whole thing more variety.

The real Miss Seegen wears an enormous hat made of straw with fake violets on it. Sometimes the boys bump into it, then it's crooked.

Good marks and hard work in Writing or Arithmetic are rewarded with stamps: "Deutsch-Neu-Guinea 3 Mk," black-and-purple.

When all the *i*'s stand in a row, perfectly even, and not a single dot is even half a millimeter larger than any other—the girls are better at that—and when the squared arithmetic pages have been calculated exactly, leaving a margin at top and bottom (whether the answers are correct is less important), such stamps make their appearance. You have to go up to the front, step onto the dais, and Miss Seegen will open her desk and bring out the little stamp tin, close her uplifted eyes, and fish for one of those coveted little colored objects.

Unite, unite, all ye unite!

Sometimes she fishes out a barrette instead of a stamp, it's meant to be a little joke, and you're supposed to laugh, Miss Seegen expects that, but not too uproariously, otherwise the little tin is snapped shut and there will "never again" be any stamps because you have been so impudent and cheeky. Understand?

The album comes as a birthday surprise at home. Maps are inserted to show the location of the recently acquired German colonies: German Southwest Africa, Togo, and Cameroon on the left, German East Africa on the right. Strange, those borders drawn as if with a ruler . . .

The German colonies, where the stupid natives are told about the Savior, how He has redeemed them from their sins, and how they must believe in Him, then all will be well.

In the Pacific, too, there are German colonies. New Pomerania and New Mecklenburg. In vain the map was searched in the hope of finding a "New Rostock."

When "Korli" has been awarded a stamp—"Korli" is Karl's nickname—he trots home with the pencil box rattling in his satchel, and the men twisting ropes on the Reiferbahn turn to look.

As for Reading: despite the lure of the stamps, Karl displays not the slightest ambition. Eventually he is sent with the governess every afternoon—after lunch when the parents have retired to their rooms with their magazines for a rest—to Fishermen's Bastion with its old cannons that you are allowed to sit astride—no doubt there are also sparrows nesting in their muzzles—to Fishermen's Bastion where old salts sit overlooking the harbor, the schooners, barges, and steamers, spinning yarns that are nothing but pure invention. By counting the mast tips they can tell how many ships are in port.

On Fishermen's Bastion Korli has laboriously to read aloud to his governess, and they had the bright idea of using Cooper's *Leatherstocking*. This method is successful, he has soon figured out the names Chingachgook and Natty Bumppo, and before long he is reading the rest of *Leatherstocking* all by himself.

. . .

On Sundays the governess doesn't go to Fishermen's Bastion, although she is supposed to, on Sundays they go to Schuster's, a honky-tonk where workmen with tattooed arms sit around smoking cheap cigarettes. Schuster's is not for reading, Schuster's is for dancing.

> Lottie's dying, Lottie's dying,
> Julie's almost dead.
> Let them go, let them go,
> There's nothing to be had.

Of course Korli mustn't let on that his governess comes here to dance. He sits in a corner and is stuffed with chocolate pennies and cat's tongues, so many, in fact, that he can't eat his supper.

One day the secret is out: the governess has to go. "We are very disappointed in you!" she is told, and the family stands at the door watching her departure. One almost expected them to point commandingly in the direction she had to take.

There is quite a turnover in servants. That's the way things are at Anna Kempowski's. As one comes out, the next goes in. Staying out too late is cause for dismissal, so is impertinence. One of them even stole: she pinched some of the cold roast and gave it to her boy friend at the barracks.

Most of the maids are country-bred, broad-hipped, and with red fingers. They have just turned fourteen when they are employed. Giesing Köhler is so homesick she cries all day long, she thinks of the geese she herded and of her Grandpa. Every day she has to drink a glass of red wine after her dinner since she is thought to be "anemic," or is she sure she doesn't have worms? she is asked.

Rostock in the summer of 1904?
     Those are the days when Korli waits outside the Kröpeliner Gate for the big yellow mail coach. He wears long stockings, and a sailor hat on his close-cropped head. The long stockings are fastened to

a bodice with elastic; if one of them breaks, his stockings slip down, and that's embarrassing.

The postilion is called Kassebohm, he wears a uniform, and his varnished top hat sports a tuft of feathers. Beside him is a curved whip in its holder.

Karl is allowed to sit beside him on the coach box. He holds on tight as the coach sways under the weight of all the trunks and parcels. They drive through the Kröpeliner Gate, where the hooves resound, then along Kröpeliner-Strasse, past the University and past the colonnaded palace where the Grand Duke once spent a few weeks. Now a bucolic-looking soldier walks his six steps there, ticktock, endlessly back and forth.

Just before the post office, at the Schwaansche Gate, right by the monastery of the "Brothers of the Communal Life," Karl has to jump off, otherwise Kassebohm will get into trouble.

The horses are unharnessed and led to the stable. Coachman Kassebohm goes to the tavern—the Wooden Doorknob, the door inscribed with the words: "Come in, you can look out!"—where other coachmen are sitting talking to each other, "Why" and "What for?"

Near the post office, beside the Rose Garden where the nursemaids push their high baby carriages, some three-wheeled, and gossip about their employers, is Welp's tobacco shop.

> Give yourself a treat!
> Smoke Welp's cigars!

Karl goes inside to watch the gentlemen selecting their cigars. He likes the atmosphere, and there is a nice smell too. Outside the open door, sparrows are quarreling.

The favorite brand is "Compasión." On the lid, below the usual gold medals—some shown from the back and some from the front—there is a woman slicing bread for hungry children: Compassion.

"One of these and two of those," the gentlemen say, and the holders are thrown in. And when a workman enters to buy cigarette paper or some curly cut for his pipe, they break off their conversation and remain silent until he has left again.

When Karl has stood there long enough, looking on, his hands clasped behind his back like one of those old gentlemen, Mr. Welp comes out from behind his counter and, gently but firmly, propels him out of the shop with little nudges of his barrel stomach. But sometimes Karl is given empty cigar boxes containing shreds of tobacco. These are useful for keeping stamps in, duplicates, or those to be soaked off, on Sunday, in a soup plate.

Two streets farther on is Meyer's margarine factory, where you can look through the window and see how margarine is manufactured. In a large, well-lit room with white-tiled walls stands a great wooden tub in which several workmen wearing Dutch clogs are kneading the margarine. It looks delicious, and Karl likes to watch, until one day he sees a workman spitting into the mixture.

At home on Stephan-Strasse, in the white villa bought with the *Henriette Schüssler* money, with stuccoed ceilings but no fireplace— full of heavy brocade drapes with tasseled cords, with the unframed portrait of Bismarck, that greatest diplomat of all time, on a carved easel, with holly and quantities of bric-a-brac, albums, little boxes, round or oblong, lying around as if just used or about to be used— in this drape-shrouded domesticity stands his mother, looking into the ornate mirror and patting her waist smooth. She has a cold face and wears her black hair pinned high: it's time the dressmaker came again, one really hasn't "a thing to wear."

"You were only an accident, you know," she will one day tell her son when he is already playing tennis and writing letters to Wandsbek. Around her shoulders is a feather boa, and up on the curtain rod the parakeet is pulling pins out of the drapes, one by one: Anna Kempowski, the "Queen Mother" as the actors of the Civic Theater call her because that's the way she looks and because she likes to send wine and cold chicken backstage during a premiere. "Forsooth, this chicken is fit for a king!" they say as they tear it apart, and they drink her health in wine.

When the curtain is finally lowered, they drive off in cabs to Stephan-Strasse, the Queen Mother in her carriage leading the way. Müller, the tenor from Hamburg, rides in the carriage with her; the side curtains are drawn shut: "The young Linz woman was atrocious again, don't you agree . . . ?"

On Stephan-Strasse the rooms are brightly lit: the maids wear black dresses and starched white aprons. The dining room has been cleared for dancing, the cold buffet has been set up in the drawing room: cold roasts and fruit salad from Krüger's, the table dotted with gay crepe-paper crackers. All the artists are telling each other, on the one hand, how good they were today and, on the other, that actually the premiere came close to being a disaster, and they all say this at once and at length. And then Strahlenbeck sits down at the grand piano and plays waltzes:

> Once again, once again, once again,
> Sing, oh sing, nightingale . . .

And he is so good at it that the assembled company are swept right out of their armchairs. And the maids downstairs in the basement kitchen, beside the dumbwaiter shaft, listen, and dance every bit as well as the people upstairs.

The master of the house sits with old Mr. Ahlers, his friend who "has come down in the world" and is in need of a helping hand. He sits close to the stove, drinking his claret and chuckling over those crazy specimens dancing around, trying to outsing each other in his house and asking behind his back: "Aren't the Kempowskis going to have any champagne tonight?"

> Nero the Watchdog!

sung in a light soprano by the young Linz woman, a wringing wet handkerchief in her hand. And when she has finished she runs out of the room in tears. And from outside she can hear them laughing inside.

(Old Mr. Kempowski is not yet an invalid, although the bacteria he has picked up God knows where are already doing their work.)

. . .

Karl sits in the basement kitchen with the maids, who are listening at the dumbwaiter:

Year after year a dove descends from Heaven!

They don't miss a thing of what's going on up above; the house-keeper replenishes platters to be sent upstairs, and softly sings along:

. . . once more His wondrous powers to renew . . .

When the bell rings three times she places the platters in the dumb-waiter and hauls on the rope to send them up. Stop! Bring it back for a moment, pop on a bit of parsley and some chopped aspic.

"Get along in there too, dearie," she tells Korli, pretending she is going to stuff him into the dumbwaiter, and when he has fought her off enough she presses his head to her bosom: right in between her great country breasts.

Pale little Gisela has given up crying long ago. Sometimes she pulls young Karl onto her lap and cuddles him. At first he didn't like that at all, but now he is used to it.

"My, you're a sweetie!" she tells him; and when it's time for him to go to bed and toys are still lying around all over his room, she helps him put them away. For instance, she helps him put away the "Anchor" building blocks with which you can build grand houses like Privy Counselor Öhlschläger's or forts for tin soldiers, and to do this she kneels on the floor beside him. There are red blocks and white blocks. RICHTER'S ANCHOR BLOCKS. The turrets and roofs are blue.

Strictly speaking, tonight Karl should have "gone bye-byes," as Gisela likes to say, long ago, but such things aren't taken too seriously in this household.

Si può? . . . Si può? . . .
Signore! . . . Signori! . . .
Scusatemi se da sol mi presento.
Io sono il Prologo!

someone is now singing.

Karl is absorbing everything Müller the tenor is singing upstairs, and later, when he has his own family, twenty years later, he will be sitting at the piano in his apartment playing excerpts from operas, and wincing when he is interrupted.

4 The Housekeeper

My name is Gertrud Grewe, and I was born in Parchim, and that was eighty-five years ago!

How nice of you to come and see me! I could write a book about the Kempowskis. Ten years I was in that job, ten years and three months; in those days my name was still Obermeyer. Obermeyer with a *y*.

One day a man said to me—he had a hairdressing business—"Trudchen, come over here, d'you know what it says in the paper? Kempowski the shipowner is looking for a housekeeper; you'd better go there at once. Get ready right away!"

I dressed quickly, a simple navy-blue suit and a white hat, and off I hurried. My heart was really beating fast, for the Kempowskis were prominent people and lived in a high-class neighborhood.

So I went there and rang the bell, and I'm standing there in the front hall when she comes sailing down the staircase, Madam herself. "Is it starting all over again this morning?" she said, for seventy-five girls had answered the advertisement, and they had been besieging the house for days. "Is it really starting all over again this morning?" she said, and: "Would you mind going into the drawing room, my husband has to have his breakfast first."

So down I sat in the Biedermeier drawing room—I've gone Biedermeier myself now—and looked at their stuff: the chandelier and the lovely furniture, all polished. The alcove had a heavy green velvet curtain across it, and there were photos everywhere, on the sewing table and on the chest of drawers, photos of relatives and friends and of Madam herself, taken at a spa, in the park, leaning against a birch tree wearing a straw hat . . .

So I sat there and waited, and when her husband had finished his breakfast she saw him off, the cab was already waiting at the door.

And then she swept in again and said: "Well, now it's *your* turn . . ."

So there I am, standing there in my navy-blue suit and my white hat, and she undid my jacket, had a good look at my suit, and said: "Mm, I like *that*, I *do* like that."

Then we sat in the alcove, and she rattled away about all sorts of things, about her husband and about the children. "Ohmygod," I'm thinking, "what's all this leading up to?" and finally I had the job, on May 3, 1907, out of seventy-five applicants! I still don't know why. "There's no escaping Destiny," my mother used to say, and I suppose that's how it is.

On my very first day there was a terrific row. The Kempowskis had a huge staff, you know, sometimes there were eight of us! Coachman and gardener and two housemaids, a cook, and then the ironing woman once a week, and every two weeks two women to do the laundry. It was the cook's afternoon off, and she hadn't shown up in time for supper: "You can pack your things right away," she was told, so I had to fry the duck legs.

"I really enjoyed that," said Mr. Kempowski, wiping his mouth with his serviette. "I couldn't have done them better myself!"

As housekeeper I was responsible for the household accounts, and I had to be a sort of go-between from upstairs to downstairs. I was s'posed to be a kind of spy, they were all scared stiff of me. It wasn't often that I had to do any cooking.

Old Mr. Kempowski was always very careful with his money, of course he was a businessman (how else would he have got where he was?). When I had to do the accounts with him, I used to feel quite nervous.

"Radishes?" he'd say. "I didn't get any radishes . . ."

I much preferred doing the accounts with *her*. "Just hand them to me," she would say, and sign them all, and then I could go and get a new supply of money. I could've cheated *her* right and left.

. . .

Those Kempowskis: I could write a book about them, and all my experiences.

As I said, there was a large staff, even by the standards of those days, but to keep nine rooms clean is certainly no easy job! (No one had even dreamed of vacuum cleaners at that time!)

Just take all those kerosene lamps! Every afternoon they all stood on the kitchen table, the big ones and the little ones, and the brass reflectors had to be polished and the glass chimneys, and the wicks had to be trimmed. Every single day.

Before we had gas lamps ("Auerlicht" brand), the larger rooms were lit by hanging lamps with bulbous chimneys. They cast a lovely light. But oh my, if you weren't there to watch them! When the wick started to smoke, the whole room became filled with black flakes, and *then* the fat was in the fire. Those beautiful cushions, those tablecloths and curtains—everything covered with a thick black layer. Believe you me, many a time there were tears!

We were always busy, never idle. Almost every household did its own preserving in those days. The fruit was bought at the market, from the farmer, and the mistress always did the choosing herself. Then it was washed and boiled and put into crocks or glass jars, each covered by a piece of white cloth soaked in salicyl. In winter, when the fruit was eaten, it had a thick layer of jelly on top.

The most exhausting job of all was making plum jam. For that we had polished brass cauldrons, and the stuff had to be stirred and stirred, hour after hour, otherwise it would overheat and stick to the bottom. Oh my, when I think of that . . . But the flavor was worth it.

We used to cook up a whole laundry basket of plums every year! And what a mountain of lingonberries! Whole tubfuls. The master wanted a helping of lingonberries every day, regardless of what else there was to eat.

Sausage-making was also a big affair. Everyone had to pitch in, the coachman cranked the sausage machine, and the mistress did the tasting. She didn't use a recipe, she went more by her own ideas. The casings had to be filled tightly, and if there was a bubble of air she would take a darning needle and prick it. (The needle hung on a string around her neck so she wouldn't lose it.) Oh, what good sausage we had!

The master was really quite nice, except: he had a weakness for the fair sex. That very first day our ironing woman told me: "When you go to Mr. Kempowski, don't let it worry you, he always wants to know what kind of a dress you're wearing: 'Is it wool or is it silk?' Don't let it worry you."

He even did it to my aunt when she came to see me one time. He used to really paw you: "Come a little closer," he'd say, "I just want to have a look at the material—I can tell at once whether it's good or not . . ." He'd grab you right here by the arm and pinch.

Sometimes he'd ask in young girls from the neighborhood—he used to sit a lot in the alcove and watch what was going on outside —he wanted them to have coffee with him, and cake. He'd make them lift their arms to see whether there was anything sprouting yet under there. The giggling that went on! He was always making jokes!

Every morning at seven I had to take a cup of cocoa to his bedside. The mistress got coffee, he got cocoa. And as I left the room he would say: "Well, Gertrud Elisabeth Hedwig? Still a good girl?"

"Oh yes, sir!"

"Well, keep it up!"

The couple had separate bedrooms, of course, and between them was the library. He would push open the door with his cane and call out across the library: "Well, Anna? How are you this morning?"

"Oh dear, I don't feel well at all, Robbie . . ."

"My wife has three hundred and sixty-five diseases, one for every day," he sometimes said to me.

She made life miserable for the staff, she really did, it was more than a body could stand. Sometimes the master would say: "And whose turn is it now?"

Before my time there were often staff changes every month, and what head of the household would care for that, I'd like to know?

Old Mr. Ahlers—a bachelor with a white beard and a bowler hat —he always said: "Well, Trudelchen, what's the weather in there like today?" He came every day to eat the bread of charity.

In the morning, when Madam came downstairs, the housemaid would often say: "Watch out, girls! The old girl's wearing her dark dress today!"

What she really couldn't stand was for one of the maids to be pretty. At one time we had a girl who was only fourteen. Gisela was her name, and she said to me: "Just imagine, she has a true Greek nose! Are her parents that good-looking?"

"Madam," I said, "I don't know her parents, she's from Grabow."

Another time we had a girl who never said "Madam" but simply: "Mrs. Kempowski." So she said to her: "I would have you know that for you I am still Madam!" And with that she swept out of the room. (In those days there were still dresses with trains.)

From the dining room a dumbwaiter went down to the basement kitchen, and sometimes she would listen at the shaft.

"They always say 'the old girl'!" she told me once.

"I have *never* said that!" I replied.

"No, that's true, I've never heard it from you."

When the master had finished his cocoa in the morning, the barber, Mr. Risse, would arrive, and that was the signal for the jokes to begin, and some of them were quite off-color! How they laughed!

The barber was paid exactly eight pfennigs for a shave. Yes indeed, I still remember that. And he supplied the soap himself.

On the dot of eight the carriage would arrive to take him to the office. One of the cabbies was called Siedow and the other one Bach. He always used to joke with them too. He really was a card, was the old gent.

"But don't tell my wife!" he would always say, and she'd say: "Robbie, how could you!" when she happened to catch something.

We got along much better with the old gent, of course, than with her. "That's right, dance around the golden calf," she would say whenever we tried to be nice to him. "But I would have you know that even when I'm in my coffin I'll knock on the lid and say: 'It's going to be done *my* way, like it or not!' "

So at eight o'clock he'd drive off in the cab, and at one he'd come home again. The midday meal was served at a big table, and the table was always extended and fully set for those four people. Each person had two glasses for two different wines, and in the middle stood a candelabra with seven candles.

The drapes were pulled shut, even on a bright summer's day, so the candles would show up better.

The meal began every day with soup or bouillon, then came the main course, meat or fish, whatever they happened to fancy. And after that a vanilla or chocolate pudding. With the chocolate pudding went a frothy wine sauce made by the mistress herself, over an open fire.

Meatballs were the master's favorite. They had to be made of pure pork. Before leaving in the morning he would say: "Gertrud Elisabeth Hedwig! Today we're going to have meatballs, make sure they're nice and brown!" And when he had finished his lunch he would undo his napkin and say: "Well! . . . I really enjoyed that. I couldn't have made them better myself!"

The fish came from Max Müller on Grüner-Weg, I always had to order it ahead, herring with roe, nothing else would do, it had to be with roe.

I could write a whole book about the Kempowskis. Just take the pudding, I only have to think of the pudding! "Poocking," the old man called it, and she'd say: "The pudding must be whipped, and when it says phew! it's ready." Twenty eggs was nothing.

Some days there were ten people around the table! Students and opera singers from the theater, a proper bunch of spongers. The worse the times were, the more used to turn up. There were two maids to serve, black dresses, white caps, and the guests really tucked in.

"What an exquisite bouillon," one of them once said. "I could make a whole meal of it."

"Yes, but only if you drank a pailful of it," said the other.

Old Mr. Ahlers usually came only in the evening. Whatever we had for lunch he was served in the evening. He always called me "Trudelchen," "Well, Trudelchen? All in white today?" Or: "Oh Trudelchen, looks like Blue Monday today. We're in a bad mood today, are we?" To tell the truth, the mistress was always in a bad mood. One time I upset a box of pins. *"Must* you upset the pins?" she said. "Isn't there enough racket in the house?" On Saturdays she'd have her hair marcelled, and she would look quite nice. Once she had a new dressing table, so she sits down at it, looks in the mirror, and says: "You don't know me yet, any of you. I am the greatest actress in the world."

When one of her admirers crossed her, she'd fly into a rage. "Oh my God, I could smash everything in sight!" Then she'd just pick up a flower vase and smash it on the floor.

One of them once gave her a white rose for her birthday, a white rose in a pot. She immediately put on her coat: "Oh, that means Death!" and took the rose to a neighbor, to Mrs. Jesse across the street. She must have been amazed.

"White roses mean Death! How dare he give me a white rose for my birthday!"

Daffodils, her favorite flowers were daffodils, she often sent out for some from a nursery.

Oh, such goings-on! The ironing woman used to say to me: "Miss Obermeyer, if you ever leave the Kempowskis you'll never find another job in Rostock."

Those Kempowskis—that was the liveliest house in all Rostock.

When the mistress was away on a trip, the old gentleman really had himself a good time. In the evening he would have us girls come upstairs to his room and there would be music, he had a phonograph and some records. And then we had to dance. He got a kick out of that: "Oh that Miss Obermeyer, she's a great little dancer!"

Old Mr. Ahlers was sometimes there too, and they'd get him drunk, and then all of us had to help him into bed.

. . .

The mistress was extremely fond of the theater—she went every week—and she was just as fond of the performers. She'd send baskets of flowers backstage, and wine; the actors and singers could then drink each other's health.

Müller, he was her favorite, he was from Hamburg. When he came the housemaid would say to us: "Old Hamburger's there."

"The Lotus Flower" he used to sing, it was his best song. Sometimes even the master would listen to that, sitting in his leather armchair, his cane between his knees, and we'd stand down below at the dumbwaiter, like listening to the radio.

The pianist's name was Strahlenbeck, he used to accompany the singers, they couldn't have managed without him.

When the mistress was in a good mood she would sit down at the piano herself.

La donna è mobile

and:

Wer uns getraut . . .

she would play, and the kitchenmaid would stand by the shaft downstairs and during a pause sing: "Love is a celestial force." Then the mistress upstairs would laugh and call out: "Quiet!"

One morning she rang for me: "Would you please go and look at the name of my piano?" The name was "Ibach." I remember it to this day. I had to rush downstairs specially, she couldn't remember the name.

"Would you please go and look at the name of my piano?"

I used to like to sing too, and then I quit for a few weeks, I got mad at her, and then she wrote me letters, one letter after another, asking me to come back. And then she wrote: "And we've been missing you and your singing so much."

Once she said to me: "You know what?"—I had such a pretty blouse—"Next time I'll take you with me to the theater, and you'll sit in my box wearing your white blouse, and people will look and they'll say: 'I wonder who that is with Mrs. Kempowski today?' "

. . .

I still have a ring she gave me, this one here, that was hers. She was sitting at her desk, and she must have just thought about it for she suddenly says: "Would you like to have this ring?"

"Why not?" I think, and say: "Yes, I'd love to." And so she gave it to me, this one here, and I still have it.

Otherwise she wasn't all that generous, and she never once praised me.

On fine Sundays outings are organized. In the morning, a first glance through a gap in the curtains: Thank heaven, no clouds . . .

Siedow the coachman drives up . . . "Whoah!" He tightens the brake and twists the reins round the crank. The carriage with its red wheels has just been washed, and the horses have been groomed to perfection, their hooves polished and oiled.

Despite the early hour, Mrs. Jesse also emerges from her front door and sits down on the bench, her parrot on her wrist.

Into the carriage go hampers packed with smoked eels, soft-boiled eggs (still warm), fresh rolls, wieners, and chunks of ham. Coachman Siedow takes a preliminary swig from his bottle, it's going to be a hot day, and looks around to see whether they've finished loading yet.

At last they are ready, the family party has settled in, the coachman cracks his whip, and the horses pull away.

"Ohmygoodnessme!" shrieks Mrs. Jesse's parrot, spreading its wings.

Korli is allowed to sit on the coach box. He waves to Giesi, who is staying behind and waves back. She would love to be going along too, little Gisela would, but you've got to draw the line somewhere.

Silbi is sulking because she would rather stay home, sit in the garden and read, casting an occasional furtive look next door to see whether the boy from Berlin is still there. Now she is sitting next to old Mr. Ahlers, and old Mr. Ahlers stinks.

"Keep right on to the end of the road . . ."

The clipclop of the horses: the streets are still empty at this hour. And when someone does appear whom the coachman happens to know—Plückhahn the porter, maybe, or Kolbe the stevedore, that good-natured fellow—Siedow either cracks his whip or sticks out his tongue, depending on whether it's friend or foe.

If a housekeeper should be walking along the street, wearing her white bonnet and carrying a basket over her arm, he raises his moss-green coachman's hat.

Karl looks down onto the rumps of the horses as they swish their tails, and Karl can observe the ingenious arrangement provided by the good Lord underneath those tails.

Now Moritz, the left horse, raises his tail to discharge his droppings at a trot, isn't that interesting. Lena makes no such preparatory motion. The falling horse apples look luscious, and they smell good.

The sun sparkles through the trees: they drive through villages, past village pond, linden tree, and church, and thatched farmhouses with dark, yawning entrances—a stork's nest on the roof—dogs yapping as they race alongside. The coachman jabs at them with his whip, and Stribold has to be firmly restrained, otherwise he might jump out and tear all his fellow canines to pieces.

On they go past fields of wheat, larks rising above them. By now the smooth paving of the town has given way to a corduroy road.

Rural estates lie hidden behind tall trees, approached by tree-lined avenues, straight as arrows. The owners are known by name, and one knows whether they are middle-class or aristocrats, affluent or on the edge of the silver spoon.

Father Kempowski has two lenses that he can fasten to his cane with two clips, the big one at the tip, the little one in front, and he uses this as a telescope. He frequently resorts to this device: when he looks through it one imagines he is going to shoot with his cane.

At last they reach the forest, Rostock Heath (a jay flies off with a raucous cry), that ancient forest from which generations of ship-builders have cut their timber. It's a wonder there are still so many old beech trees, and even oak trees, left.

Rövershagen, where the delicious honey comes from: they drive along an avenue of birches, and where a path branches off they stop and get out.

"Quiet, everybody, we might see some deer."

The horses are given their nosebags, stamp their hooves because of the flies, and heave a deep sigh. Coachman Siedow spreads out the tablecloth and arranges the nourishing delicacies as if competing for a prize. Then he takes a swig from his bottle, Stribold the dog lifts one leg, and the Kempowskis, groaning and sweating, lower themselves to the ground.

Old Mr. Ahlers settles down as usual in his frock coat, keeping a grip on his "brolly," just in case: you can't be too careful, that cloud up there, he doesn't quite trust it.

At the mention of rain, someone brings out the old joke about "He reigns, her reins, it rains."

Old Mr. Ahlers has a fine, leonine head, only the red nose seems out of character, the fleshy red nose that contradicts the magnificent head.

Everyone settles down to enjoy the smoked eels and the soft-boiled eggs, the fresh rolls, wieners, and ham. The butter on a bed of ice is wrapped in lettuce leaves, it has been whipped and has a marvelous aroma.

Stribold, having attended to his business, steps right into this butter, an event that was told and retold for many years to come. Stribold, the little mongrel, and at this point even Silbi's face brightens: that boy from Berlin—perhaps he's gone by now anyway.

A civilized conversation now gets under way: what this person is doing, and that person has died . . . and Father Kempowski points his cane/telescope now in this direction and now in that. Over there, isn't that a buzzard? Or even an eagle maybe?

"Here, Ludwig, take a peek through here! Isn't that an eagle? Monarch of all he surveys, eh?"

The children—"Don't go too far, it looks like rain!"—catch June bugs, if there are any, look for raspberries, pick cornflowers, sweet peas, and poppies. The June bugs are put into cigar boxes that have been provided with air holes, the raspberries are eaten, and the bunches of flowers are immediately thrown away again, into the ditch, where they remain.

The lake, which is quite near, is strictly speaking out of bounds— "Don't fall in!"—it is completely overgrown and no one knows how deep it is.

If you fall in, the water lilies twine themselves around your legs and pull you under—so the children are told, also that there are no water sprites in it, none at all, they're told that too. In that lake many a corpse has been found, swollen and slimy.

". . . and down below the bottom is covered with skeletons," says Luden Ahlers, and Father Kempowski confirms this and makes a face like a grinning skull.

The talk then turns to suicides, to people who for whatever reason hang or shoot themselves. The Bible tells us of those whose bowels "gushed out," claims Ludwig Ahlers, also that Schlängelberg the grocer killed his wife with an ax, and that her head was actually split right down the middle.

> Meadows trim with daisies pied,
> Shallow brooks and rivers wide.
> Towers and battlements it sees
> Bosomed high in tufted trees.

The horses stand in the shade, with bowed heads, flies swarming around their nostrils. Father Kempowski smokes one cigar after another and lifts a little pitcher of milk to toast his wife, who is photographing the scene. He has already addressed himself to his double Kümmel, but of course *only* "to get rid of the taste of coffee," as is invariably said.

When it is very hot he takes off his freshly cleaned straw hat and hooks it onto a waistcoat button. Korli is then allowed to remove the dicky from the front of his sailor suit. The idea of taking off the blouse has never crossed anyone's mind, it simply isn't done.

Then they play forfeit games, blindman's buff or fox and geese. Mother lifts her skirts as she runs, and Silbi copies her: she has stopped thinking about the boy from Berlin, who, so she now finds, was really rather silly.

Oh, it's marvelous here, and very appropriate for a squirrel to run down the tree, take a piece of bread from the plate, and run up the next tree.

Silbi gets a good scolding for clapping her hands. A little creature like that is so easily scared! Who knows, it might have stopped and sat up among all the wieners and cups and plates. And maybe the whole thing could have been photographed. What a lovely picture that would have made! That's all ruined now, and the scolding goes on, to the detriment of Silbi's mood: for the rest of the day she subsides into a sulk.

The journey is resumed: Siedow, after quickly downing one more good swig, packs up the remains of the picnic and collects baskets and pitchers.

"Hurry up, everybody!"

Their route takes them along woodland roads. Groups of ramblers with guitars and pennants cross their path singing, and other picnic groups are lying around in the grass, men in suspenders, women in hats, likewise singing and calling out: "Yoohoo!"

To one side some men are passing their water, which is rather less pleasant. Why do they have to stand right by the side of the road . . . ?

As for the ramblers, who call themselves *Wandervögel:* a strange phenomenon of the times. They are said to sleep in the straw, in barns, and eat the pea soup they have made themselves. Like the Hottentots. Without manners or morals.

Really, one can only shake one's head. This isn't just any old place, after all! And stern eyes are turned on Karl, and the hope is expressed that he won't "run away with the gypsies" when he's a big boy. Instead he should work hard in school, as hard as he can, and be a credit to his parents.

On they go in a jog trot.

By this time Siedow's face is very red, and his eyes are watery; his spittle blows back, and old Ahlers has fallen asleep, his head slipping onto Silbi's shoulder; Silbi moves farther and farther into her corner, now nursing her grievance to the full.

"The best thing is to ignore her!"

The journey continues along the wide, sandy roads, beneath towering pines and spreading beech trees. They pause for a moment at Brandt's Cross, a tall, frequently renovated wooden cross erected in memory of Brandt, the forester who was gored to death at this spot a hundred years ago by a wild boar. The ferns are shoulder-high, almost completely obscuring the cross.

Karl asks whether there are any wild boar like that nowadays right here. He is concerned about this and wants to know whether the boar slit open the forester's belly.

His father reassures him, which does not alter the fact that both have to think of bowels, the bowels that gushed out.

If there is time they visit Borwin's Oak, or they go straight on to the forest inn called The Margrave's Heath, a thatched building almost completely overgrown by an ancient wisteria. Outside the door stands a wire cage with an old raven sitting in it.

In the orchard there is a swing for the whole family, a box swing, also some quoits and a "giant stride." There is a bowling alley too, but there are no bowls. The swing has rusted through, and the giant stride lacks its rope, but that doesn't matter at all for by this time you are much too tired for such things. Besides—"Don't fall down!"

—it worries his parents. No sense wearing yourself out there. And: many a child has lost a finger on that kind of equipment.

Indoors, the wooden floors have been strewn with white sand, there is a smell of cow dung and warm milk. Antlers hang on the yellowed walls, and a motto:

> Drink thy fill, and eat for six,
> But keep away from politics!

"Is there a key to this piano?" asks Father Kempowski, as he invariably does when he comes here. Yes, there is a key, and it is handed to him. "As long as I am in this place, this piano will not be played," he says loudly and in High German, and looks around the room although there isn't a soul there.

At The Margrave's Heath they are served scrambled eggs such as nowadays no one can even imagine.

> Eat and drink for a start,
> Then go for a walk and fart.

Golden-yellow, savory scrambled eggs cooked with crisp bacon; garnished with fresh chives that weren't grown in a flowerpot.

The grownups have a glass of draft beer, and the children are given cold milk.

Luise, the fat landlady, says: "I know how much the boy likes my butter cake . . ." as she sets down a plate of butter cake. She speaks Low German dialect, Grandfather Kempowski speaks it, everyone speaks it.

"Good day to ye!" they say as new guests turn up, which is somewhat frowned upon because the landlady now turns her attention toward them. The strangers are severely scrutinized, and great surprise is expressed at the curious type of Low German dialect they speak. What outlandish place could they be from?

One is tempted to aim the cane/spyglass at the woman who (people *did* notice!) has undone the tops of her buttoned boots.

That curious dialect—might they even be from Pomerania?

. . .

This is one inn they'll never come back to, it is asserted—as it is asserted each time they have been here—to an inn frequented by people who speak such an extraordinary dialect.

Now they all tuck into a good meal: but, whether scrambled eggs or butter cake, the plate must not be emptied completely, something must be left on it, one doesn't want people to think one is starving. Silbi doesn't touch her plate at all, she is not taking part in this meal. She looks morosely out the window, although there is nothing to be seen there but a shrub barely swaying to left and right.

Old Ahlers gives a hearty belch, he sits slumped in his chair, and Robert William is holding forth about Pomerania, what a strange part of the world that is, and about the "Pomeroos," that they're usually grumpy. "That's my opinion!" Crappy people with shifty eyes, they should go back where they came from. They should clear off to their crappy Pomerania, where there's not so much as a tree or a bush.

Then the bill is paid, that is to say, the money is tossed onto the table, so that it bounces and rolls among the dishes, and they leave— William leaning heavily on his wife, and it doesn't escape them that those stuck-up strangers pull out their spectacles and unabashedly watch their departure.

The drive home doesn't take off nearly as briskly. The coachman stares glassily ahead, his bottle is empty.

No. This is one inn they'll never stop at again, at an inn patronized by people who speak such an extraordinary dialect: everyone is agreed. Who knows where they could have crawled out from?

"I hear they still eat human flesh in Pomerania," says old Ahlers with his last ounce of strength, and they laugh in spite of themselves.

The horses jog along, and the farmers by the wayside ask: "With *those* horses they expect to get back to Rostock?" and shake their heads. "Well, well, those Rostockers . . ."

It seems a long time before the church spires finally show up beyond the low rise, and this briefly revives the company. They assure each other: what a view, now really, it simply bowls you over.

No one can remember how the drive ended; asleep on one's feet one sinks into the soft bed. Giesi comes in for a last look at Korli to hear what kind of a day it had been, she draws the curtains, and Mrs. Jesse across the street does the same.

6 A Schoolmate

My name is Seidel, you've heard of Heinrich Seidel, of course, the Mecklenburg author—no? *Leberecht Hühnchen?* That does surprise me. He used to be included in every fourth-grade reader . . . Anyway, my name is exactly like Seidel's, Heinrich Seidel in fact—as I say, exactly like the author, whom I can highly recommend to you.

I now live in Lübeck, I like being near Rostock, you see, in my old age. The streets with their gabled houses . . . sometimes I almost think I'm back in Rostock. And then of course *Trave*münde, being so close to Travemünde, to the sea, you know; it's called *Trave*münde because it's the mouth of the River Trave, and *Warne*münde, because that's the mouth of the River Warnow. That's how it is. Rostock and Lübeck, they are, you might say, sister cities.

As children we used to be taken by train to Warnemünde pretty well every vacation, in a compartment, the fare was fifty pfennigs, third class. During the trip the conductor would swing himself along on the running board outside from compartment to compartment, to check on the passengers and make sure they had paid. To turn on the gas lamps he even had to climb up onto the roof.

Sea-bathing in Warnemünde? The bathing area was fenced off, separate sections for ladies and gentlemen. The ladies' area was so far away from the gentlemen's that the men had to use binoculars. They had bathing cabins, narrow boardwalks leading to the water, and a pier: the braver souls would dive in headfirst.

We never bathed, we sat on the terrace at Berringer's eating éclairs, chocolate cream puffs, and cream horns, and drinking coffee at fifteen pfennigs a cup.

A slice of torte cost twenty pfennigs.

"A cup of coffee must be hot, it must boil in your mouth." We children were given a bottle of soda water. "Now children, drink up!" cried my mother. "The bubbles are the most expensive part, otherwise you might as well drink tap water!"

The fine view over the many wicker beach cabanas with their rows of pennants: blue-yellow-and-red, Mecklenburg's colors, and black-white-and-red, the colors of the German Empire. Threading his way among the cabanas was a vendor carrying a tray on a strap around his neck and wearing a tall white chef's cap:

Chocolate, candies, cookies!

he'd shout. And at "cookies!" he would shoot a lightning glance into the cabanas, startling the occupants. "Cookies!" And it sounded as if he were saying "Lookie!"

Out on the water was the ferry, its jaws wide open, really a marvelous invention, quite amazing.

My father would twirl up the ends of his moustache and keep a lookout for "acquaintances," and I would go off to play war. Below the walls of the mole, boys had built two big sand castles, one with a blue-white-and-blue flag, the other blue-and-yellow. The castles were expertly constructed, with layers of seaweed in between the sand so that they could even withstand the tide. We had swords made of reed stalks, and armbands that could be torn off to indicate who was dead.

> The Kaiser firmly grasps the helm,
> Prince Henry is the naval planner,
> And in the stern Prince Adalbert
> Waves to and fro the Imperial banner.
>
> So here we stand beneath the throne,
> Declaring our undying loyalty,
> Prepared to utter loud Hurrahs
> In honor of our noble royalty.

In charge of these maneuvers was a gentleman from Berlin who had fought in the Franco-Prussian War of 1870: the Frenchmen in their red trousers and how they ran away, that's what he told us about, and about Timm, the Mecklenburg hussar who was the only man during the Napoleonic Wars to capture a French eagle standard.

"Look at the dickybird!" he had said on that occasion.

In 1903 the Kaiser paid a surprise visit to Warnemünde. There was a regatta, and he took part in it. That's seventy years ago now, it's hard to believe. I was all of four years old then, and my father was still alive.

"What? The Kaiser's coming?" the word spread through Rostock. "It can't be true . . ."

But after the newspapers had published "extras," a veritable tide of humanity poured into Warnemünde, no one wanted to miss out. Steamers and trains brought thousands, they arrived on bicycles and in carriages and from all over.

"The Kaiser's coming!" the cry went out, and they all came pouring in.

We took the train because my mother was reluctant to expose herself to the crowds on a steamer, which, of course, would have been cheaper, for she had a new summer hat, one of those huge things with fruit and vegetables on it, a veritable monster of a hat, one of Fashion's follies, as they say.

But at the railway station the crush was if anything even worse. The wickets were besieged by impatient hordes. Everyone was afraid they might miss the Kaiser. There were no holds barred, as you might say today.

Those who finally had their tickets rushed to the train, all available passenger cars having been assembled for special trains, first, second, third, and even fourth class (which still existed in those days), it didn't make any difference. Even freight cars weren't scorned.

Tragedy befell me right at the start. As I was boarding the train, someone broke the stick of the little black-white-and-red paper flag my father had bought for me to wave; I bawled my head off!

For such occasions my mother always kept something on hand.

From her "reticule" she pulled out a bag of chocolate drops and gave me two. Her beautiful new straw hat, by the way, was so large that she had to tilt her head sideways on boarding the train, otherwise she wouldn't have got it through the door. In those days there was nothing ridiculous about that, and anyway the grownups were held in respect, not a bit like today. My father, with his martial expression, was never one to mince matters, and the slaps I received from him I'll remember to my dying day.

In Warnemünde I was given a new flag, for the people of Warnemünde had turned the Kaiser's visit into a big business. Booths had been set up selling marvelous knackwurst, bakers' boys carried baskets of fresh rolls through the crowds, and fishwives were selling smoked eels. Even postcards were being hawked: "The Kaiser as a sailor! The Kaiser at the helm! Their Imperial Majesties, latest photo!" And, of course, little flags too. Every peddler was doing well, everything sold like hot cakes.

Those were the days when people collected pictures of the Kaiser. Everyone knew the entire family tree of the Hohenzollerns by heart, and not only of the Hohenzollerns. The newspapers had a special column for "Court News" that always reported in detail who had had a baby and where the royal personages were spending their vacations. What annoyed my father that particular day was that the people of Warnemünde hadn't cleaned up the place, it was littered with fish crates and tar barrels, which really wasn't appropriate to the festive occasion. Why, it came close to *lèse-majesté*.

One man whom he challenged about this said: "Tommyrot! A fellow'll at least have a chance to say hello to him!"

The west mole was swarming with people, but my father managed to secure places for us from which we could look down on the whole scene. Countless rowboats and sailboats dotted the water, and one passenger steamer after another, jam-packed with people, was arriving from Rostock.

Some of the bigger steamers, like the *Fürst Blücher* for instance, would make a sortie out to sea to keep a lookout for the Kaiser.

The Baltic was a bit choppy that day, but there were no whitecaps, and the air was gray and opaque. Suddenly the veils parted, and the sun broke through: dark dots on the horizon—the outlines of large warships. Among them, billowing in the fresh breeze, the first white sails of the racing yachts.

"The Kaiser's in sight!" the cry reverberated through the crowds and into the town, and whoever was still walking about on the streets came running to the mole. Thieves could have had a field day.

We held on grimly to our places, and didn't regret it.

The ships swiftly approached. At first the colossus of the battleship *Mecklenburg*, a majestic sight. The sailors in their white uniforms were lined up, and thick black smoke belched from the funnels: the ship rose and fell gently in the swell.

Then we made out the Imperial standard on the center mast of the next vessel: it was the Imperial yacht *Hohenzollern*, and beside it, as escort, the light cruiser *Nymphe*.

We could also make out the *Sleipnir*, and while the four ships—by now quite close—dropped anchor in the roadstead, the racing yachts approached, bobbing gently in a widely scattered line. We counted more than thirty yachts, each one handsomer than the next.

Finally the whole harbor was crowded with vessels of all kinds. Among black, smoking tugs, pilot boats, and passenger ships entering and leaving, the graceful yachts glided into the harbor, each bent on outdoing the others in elegance and skill.

Just before seven the pinnace of the *Hohenzollern* also veered off into the harbor. Now the crowds were rewarded for their long wait. I sat on my father's shoulders, the flag in one hand and a knackwurst in the other, and my mother was holding onto me, too. From far away we heard the cheers and hurrahs: "The Kaiser! The Empress!" and we also shouted: "Hurrah! The Kaiser!"—although we couldn't see a thing yet.

More and more people were surging toward the mole, which was already densely packed. We had to stand our ground against them, at least my father did, I, of course, being in a safe spot up on his shoulders.

"Don't push, sir!"

The pinnace was rapidly approaching, and already we could make out the Kaiser with his familiar upswept moustache. Hats and caps were flourished, flags were waved, and thousands of voices roared "Hurrah!"

The Kaiser acknowledged the cheering, and the Empress beside him waved and smiled.

The pinnace now went alongside the *Iduna*, and the Imperial couple went on board. Waves of hurrahs continued to reverberate, and their Imperial Majesties smiled and bowed, gracious and affable, just like in their photographs: the Kaiser in nautical gear, yachting cap, navy blazer, and white trousers. He walked up and down in lively conversation with some of the members of his entourage. The Empress, all in white, chatted animatedly with another group.

"Hurrah! Hurrah! Hurrah!"

Then we saw the Kaiser pointing up to the sky: a wall of black clouds was advancing. Already the wind was churning leaves and dust through the air. The colorful vision of bright summer dresses disappeared beneath a black roof of umbrellas. *Sauve qui peut* . . . Down came the rain and hail: their Majesties went below into the cabin. The show was over, and the crowds gradually dispersed.

That was in June of 1903, and I remember it as if it were yesterday!

"Did *you* see the Kaiser?" everyone was asking. Yes, we had seen the Kaiser, Wilhelm "the One and Only," and we all felt cheered, as if now nothing could go wrong.

7

A sepia class picture has survived from Karl's schooldays: twenty-five boys in school caps harmoniously lined up, their hands linked in brotherly fashion. Up front, on the right, stands Korli, at the very end of the second row. There is a penciled *x* above his head, with "Korli" beside it. He wears unflattering steel-rimmed spectacles because, like his father, he is extremely shortsighted.

> *Gutta cavat lapidem non vi*
> *sed saepe cadenda.*

On his last day Miss Seegen wept. "You'll come and see me sometime, won't you, dear boy?" for he was a nice boy, a true Rostock boy, as Miss Seegen put it, a boy with a sense of fun.

"Korl, I can see you!"

"I can see you too!"

But when not long after that he meets her in town, she doesn't even recognize him. He is now one of the "back numbers," his case is closed.

The sealskin satchel lies in the attic; a simple strap is now fastened around the bundle of books that Karl slings over his shoulder.

In the morning four lessons, in the afternoon three. History dates have to be learned by heart, forward and, strangely enough, backward too. 1710 the War of the Spanish Succession.

"Iller, Lech, Isar, Inn, flow to fill the Danube in . . ."

Rivers with their tributaries, plant families, and long poems.

'Tis dangerous to rouse the lion,
'Tis grimmer yet the tiger's tooth,
But horrifying more than they
Is Man's perversion of the truth.

Schiller's *The Bell* with all its familiar quotes, *The Diver* of course, and *The Pledge*. Mostly Schiller, therefore. Not so much of Goethe.

Play reading of *William Tell*. One boy declaims: "Ye men from Unterwall!" instead of "Ye men from Unterwalden!"

And these days no one understands why that made the class laugh, for no one remembers the Unterwall, the lower ramparts of the city, with its swans and the great weeping willow and the quack-ducks being pelted with crusts by toddlers—"Ye men from Unter-wall!"—where the old sea captains sat beneath the elms playing skat, their pipes secured with a rubber ring to keep them from falling out of the toothless mouths: "I should've played my ace after all!"

In the morning four lessons, in the afternoon three, even in the heat of summer, in a dark classroom with an oiled wooden floor.

"Open all the windows! Who was that?"

Flies buzz behind the dusty drapes and bang their heads against the windowpane.

Outside, water carts sprinkle the pavement to keep down the dust, accompanied by yelling street urchins who wear patched trousers and don't have to learn Latin vocabularies.

"Please sir, can I be excused?"

"No doubt you *can*, but whether you *may* is another matter." Their teacher is Paul Wolff: "Own up, and you'll only get half!" He sits at his raised desk, from time to time lifting the lid to cut off a quid of tobacco. He has removed his starched cuffs and placed them beside the inkwell. Dr. Wolff, a genial soul who carries his bald head like a dome through all of Rostock.

Beside the door stands the polished spittoon, filled with sawdust.

At regular intervals Paul Wolff stands up, stretches, and spits into the bowl: his saliva is brown.

"Kempowski will stay behind for an hour."

". . . but sir!"

"Kempowski will stay behind for *two* hours!"

". . . but sir!"

"Kempowski will stay behind *three* hours!"

Calm as you please. Besides, there on the desk lies the class book in which, if necessary, it is always possible to write: "Kempowski merits a severe rebuke."

For the gravest cases, the most hardened sinners, there is a thin yellow cane lying on top of the cupboard; fortunately it is rarely used.

The hours crawl sluggishly by. Mumbling and droning, the class repeat their lessons. Sometimes the janitor in the corridor looks through a peephole into the room to see if everything is in order, whether he should bring some more chalk or turn up the lamps: the boys gesture their desire for this more often than is necessary: "Turn 'em up!" For in this room, which faces north, the lights must always be on: and turning up the lamps at least means a break in the monotony.

Sometimes the janitor happens to peek through the hole when there is a caning going on and a boy is rubbing his bottom. "You see? You see?" says Paul Wolff, wiping the cane as if it had been soiled. When the janitor sees that he shakes his head: What are young people coming to, it's hard to believe. Things had certainly been different in his day.

During the long recess his wife doles out cold milk in the basement. Such a nice woman, it's a pleasure to be with her: sometimes her little girl Marianne sits beside her on the table, barefoot. She is cheeky, and that's rather fun.

"Third person plural passive imperfect conjunctive of *amare?*— Kempowski, don't let me down."

Twice Korli fails his year, he has to do two "extra laps," but in those days that only meant six months each.

He intercepts bad report cards and forges the signature: "Noted with regret. K."

Old Ludwig Ahlers is persuaded to undertake some tutoring, "Maybe I will, maybe I won't . . ." Since he gets his dinner at Stephan-Strasse every day and all that brandy and all those cigars, surely he could do a bit to show his appreciation.

Old Ahlers? He is a man who never answers the telephone and never wears an overcoat, or socks, just army boots, and invariably a bowler hat.

Old Ahlers, who commands the vestiges of an education (a university education that had to be abandoned for lack of funds)—so Ludwig Ahlers tutors him, down there on Eselföter-Strasse, in his smoke-saturated bachelor's den where there is so little room that he has to tie up the few books he still owns with string so they can hang over the edge of the desk.

His shirt open, Ludwig Ahlers lies on his bed stroking his beard. *"Caesar adsum jam forte,"* he says for the tenth time and immediately provides the explanation: "Caesar 'ad some jam for tea."

The only window of his room looks out onto a courtyard where two men are sawing wood.

Sometimes he gets heavily to his feet and goes to the chest of drawers. In the top drawer he keeps his bread and some onions, the middle one is inhabited by the cat, and the bottom one contains coal. He pulls open the top one, cuts off a piece of bread, and bites into an onion.

He did once go to university, it's true, but that's a long time ago. He's been to sea, and he remembers that considerably better. That's why he unfortunately talks more about "When I was in

Antofagasta" than about Latin conjugations: how in Antofagasta
he knocked down a man who went for him with a knife, that's what
he talks about, and about sailing around the Horn, where unfortunately he happened to be sick in bed and consequently did not
sail around Cape Horn at all, as his friends of the Jolly Teapot
maintain. He tells the story over and over, and he says: "Just open
that cupboard . . ." (there's a bottle in there also), and: "D'you
want one too?" And that's why Korli's visits to Eselföter-Strasse are
soon discontinued.

Mr. Lehmann, a high-school teacher living on Kaiser-Wilhelm-
Strasse, has to come to the rescue, a vigorous type with dueling
scars. The first savage slap Karl received from him nonplussed Karl
for the rest of his life.
  "After that there was no more trouble," it was said.

Mr. Lehmann doesn't waste time explaining that *"Pompeius et
erat"* means "Pompeius ate a rat," something that old Ahlers had
considered essential to one's education. Mr. Lehmann teaches Latin
grammar in the dining room of his apartment as if on the parade
ground.
  "Utinam ne?"
  "Oh, may it not, if not! Takes the conjunctive!" Karl has to sit
up very straight, keeping his hands on his knees and, strangely
enough, the more he improves at this language drill the more he
enjoys it, and he can't get enough of it.

At school Paul Wolff takes off his pince-nez and muses out loud:
"It must have been there all along." He walks to the door, spits
into the spittoon, and says that Karl must be the type that needs
the strap, a good hiding, hmm?

On dusky evenings Lehmann breaks off his drill early. Walking up
and down by the curved buffet (which sets up a tinkle), he tells
Karl about the ups and downs of the German Empire: invariably

when everything is going smoothly, along come the French or the Pope . . . Or a weak ruler messes everything up.

He also tells him about Bismarck, the Iron Chancellor, how astute he was, that business of tightening up the Ems Dispatch, and what the venerable King Wilhelm of Prussia must have thought, that unassuming, dedicated German prince, when the French Ambassador buttonholed him on the spa promenade. There he is strolling up and down, all unsuspecting, and the next thing he knows he is being accosted by this absurd Frenchman! Who does the fellow think he's talking to?

And then the last thing the French would have expected—Sedan: eighty thousand prisoners! And Napoleon III among them, a prisoner! How he must have regretted writing to his ambassador in Bad Ems, telling him to accost King Wilhelm.

(Mr. Lehmann pours himself a glass of water from a carafe and drinks it down.)

Napoleon with his crazy little beard. How can anyone wear such a crazy beard? And an emperor captured in battle, when has that ever happened before, surely one has to go back to the Middle Ages to dig up a captured emperor. (Another glass.) Who did they think they were anyway!

He brings in books from the next room and lays them on the dining-room table: *Days of Greatness*, with woodcuts after Rethel and Schnorr von Carolsfeld, "Charles Martel defeating the Moors."

And he unfolds maps, the Battle of Leuthen, and explains the diagonal battle order, or the Battle of the Nations at Leipzig and what a devastating effect even the tiniest river can have if it happens to flow at the right point, in that case the Elster, almost like the Berezina.

With ruler and compasses the battles are reenacted on squared paper, not Kunersdorf obviously, or Auerstedt either, but Rossbach more likely, or even better Waterloo. Yes, Waterloo: "Blücher or night!" those moving words of Wellington's that he may never have spoken at all. And meanwhile the Prussians, pushing their cannons with their bare fists through the knee-deep mud, such faithfulness!

They might well not have bothered, like Schwarzenberg, that volatile Austrian. No, cost what it might, faithfully through mud and rain.

All the more inexplicable that Wellington should later have said all kinds of extraordinary things, and strange that he should have insisted on calling it the Battle "of Waterloo" rather than "of Belle Alliance," which, after all, would have been symbolic in every respect.

Lehmann also shows his pupil the bound volumes of the *Berliner Illustrirte*, with pictures of the new battleships and cruisers. Without being asked Karl learns the names of these ships by heart, and soon he can rattle them off with the same ease as the irregular verbs.

"Germany needs *Lebensraum*, my boy," says Mr. Lehmann, when it is already dark and the smoke of his cigar curls under the lampshade, "and *Lebensraum* is only to be found in the east." And as far as the fleet is concerned, you can't be expected to ask every Tom, Dick, and Harry for permission to build one. That's strictly one's own business. "Do the British ask us?"

It should start with the emigrants. If it were up to *him*, this is what *he* would do: Have the emigrants step up to his desk, state name, date of birth, and so on, and then: "You want to emigrate? By all means! But go to Posen or to Kurland or the eastern parts of Austria . . ." That's what he would say to the emigrants. And what's more he'd give them money. A hundred marks per head. And before the Poles can turn around, all those areas are German, German to the core. By infiltration.

Right there on his desk he'd stack up the bank notes, so they could see: We'll get some of that right away if we say "Yes—yes we'll go east." And then: off they go to Posen and immediately into key areas.

The colonies? All very well, but they're a bit far off. Old Bismarck, he knew what he was doing when he opposed the idea.

· · ·

He gives his pupil the books of Paul de Lagarde to read, they put the whole thing much clearer than he can.

"Read this, my boy!" he tells Karl.

Apart from that: piano lessons with Mrs. Lübbers, a needy widow on Schiessbahn-Strasse, whose room is crammed with greenish plush furniture.

> Ding dong bell,
> Pussy's in the well!

When Karl rings her front doorbell, at four in the afternoon, she is just getting out of bed; she wears a dressing gown and an ancient boudoir cap.

First she has to make coffee: "Go and sit down, my boy!" Mrs. Lübbers wears a false braid, she has to attach that and, no matter how quick she is, Karl always sees it, and he seriously wonders whether Mrs. Lübbers hasn't a little nail on her head to hang the braid on.

At last she comes in, wafting a miasma of stale air. She places the cup of coffee on the treble keys and a plate of cookies beside it.

Now comes "The Jolly Peasant," a piece never to be forgotten even if heard but a single time—it is not played but hammered because the worn, yellowed keys hardly produce any sound—and then "The Parade of the Little Tin Soldiers" in which all the tin soldiers fall down at the end. One is supposed to laugh every time: at their falling down, and one does laugh. That's part of the performance.

There are also pieces to be played with the left hand on the right and with the right hand on the left: that seems funny to the boy.

When he is tired of playing he asks Mrs. Lübbers to play him something.

He is allowed to sit on the green sofa, under Leonardo's "Last Supper," and listen while she plays the Rubinstein, which reminds her of her youth, or Schumann's "Aufschwung": how everything was going to be different in those days, and then things didn't work out.

Comfortably ensconced, Karl looks around the room: the greenish, somewhat faded plush furniture with fringes at the bottom, the mahogany table whose split veneer he can't stop picking at. The cabinet with the Beethoven bust and the flower made of real human hair: now that really is a work of art, he couldn't imagine how such a thing could ever be made. (It must have cost at least a thousand marks?)

"Karl, are you listening, Karl?" she calls out. "Isn't this sweet?"

Yes, Karl is listening to the music being performed for him. That's how he'd like to be able to play one day, he thinks, with someone else sitting on the sofa and listening.

Mrs. Lübbers ends by playing Paderewski's minuet, clicking with her fingernails and swaying in time to the music, and Karl stares at her false braid, hoping that it will come loose and maybe fall off.

As for her having a nail in her head, he doesn't seriously believe that, but he likes to think it.

Father Kempowski, too, at one time practiced scales, many years ago, together with old Ahlers, four hands: Up, down, a schnapps! Up, down, a schnapps! Then they poured beer into the piano, and "Back in Antofagasta," and that was that.

Silbi, with red and white peppermint brittle in her pocket, takes singing lessons.

Oh lilala, oh lulala, oh Laila!

She is accompanied by her mother on the grand piano. Difficult passages are simplified, and when a wrong note is sung or struck they laugh. A cut-glass bowl filled with shredded coconut, pink and green, stands on the instrument. Above it hangs the picture: "The Germans to the front!"

Visits to the dentist are less popular.

Up, down, a schnapps! In 1910 the inevitable happened: Father Kempowski is suddenly unable to walk, he is stricken in the theater when he is about to drink a beer, in the refreshment room: his legs give way under him, oh my! There had been intimations of this for some time, and he had been to see the doctor—but probably not the right one and not soon enough.

For the people of Rostock he has now become a spinal case, of which there are several others. He is pushed along the streets in a wheelchair and bows to other spinal cases—"That's old Mr. Kempowski"—and at night his wife puts him to bed, *every* night, and he really isn't that old . . .

He likes to sit in the alcove, orders up a bottle of good wine and a cigar from Welp's or from Loeser & Wolff in Elbing ("You can't lose with Wolff," he likes to say), and then he looks out the window to see who is passing by on the street. Mrs. von Wondring, for instance, with her long widow's veil billowing behind her: "The Ride of the Valkyrie," he calls her.

Or Gütschow, coming from the other direction: from Orleans-Strasse where he has a furnished room. He pokes his walking stick into the paving so hard that sparks fly.

"Kempowski! Keep out of my way!" That's what he had said all those years ago, when his big deal had gone wrong and he had soon had to declare bankruptcy, and the fine house that was to have been paid for out of the deal went down the drain. And now that upstart Kempowski sits there in *his* alcove and has the nerve to wave at him and smile . . .

When William Kempowski happens to be alone, which is often, and when he happens not to be in pain, which is seldom, he plays the violin that he still has from his Königsberg days. He fiddles

away a bit, and the dogs set up a howl, Phylax the German shepherd, Nero the airedale, and Stribold the little mongrel who stepped
in the butter at the picnic, bought at the fair for thirty pfennigs.

Sometimes he asks young girls in, does Mr. Kempowski, girls from
the neighborhood who happen to be passing by and curtsey nicely.
If his wife is not there he asks them in. Then coffee is served and
cakes from Fall's, the Konditorei.

8 Young Blood

My name is Christel Kranz, I was born in Rostock and have been living in Vancouver since 1928, but whenever possible I come to Germany every two years, and then of course I always go to Rostock.

I never have any trouble getting a visa. The first few years the East German authorities kept trying to convince me, they had me come to City Hall or to the Cultural Association, but then they must have realized they were wasting their time. My sister, who still lives over there, is always overjoyed, and of course I'm happy to see my old home town. But what a sad sight it is now! The buildings peeling and gray, the pavement crooked and uneven, and the front yards bedraggled and trampled over. You have the feeling that time has stood still over there. Everything is exactly the way it was forty years ago! The store sign of Meissner the grocer on Alexandrinen-Strasse, who emigrated to Buenos Aires back in 1936, it's still there, and you can still read the sign "Photo Lasswitz" on Friedrich-Franz-Strasse, although Mr. Lasswitz has been dead for years. (He always had a signed photo of the Crown Prince hanging in his showcase.)

We children always had to do the grocery shopping at Meissner's, and one day we discovered that we could also get candies, we only had to ask for them, since everything was charged to the account. My mother didn't tumble to it for a long time, until one day the grocer refused to give us any candies. Then we knew: Aha! They've caught on. But nothing was said.

My father was a high-school principal, we lived on Adolf-Wilbrandt-Strasse, three houses away from the Kempowskis. Our gardens were back to back.

My first memory of the Kempowskis is a children's party, it must have been Silbi's birthday. We were playing forfeit games in the garden, and there was lots of cake. Mrs. Kempowski put a glass of hot milk in front of me, no doubt she meant well, but hot milk was something I simply can't stand, and I gulped down that milk at one go and mentally holding my nose. And that must have made her think I had enjoyed it, so she filled up my glass again.

Karl wore thick glasses and always spoke very earnestly, with an air of importance. We never really took him seriously. I rather think his strangely solemn nature could be explained by his home atmosphere, for he never had any tender loving care (as one says nowadays). His father was an invalid, he had something the matter with his spine, and his mother was really only interested in the theater.

I always had the feeling that Karl Kempowski mentally rejected his father. I don't know. While the old man was never anything but nice to him, Karl always displayed a certain reserve toward him.

The old gentleman spent most of his time sitting in the alcove, like a spider in its web, but in the best sense of the words: so as not to miss a thing. As I got a bit older, I would often walk past there on purpose, around teatime, and then I would curtsey, and he'd knock on the windowpane and call me in.

The alcove was very pretty, separated from the room by a white balustrade.

I would curtsey and shake hands with him, and the old fellow would tell tales from his past and admonish me always to be a good girl and not to "get into trouble," though naturally the implications of this meant nothing to me as a child. Then he would do magic tricks with his pocket watch or read aloud from the works of Fritz Reuter, he was good at that. Or, when the poetic urge was upon him, he would recite old poems with pathos and gestures:

> A man should not love
> Unless he's sincere.
> For hearts may be broken
> Through many a tear.

His *pièce de résistance* was a long ballad called "Heini von Steyr." I found it most touching, and tears would immediately start to run down my cheeks.

Sometimes Silbi would sit with us, reading or knitting. She must have been about fifteen at the time. Oh, how cozy it all was!

On one occasion she said: "Today I read in a book, 'The lindens are hung with blossoms, they look like Brabant lace . . .' Can you see Brabant lace in the trees? I can't."

Then, shortly before four, the old gentleman would say (we were waiting for that!) : "Silbi? Fall's!"

Then she would jump up and phone Café Fall, and half an hour later a boy would arrive on a bicycle bringing a tray of cakes: chocolate cream puffs or lemon slices. Beautifully light and much better than nowadays. Nowadays all they have is synthetic flavors, and the cream torte comes out of the cooler, how *can* it taste good?

"In Spring, a Mr. Fall buys a Summer topcoat from Mr. Winter the tailor," the old gentleman repeated this little joke more than once, and: "Silbi? Fall's!" I did love that. In our house there was never anything but pound cake—and as for real coffee, that was unthinkable, it was usually mixed, half and half. With a few grains of chicory in it.

Now and again he would invite me to lunch, when his wife wasn't there. Then we'd have "roast pork with music," with cinnamon and sugar on it. That was a treat. Served with cabbage.

Mrs. Kempowski always looked a bit wistful, she was what you might call a "faded beauty," whereas he was a "very colorful person," as they say in America. It wasn't in his nature to be gloomy. He drank a good deal, and then he'd be very lively and get red in the face. You could laugh yourself sick over him. Sometimes he would pick up a hair brush and look into the back of it as if it were a mirror, and then he'd twirl his moustache and smooth his hair. And he was always good fun. Whether everything he told us was true I can't judge. Silbi would sometimes mutter: "That's not so, that's simply not true!"

Then he'd say. "What was that?"

"I was just counting my stitches . . ."

We had a lot of fun, and we used to laugh a lot. My children have often said: "Do tell us again about Kempowski."

The people who passed by the house intrigued him: "Look at that one!" he would say then, or: "Look at her!"

An old colonel with sticking plaster on his nose, a little shriveled old person. Well! You should have heard the old man's comments about *that*, what was the idea of that plaster and why was he running around with it and all that kind of thing.

"Look! There he comes again!"

Or Mrs. von Wondring, the old woman with the flapping skirt. As children we used to jeer at her as she passed because she was a bit off her rocker. She wore a full black skirt, "The Ride of the Valkyrie," as Mr. Kempowski used to call her.

He could curse like a trooper. It could take your ear off. One time a fat dachshund belonging to a woman in the neighborhood died on his front door mat. My heavens, the language he used! He couldn't stand that woman in the first place, she used to walk past every day with her fat dachshund, and now the dog had to breathe its last on *his* door mat of all places!

He was always sitting in the alcove, looking out. Across the street lived a Mrs. Jessow, the widow of a veterinarian, she had a parrot that sat on the fence, a stupid creature. She used to annoy him too: "Look at that old bag!" he'd say. It annoyed him that she looked out onto the street just like he did and, above all, that she was forever looking across at him.

When he had to go to the bathroom he would say: "I hear a distant thunder," then he would ring the bell and someone would have to come and maneuver his wheelchair into the bedroom, where his potty-chair stood.

In a way, you had to admire his attitude: it must have been obvious to him, mustn't it, the way he was deteriorating? He was often in pain, then he would clench his hands on the arms of his chair and say: "Silbi, give Dr. Kranich a call," and he would give him an injection, morphine, you know. He really should have had a different doctor, they say Kranich pretty well messed him up instead of curing him. That's probably why he gave the old fellow whatever he wanted: he seems to have let him have all the morphine he asked for.

As time went on, Mr. Kempowski's condition got pretty bad. I've heard people say: "What a dreadful old fellow, that Kempowski," but those were people who didn't know him. I could never understand that. In his own gruff way he did a great deal of good. For a young couple he once gave a wedding in his house, with all the trimmings. The altar was set up in the alcove, and then there was a dinner after, with music, the whole works.

And there were always visitors in the house. He had the strangest friends. Once there was one who must've been quite an old goat. He said: "Well Robert, now show me Rostock," and then they drove off in a cab through the town, and he'd always have some bits of paper that he'd throw out of the cab here and there whenever a pretty girl happened to be passing by.

> Come and see me,
> I am staying at 11, Stephan-Strasse,
> at Kempowski's.

And then the girls would turn up, reeking of powder. When the old trout caught on, they were out on their ear, of course. And the old goat, too.

Another time there was a man who left again in a hurry. He said there were cat hairs in his cocoa, he couldn't stand that.

Then there was a steady guest, old Mr. Ahlers, a friend from the early days, no doubt. He would sometimes join us for a cup of coffee. And when his coffee was being poured he'd take off his pince-nez, rise, and, as soon as the cup was full, sit down again and say with a look of doglike devotion: "Much obliged, I'm sure." A gentleman of the old school who had seen better days. Here he ate the bread of charity.

Mrs. Kempowski had her friends, too, but those were theatrical types who came in the evening, I wasn't really in on that. She was a faded beauty, you might say. There was something tragic in her expression, something veiled and wistful. My mother used to claim she had a "kink."

The only time she was nice was when you were alone with her. The library upstairs, that was her domain. She'd take me up sometimes and lend me books, not at all like those my father had, lighter, more sentimental, you might say. It was a small room with a chaise longue and a little white table, and between the windows an ornamental clock under a glass dome. It was just charming.

I remember borrowing Cäsar Flaischlen there, I was thirteen— thirteen or fourteen.

When I was still in my baby carriage she's supposed to have said I had a peachlike complexion. My father used to say to me later: "My golden nugget with the peach-bloom complexion."

But my mother would say: "That Mrs. Kempowski certainly has a kink."

In 1911 Karl is given his first bicycle, a "velocipede," as it is still called in those days. It comes from Vollquartz's, on the Hop Market, a secondhand Brennabor bike costing twenty marks.

("One free lesson was thrown in. There were these fellows there who would give you a push.")

It has a lamp lit by a candle, his request for a carbide lamp is turned down, that's really too expensive, and the gift is kept a secret from Father, who is against bicycles, who in fact is against any kind of exercise because in his opinion it's overdone and can only lead to harm.

It is a beautiful bicycle, with only a candle lamp, true, but with a loud bell and a luggage carrier. On the back axle there is a spur for a passenger to stand on, he has to hold onto the rider's back.

This is how Karl rides around town with his fair-haired friend Erich Woltersen—known as "Erex" because of his habit of hanging an "ex" onto the words of ordinary speech—in knickerbockers and stiff collar. A playing card is fastened into the spokes, and it goes "Brrrrt!" whenever an old woman happens to come along.

On Schiller-Platz they go careering around under the fountain as it blows across the street, and at Lloyd Station they annoy the cab drivers by shouting "Giddy-up!" The horses pull away, and the cabbie wakes up from his doze.

It is wiser not to shout at the street cleaners who happen to be on their way to work, shouldering brooms and pushing their two-wheeled carts—the "cane brigade," as they are also called.

Back and forth they ride around their home town, incessantly ringing the bell or making the playing card clatter or braking so hard that they leave tracks on the roadway. By the Wool Depot there is a tall walnut tree, they throw sticks into it, and at St. Georgs-Platz they place Bengal flares on the tracks of the newly installed electric streetcar. They go off with a bang, and the driver, who is not yet fully familiar with his new vehicle, stops to see what the devil is the matter now.

In the Old Town, where iron urinals—piss shelters painted green and black—are set up at regular intervals along the sidewalks, where there are streets with strange names—"Thieves' Lane" and "At the Bagehl"—there is a smell of wool and Norwegian *flom* herrings, and on Stein-Strasse it smells of asphalt, this being the time when the first streets are paved with asphalt in Rostock. The steaming asphalt, still powdery, is tipped from a wheelbarrow onto the old paving stones. Workmen drop tampers with round iron plates onto the hot asphalt. This rhythmic tamping and the smell—what a pleasure to watch.

The weekly market is also interesting, with its booths and stalls, its big ponderous farm carts and fluttering canvas awnings against sun and rain. The boys lean the bicycle against the public fountain and join the crowds.

A thousand sparrows shoot like buckshot across the paving where the steaming horse apples lie which they'd set their hearts on.

Herring, green herring, and cod!

Right in front of City Hall is where the Warnemünde fishwives have their stands, as they have since time immemorial. There they sit in their great black shawls and black bonnets, surrounded by shallow wooden tubs of fish. The men catch the fish and the women sell them, and the money goes into the big leather pouch under the apron, and there it stays, it definitely won't be spent on drink.

. . .

The butter cart from Pastow carrying only butter, Jean Tondera with bananas and Valencia oranges (five pounds for eighty pfennigs). New-laid eggs in chopped straw (a score for a mark), country sausages laid out on white cloths, plucked poultry, and fruit.

"Straight from the farm! Straight from the farm!"

Mrs. Baade from Allershagen, who must surely soon be a hundred years old, sits there every market day selling honey.

The day's main attraction is Samuel, the little Jew with the big head. At the approach of his cart along Grosse-Wasser-Strasse, all the pigeons take flight. His shouts are heard away in the distance, long before he comes into view, ranting in a raucous voice because he knows that ballyhoo is part of the trade, and, when he turns his cart into the market, naturally everybody is curious and comes running up to see if it's really Samuel the little Jew with the oversize head and what he's selling today, that's what they want to see. He talks and rants without pause until he has at last found his spot, attended by a crowd: today it's red-and-white peppermint brittle, nothing special, but the Rostockers buy just the same. (His eyes flit back and forth: taking without paying—he doesn't care for that.)

Karl and Erex don't buy any peppermint brittle, they accept "samples" from the farmers, just like the pensioners who carry around a little cloth bag to take home whatever they manage to cadge because that's what they live on.

When the two boys have eaten enough samples, and when they have watched the chickens being slaughtered back in the lane beside City Hall—they ruffle their feathers and make a weird cooing sound, that's the death-coo—they ride off again on their Brennabor. They ring the bell because of the marvelously loud tinkle, and they make the playing card in front purr whenever an old woman comes along. But riding on the sidewalk is more than they dare in case one of the two policemen who are responsible for keeping order here shows up.

They ride along Alexandrinen-Strasse, at top speed, then down Tal-Strasse, past the waterworks where the brake is jammed on because through the windows you can see the huge shining pumps moving steadily back and forth: an interesting and reassuring sight that can enthrall a boy for a long time.

The barrier at the railway crossing is down, of course, and there is often a very long wait. "How often do they close the barrier here?" they wonder, and they count the railway cars being shunted from right to left and then from left to right.

At last the barrier is raised, pink-pink, pink-pink, and they hurry across so the barrier doesn't come pinking down again before they reach the other side. Then they ride along Willoway, a leafy walk for elderly and very young citizens, for whose benefit there are benches at regular intervals and a sign saying "No Cycling." They *ride* along it, and they take Stribold along in a cardboard box, he enjoys that.

In the meadows beside the Warnow all is quiet, here Nature is waiting for what is yet to come. A painter would need only a few horizontal lines.

You can look for plovers' eggs here, and swim too, for the Warnow, the black, quiet Warnow that meanders through the meadows in long loops, is just thirty yards wide here, and the river is tranquillity itself, just as the countryside from which it flows is calm, the Mecklenburg farmlands, without guile and without turmoil.

You can swim in the Warnow, but it isn't all that attractive as the water is muddy and you've been spoiled by the Baltic. If you do swim, it's a good idea to get dressed again quickly, for there are horseflies around here that you don't feel on your skin until it's too late.

There is always something of interest in the Warnow meadows. In the low-lying areas there are places where arms of the river have been closed off, as well as squelchy patches yellow with marsh marigolds. Reed warblers pipe in the heat, and yellowhammers chirrup: here the boys catch tadpoles and carve willow whistles.

. . .

One day they come upon a man standing by his beehives, a veil over his head and puffing smoke from a large pipe; they approach him cautiously. They watch what he is doing with his bees, and he tells them he is a village schoolteacher and that he has a whole stableful of "young rascals" just like them.

That the queen bee sits in the center and lays eggs all day long—he tells them that too, and that the worker bees in the hive have never heard of the eight-hour day and "such newfangled ideas." He talks about the soldier bees who keep order—"order is half the battle"—and he says that it gets "good and hot in there," and asks them whether they'd like to stick their noses into the hive, to find out if it smells of honey. "No? You wouldn't?" He can understand their not wanting to stick their noses in, he says, for the village children won't do it either when he suggests it to them.

Even more interesting than the beekeeper are the alder bushes. For the alder bushes are favorite spots for lovers. If you're lucky you can spot a couple: the man's face pale and the woman's red.

For some reason or other it's always a bit scary in the Warnow meadows: when the local constable shows up you have to make a dash for it or he'll take down your name, ask what you're up to, and don't you know you're not allowed to cycle along here? What kind of a cheeky ruffian d'you think you are? And there's no end of trouble at home, whatever got into you, is it a thrashing you're after?

> Don't care was made to care,
> Don't care was hung.
> Don't care was put in a pot .
> And boiled till he was done.

One day they find a waterlogged black rowboat, they bail it out with empty cans and get it afloat again by stuffing up the leak with rags. Stribold stands in the bow while the boys paddle across to the other side, where the cows raise their heads and the calves come running up.

. . .

When they are halfway across, the leak springs open again and the boat fills with water. What a scare that gives them, especially as behind them the constable is hopping from tussock to tussock, shouting abuse at those damned ruffians.

A mercy he didn't find the bicycle.

In an old willow tree they build themselves a cave and line it to make it soft and snug. Through the opening they can see the rowboat, the river, and their town: clouds are gathering above the church of St. Nicholas, and they have a good view of the big "1 8 8 8" set into the roof tiles by the roofers as both commemoration and decoration.

They take out their clay pipes and smoke workmen's tobacco— the smoke comes billowing out of the top of the willow tree—and they discuss murder and sudden death. They talk about Schlängelberg the grocer, who split his wife's skull with an ax, and about suicides who hang themselves till their eyes bulge out of their sockets or who let their bowels gush forth.

"Much stone there was and little bread"—they are reminded of this poem in their reader, the one about the Teuton warrior who took his sword and split a Turk right down the middle so that half a Turk fell off each side of his horse.

> And off the horse on either side
> A half-a-Turk is seen to slide . . .

They hadn't had to learn this poem by heart, yet they knew it anyway, without a moment's hesitation. It makes you wonder, doesn't it, that Germans should be so strong, so much stronger than any other people in the world.

They look at the boat, the river, and Rostock. And at the gasworks, with its tall iron structure on which a coal cart is hoisted up and, at the very top, emptied out: you can even hear it, although a second or two later. Then the cart descends again and returns with a new load. This goes on hour after hour. The boys believe they can actually see the huge gasometer rising in the distance. This evening, when the lamplighters turn on the brand-new street lighting, it will sink again.

Marvelous, the way it works.

Looking south they can see the highway with a mail coach driving along it. They wonder where it's going. To Kessin? Where the village schoolteacher with his bees comes from? Yes, but then? Where then? To Berlin? Leipzig? Dresden? They don't know any of those places yet, and wish so much they could go there.

The boys lie in the meadow, dreaming of the future, of all the experiences in store for them. They want to be friends forever, and to travel, as far away as possible. Berlin, Leipzig, Dresden. But how to pay for it? Travel costs money.

Money: it'll be found somehow. These are things that will somehow take care of themselves.

Down there on the river a heavy barge is moving toward the city, carrying rye from peaceful Mecklenburg. Silently it glides along, and the bargee's wife is hanging out her wash.

"We'll simply take a trip on our *Consul*," says Karl. What could be more obvious? And Erex is always out to please Karl so that one day he will actually be allowed to go along. ("Kempowski always wants to be king of the castle.")

"How fast can a ship like that go?"

What the two boys can't know is that down there in the harbor things aren't going so well at the moment. The dock workers are on strike, for some reason or other. Robert William Kempowski, who has six ships lying in the harbor whose captains trample around every day in his office, cursing in a variety of languages, how long are they supposed to be laid up in this filthy hole? Robert Kempowski has to bring in workers from Hamburg in one of the Bohrmann Company's furniture vans. The doors of the van stand wide open, on the coach box, inside the van itself, and behind the van stand policemen with drawn swords: rocks fly through the air!

. . .

There was never anything like this in the old days. In the old days those fellows would have been put in jail, those "strikers," or, longer ago still, even beheaded and quartered, like that rebellious Runge whose dismembered body was displayed like chunks of meat in iron cages beside Stone Gate.

Strike? That's downright blackmail.

10 Another Schoolmate

My name is Schlünz, Richard Schlünz, and I can't really say from Rostock, I was born in Bad Doberan, the place with the beautiful cathedral. "Bad Dobe*rau*," as Karl Kempowski used to say. Whom I know, of course! There is a class picture of us, we're standing side by side, hand in hand, Karl Kempowski, known as Korli, wearing thick glasses.

We used to play football, wearing stiff collars and long pants, that's right, on Schiller-Platz. I was looking for the photo, I wanted to show it to you—my daughter-in-law always tidies everything away—if I find it I'll send it to you. A big brown photo, the old-fashioned kind, mounted on cardboard.

Rostock, those were the days! For us boys? A happy, carefree time.

In the fall we flew kites, along by the railway embankment always in fear of the "bull," of course, who in those days still commanded respect. In those days the uniform still meant something. Whenever we boys saw the gleam of a police helmet, we would shoot around the corner even if we hadn't been up to anything. Kufahl and Rosenberg, I remember the names of the policemen. Nowadays you never even see a policeman, although there's every need. The other day I was going for a walk with my dog, or rather, he was going for a walk with me, and along come some young punks on bicycles and swish! one of them snatches my hat off. That's right! There was never anything like that in our day. Sure, we played a few tricks, but nothing like that.

Every year there were the different seasons, tobogganing, swimming, top-spinning; kite-flying was one of them too—when the time came around it had to be done. Every season had its games.

Another seasonal event was *"mundus vult decipi,"* meaning the Spring Fair. That was really something! It dated from 1519, according to the records, and always took place at the harbor, until the Nazis came—they had to change it, of course, and today those bandits over there, they simply put an end to it. Why? Don't ask me.

Rostock was unthinkable without the Spring Fair. The biggest event of the year. Days before we'd go to Friedrich-Franz-Station in the hope of seeing the booths and merry-go-rounds arrive, we were always curious as to what sensation the fair would bring each year. You could guess at a few things from the inscriptions on the caravans and carts. And when the big booths and scaffoldings were set up on Strand-Allee, we Rostock boys were right there, helping to carry planks and whatever else there was, often till late at night. Our homework suffered greatly during those three weeks, but the resolve to catch up with everything after the fair was enough to salve our consciences.

On Whit-Monday, at the stroke of four (no earlier!) the noise of the fair would start up: on New Market you were already met by the waves of barrel-organ music. And the next thing was "Cheap Jack's" stall. He had tattooed arms and wore seaman's pants.

There he was, standing on a low table and shouting out his wares. First he'd pick up a cake of soap and say: "Five marks!" Since no one, needless to say, wanted to buy a cake of soap for five marks, he would look around in surprise and say: "Too much?" All right, so he'd throw in a clothes brush and a shoe brush. "What? *Still* not enough? Am I supposed to *give* it away?" He would add a bundle of pencils, an account book, and a notebook. "And all this for ten, no, for nine, well today I'll let you have it for seven marks! Right, and if you buy now you'll get the lot (and he would reel off the individual items) for—and that's final—five marks!"

This went on throughout the entire afternoon. Sweat poured from the fellow's forehead and back, his voice was hoarse and rusty, but he never let up. There was no need to go any farther, just to stand here was entertaining enough, especially as the fellow also made jokes that you didn't get to hear anywhere else.

"Come along, Helga, we're leaving," a man once said. "This fellow's too coarse for our liking."

From the market square the booths led down to the harbor, where the long cake booth stood with batter cakes, doughnuts, and lard cakes.

"I wouldn't swear to it," said Langbehn the pastry baker, whose café was right beside it—he would stand in the doorway glowering at the competition—"I wouldn't swear to it, but I hear the doughnuts are fried in horse fat!"

The booths stood so close together that it was hard to find a passageway between them. Notions, textiles, hats, trinkets, fancy goods, crockery, stoneware, Bunzlau pots, glassware, crochet goods, and all the rest of it. (At the antique dealer's in Pöseldorf you can now buy Bunzlau ware for a hundred marks a cup. In those days it cost thirty pfennigs.)

The booths stretched all the way to Monks' Gate, where the crowds were so dense that one found oneself carried along: this is where the real excitement began. The droning of the barrel organs and the calliopes intensified, and through the archway of Monks' Gate Kietzmann's roller coaster, the "necking express," stood out against the sky, at the same spot every year. With its decorative, almost baroque façade, "Kietzmann" was a familiar yet ever-new spectacle. The same old calliope, "Made in Waldkirch," with its animated conductor in rococo costume up front, his head jerking left and right, with its drums and cymbals struck by ghostly hands, blared out the latest hits from *Spring Fever* or *May Time* and joined forces with the calliope from Haberjahn's Hippodrome, with the cracking of whips and whinnying of the horses.

> You never need to take a course
> To ride a Haberjahny horse . . .

Kietzmann's roller coaster was a tradition, and it was permanently besieged by young people bombarding each other with confetti. Here you could stay hour after hour, here friendship and love were born.

My father was a tram conductor
On the tracks of old Berlin.
My mother is a washerwoman
Taking soldiers' laundry in.

On Gruben-Strasse a man had set up his barrel organ, with a little monkey hopping around on it. The monkey wore a red pillbox hat with a chin strap. Over and over again it would take off its little hat, peer into it, roll its eyes, then push its chin back into the strap and replace the hat on its head. It didn't keep still for a single second. For many, many years it was to be seen there.

The boys standing around would sometimes tease the monkey into a fit of rage. It would then clutch the barrel organ with all four paws, shaking the whole box and baring its teeth and giving the onlookers a good scare. Although it was attached by a chain, the latter was still long enough for the monkey to be able to snatch a hat or cap off one of the onlookers, which, of course, made everyone laugh.

Regardless of where you stopped at the Spring Fair, there was no need to spend any money; there was something to see or hear everywhere, something funny or entertaining. Next to St. Peter's Gate the disabled miners had their stall. Wearing their traditional garb they displayed a miniature mine: the interior was an exact replica in every detail. Little cages descended into or rose up from the shaft. Dump carts moved back and forth along the tunnels, which were lit by electric-light bulbs: interesting and educational and, what's more, all in a good cause, for the pennies spent here benefited the disabled miners, who in those days probably had a hard time making ends meet. If there was any space left between two stalls, a "Test Your Strength" machine had been erected. This was where the farm boys tested their muscles. With a mighty wooden hammer you had to strike an iron stud, which, depending on the force of the blow, dispatched a metal slug up a vertical pole, and if the slug reached the very top it would trigger an explosion. It had to be a pretty hefty blow, delivered with force. Those who succeeded had a colored paper flower pinned onto them, and those who didn't were consoled with the words: "At least it went in the right direction!"

A little farther on, bound in gleaming, heavy chains, stood or lay the most renowned escape artist of all time, "Houdini," who in no time at all practically shook himself free from what appeared to be inextricably entwined chains. The spectators were free to do the shackling themselves.

"And here you see the medals, awards, and letters of eulogy bestowed upon him by the highest in the land!"

Thus one booth followed another, all the way to Wenden-Strasse, which leads into Old Market. Beyond St. Peter's Gate the *Moritat* singer had his platform. With a long stick he pointed to large, crudely colored pictures, which, in a singsong voice, he explained in detail: a cobbler with many children who had killed his wife with a hammer. Or vice versa: the cobbler's wife who had poisoned her drunken sot of a husband. Certainly very grisly, and well worth the few pfennigs dropped into the plate handed around by the singer's wife. But it was always the same thing: as soon as the woman approached with the plate, the circle of spectators thinned out and melted away. The appearance of the woman with the plate acted like an electric shock on the crowd.

There was never a Spring Fair without a panorama. Every year you could look through little windows the size of portholes and observe instructive and gory pictures.

There was the passage of the children of Israel through the Red Sea, the waves standing erect on either side, like an avenue (and on the ocean floor little puddles with starfish). And then there was Moses on Mount Sinai, holding the tablets of the Ten Commandments, and the burning of Savonarola the monk. The storming of the Bastille and of the ramparts of Düppel filled you with a delicious horror of revolution and war. The depiction of the "Last Judgment" that came next served to frighten off sinners bent on vice but to comfort the souls of the pious.

That kind of panorama booth had a separate, curtained-off partition upstairs. "Adults Only! Admission 10 Pfennigs." For many years we boys in our short pants had to forgo this "experience," until as twelfth graders we were at last accepted as adults and allowed to go in too.

In the waxworks display elaborate scenes had been set up such as "Death of a Poacher" and "Jack the Ripper," and it was all sufficiently lifelike to scare any child. Also on view was the "cancer" that had once spelled doom to the wicked Bonaparte.

On Old Market, right in front of St. Peter's Church, there was a street musician, a wizard who could play five instruments at once. His main instrument was the accordion, and in front of his mouth, held by a wire frame, was a harmonica. On his head he wore a pointed helmet with two circles of little bells. On his back he had a bass drum, with a drumstick attached to his forearm. Above the drum hung the fifth instrument, a triangle that he played by means of a string fastened to the heel of his right shoe. Assuredly a most versatile musician. He was accompanied by his wife dressed as a gypsy, who beat a tambourine and would unexpectedly invite contributions by twisting it upside down.

The later the hour (everything closed at ten o'clock), the more colorful it all became. In the blaze of the little colored lamps, the clattering roller-coaster cars raced up and down, by now garlanded with paper streamers and strewn with confetti. The cars were always full, and round about stood row upon row of teenage boys and girls.

Many a girl went home *without* a hair ribbon, and many a youth *with* one.

In the fall, upstairs in the attic behind a pile of cherry-wood planks once accepted in lieu of cash, on a discarded sofa, they read Buffalo Bill or "Captain Mors with His Metal Airship."

Flavus and Rutilus the gladiators.

In the attic they also play sixty-six, with old playing cards sticky with the remains of beer and tobacco ash. And, of course, they smoke up there, too, KLIOS cigarettes, ten for ten pfennigs.

("I think they were made of horse shit.")

Someone tips Father off about the smoking, and that evening there is a great drama: *"My son smokes . . ."* His hollow moans echo throughout the house.

Next morning at the breakfast table, solemn words are spoken, and "Peter Five-Five" is quoted, the First Epistle of Saint Peter, chapter five, verse five: Likewise, ye younger, submit yourselves unto the elder . . . Peter Five-Five, let him take that to heart, the young rapscallion. And because the boy is squirming around on his chair during this homily, he is asked: "D'you have ants in your pants?" And because he answers: "No, do you?" he gets his ears boxed.

In winter they jump ice floes in the harbor, their socks get wet: they jump from floe to floe to beat the ferry as it steams, puffing and tooting, toward Gehlsdorf. The passengers stand at the railing and berate the boys, who will surely drown. They can already see them drowning and shouting for help. Disaster is inevitable!

"Why isn't there anyone to keep them off . . . ?"

· · ·

Or they go skating, the key for the skates on a string around the neck, their gloves wet and encrusted with snow, which can be bitten off, leaving threads of blue wool on the tongue.

One year the Warnow freezes over, and it's possible to skate all the way to Warnemünde. Erex won't risk it, but Karl does one day, and when he comes home, after nine and in total darkness, he finds the whole family assembled: "Where in the world have you been?"

> The lad his tears could not contain
> When Father sternly swung his cane,
> At home . . .

Robert William sends for a cane, and as he raises it with a powerful backward swing it happens: he hits the lamp. Father and son find themselves sitting in a veritable shower of splintered glass, dumfounded.

Christmas always brings a joyous, long-awaited spending spree. Winters are colder and snowier in those years than today. Wheels are replaced by sleigh runners. The jingle of sleigh bells rings through the streets: the horses wear little bells on their harness.

The white snow, the gliding of the sleighs, the tinkling of the bells, are part and parcel of the atmosphere. Flocking into town come landowners and farmers, the latter wearing short woolen coats and green caps with earflaps.

> Jumping Jack, five pfennigs,
> Jumping Jack, ten pfennigs!

call the ragged children as they stand outside the stores with Jumping Jacks hanging from their coat buttons. The landowners buy silk ascots at Zeeck's, and the farmers' wives buy vast pairs of unmentionables (today they would be called "knickers") at Wertheim's.

> Jumping Jack! Jumping Jack!
> Pull a string behind his back!

They don't buy Jumping Jacks.

Dunski's, in the big shed down by the harbor, is selling oranges cheap.

. . .

Up from the cellar comes, instead of the bicycle, the toboggan, for which you need a good toboggan stick to push yourself along.

Watch out, keep straight!

You need practice and strength to keep those toboggans moving. Only boys do it, never girls.

Outside City Hall there is a smell of frying sausages. Stalls have been set up selling little prune men and gingerbread hearts. Next to them stand the farmers' apple carts, with sacks over the wheel hubs so that nobody gets messed up. A cutting wind blows up from the harbor, and the farmers fling away their snot with their fingers and beat their arms around their bodies. The stout marketwomen keep little brass pans of glowing coals under the trestles.

A horse-drawn van, the "Black Maria," drives up to the police station. In the whirling snow, two policemen get out, wearing spiked helmets and swords, followed by a handcuffed, middle-aged man with a reddish beard.

"Stand back! Stand back there!"

The man is wearing a fur hat that is askew, presumably clapped on his head by one of the two hefty policemen.

Korli catches only a glimpse of him. To be in jail? Now? So close to Christmas?

But maybe he's a murderer. *If* a man is arrested, there *must* be a reason . . .

He's now a serf and I'm a lord,
What change has taken place . . .

Big snowflakes float down from the sky, and high up in the tower of the blue-black church of St. Mary's stand shivering musicians, blowing their trumpets as they have done for centuries, although it's probably haunted up there, according to the old chronicles.

On Christmas Eve a visit to Grandmother has to be undertaken.

Maria Martens lives in the old ladies' Home of the Holy Spirit.

The cells of the nuns who used to shiver here in the Middle Ages are reached by wooden stairs with carved banisters leading from the cloister. The cloister is whitewashed, as are the stairwells.

"Maria Martens," it says on the little name plate, all very proper, and you have to pull on a cord that makes a little bell tinkle over the door. Then Grandmother opens the door, bows to the "young master," as she calls him, and invites him into her room, which smells of unaired bed and a whole lot of other things and is darkened by the west wall of St. Mary's.

As Korli, like Red Riding Hood, hands her the basket of Christmas presents, she says: "Thank you very much, sir!" and curtseys.

When she suddenly took to appearing among the guests dressed only in her nightgown, the situation became intolerable and she had to be sent away.

"What must people think . . .?"

Holding your breath during this visit isn't feasible, for you can't get away that fast. Grandmother insists on telling you, as she does every time, that she once had a birthday on 8.8.1888. In her gray silk dress with its black piping and innumerable folds, she really looks quite beautiful. But her face: it is the face of a child, a toothless child.

Holding your breath isn't feasible, you're not let off that fast. You have to eat a cookie, and it is an hour before you are told: "Do come and see me again, sir!" and can at last walk down the stairs, slowly, sedately, speeding up imperceptibly, for Grandmother will be watching you until you have turned the corner of the cloister just where the wooden dove hangs that looks as if it had been removed from the roller coaster.

The Kempowskis don't go to church on Christmas Eve; it is always so cold in St. Nicholas's Church, what with the old gentleman in his wheelchair, how are you supposed to manage?

First of all the family gathers in the front room for a leisurely cup of coffee. Mrs. Jesse across the street does the same and gives her parrot a piece of sponge cake.

Father Kempowski has his hot-water bottle on his lap, behind him is the tin box containing shortbreads and Königsberg marzipan, which is really meant only for him. (The tin can be locked.) He will shortly be required to hand over some of this.

Anna is crocheting, so is Silbi. The Advent wreath with all four candles burning on the table, and Karl is sitting at the piano. He plays the familiar old carols.

Adeste, fidelis! . . .

"Here, Korl," says Father when Karl has played through all the carols, and gives him the key to the tin box. Karl is allowed to unlock it and take out a marzipan ring for each person, although he doesn't like it much because it tastes so stale.

Stribold is ready and waiting, ears pricked and tail pricked: he knows he'll be getting it very soon.

They still have to wait for the bell ringers who, with lantern and halberd, will be wanting their fifty pfennigs, and there comes old Ahlers stomping through the snow, he is just passing under the yellow light from the lantern. So it's almost time for the presents. While he is knocking the snow off his bowler hat in the hall, Silbi and Karl stand close to the sliding doors, which are just about to part.

The servants also assemble, there are six maids at the moment, and Giesi is in tears again.

"Well, let's get started!" says Anna, patting her hair. "Here we go . . ." (It really won't do for her to have her mother brought over every Christmas, with the old lady being so off her rocker.) The doors slide open and there stands the lighted Christmas tree, thickly hung with colored trumpets and harps by Bobrowski, the wheelchair attendant, and each goes to his place, without further ado.

Father remains seated in the alcove, where he has his red wine and such a nice view of the street. Would there be anyone passing by at *this* hour, he wonders? And what's that fellow up to out there? He also has a good view into the room with its Christmas activities.

What will Anni say to the necklace he has bought her? He'd really like to know that, and whether he chose the right thing this time.

> Oh let us hold forever dear
> Those Christmas Eves of yesteryear!

Or is there going to be another of those emphatic scenes because once again the gift hasn't come up to expectations?

A necklace like that, of course his father could never have given such a thing to his mother. The few pieces of garnet jewelry she had?

Nice, really, to be able to.

On his gift table Korli finds a bound volume of *The New Universe*; a steam engine made of brass with nickel-plated fittings, to which belong four tin workmen who tirelessly saw, grind, hammer, and bore; and "Lehmann's Automobile of the Future (Berlin, Paris, New York): Drives Across Land and Sea!" It is made of tin and, with the aid of little paddle wheels, actually does move on the rug and in the bathtub.

There are also some new cars for the clockwork railway, one for timber loaded with varnished tree trunks. It is a pity the locomotive has to be constantly rewound, and that when rounding the curve the whole caboodle tips over.

Silbi has already put her cooking stove to work, she is frying some sugar in a doll's frypan. Her mouth waters, although there is already a strong smell of burning.

The staff stand by their gift tables with their useful objects.

Giesi the young maid sobs sporadically, thinking of home, of Parchim, of the little parlor, with Grandpa, who was then still alive.

"Did you ever hear such caterwauling!" says Anna, adjusting the tortoise-shell comb that holds up her hair.

After a decent interval, the maids gather up their knickers and stockings and disappear into the basement kitchen, where they have their own Christmas tree, also decorated by the wheelchair attendant, twelve candles, one for every month—the big one upstairs has twenty-four—and if the Kempowskis upstairs would only be quiet for a moment they would hear the old Christmas carols coming up through the dumbwaiter shaft:

Chri-hist the Savior is come . . .

Now Father Kempowski calls his son over into the alcove and lets him have a sip from the glass of red wine, it's something like Holy Communion: ". . . No more cigarette smoking, d'you hear?"

He shows him how to clip the end of a cigar: "And the band comes off first—the thing around it." And when you're offered a glass of beer, first slosh it around in your mouth so it's not too cold in your stomach. (Perhaps we should've invited that little opera singer Linz—would she be sitting all alone in her room now?)

Up, down, a schnapps!

Old Ahlers sits in his wicker chair right next to the Christmas tree, his "cog-nack" in his hand, a gift cigar in his mouth: São Paulo, that's another place he's been to. Maybe, maybe not. But he's not thinking about that at present; he's thinking about the big mistake he once made. If he hadn't made that mistake, all those years ago, everything would have turned out differently. Meanwhile he's listening to the wheelchair attendant who knows some queer verses that he is now declaiming one after the other, verses meant only for adults.

When the wedding's over,
Do it over, over, over, over . . .

(Supposed to have been a phonograph record, with a crack in it.)

"He reigns, her reins, it rains," says old Ahlers in an effort to contribute to the conversation.

After this, Karl has to turn off his buzzing railway, for the wheelchair attendant is about to perform his "Kaiser Parade," as he does every year. He puts two spoons into a beer glass and marches around the table, clinking at every step: "Company, halt!" Clink . . .

Then he makes a speech about the Kaiser, which isn't bad at

all, and finishes up with the appropriate "Hip hip hurrah!" And he does this so well that everyone has to laugh and the dogs start to bark. (The only annoying thing is that he always puts his wad of chewing tobacco on the windowsill and you get your fingers messed up; he has been told about this so many times.)

Through the dumbwaiter shaft come the sounds of the maids laughing downstairs in the basement kitchen. There's no speech about the Kaiser down there, a different performance having just ended: "The Mistress," that play is called, or "The Old Girl."
  "I can see everything!"

The real Kaiser Parade takes place on January 27, on New Market. It's a very big affair. All the streets have been cordoned off to make room for the "Ninetieth," who are due any minute, and for the local dignitaries, who are brushing the snowflakes off their top hats.

From among the crowd all the dogs come running into the middle of the square and they start sniffing each other. There are furious whistles from all sides, and the bewildered dogs don't know which way they are supposed to go.

> Do you think, do you think,
> Little Jenny Wise,
> Do you think I'll marry you
> For the sake of your blue eyes?

There is the sound of distant music, and slowly the soldiers approach from St. Nicholas's Church, where the service has been held, up through Grosse-Wasser-Strasse, gleaming spiked helmets, red cuffs, and blue uniforms. Led by the ramrod-straight drum major. But the drum major isn't quite the first after all, being preceded by the custodian of the law, a policeman wearing white gloves, his waxed moustache twirled upward, his sword dangling at his side. In *front* of him, *beside* him, and *behind* him—boys, boys everywhere, hopping along or marching with exaggerated strides, waving to the ladies who are looking out of upstairs windows.
  The soldiers mustn't bat an eyelash, nor do they.

.   .   .

Karl and Erex are also looking on and admiring the Rostock regiment: the KAISER WILHELM, it's called, and has the number 90. Hence they are known as the "Ninetieth."

At home they reenact the parade with tin soldiers, Nuremberg tin soldiers made by E. Heinrichsen, in little brown wooden boxes, "Many Awards."

Choice Tin-Composition Figures

The Battle of Sedan is fought, with blue Prussians and the French in red trousers: lying and kneeling. Thirty figures for fifty pfennigs. There are also some "falling" ones scattered among the fighting troops.

The Battle of Sedan: eighty thousand prisoners—what a turning point through God's guidance! (Forsooth, this chicken is fit for a king!) The big fort is brought down from the attic, the towers can be lit up from inside, and the galvanized moats can actually be filled with water: this kind of toy is far more interesting than the tin-figure groups that Erex is usually given by his father—"The Rustic Joys of Spring," for instance, with peasants, animals, shrubs, and trees, or "The Resort," which includes a Grand Hotel, open carriages, candelabras, and lawn furniture. Erich's father is a professor. He doesn't think much of playing soldiers.

"Do you have to do that, my boy?"

He was once even seen at a Liberal meeting.

On September 2 the victory of Sedan is commemorated. A hundred-and-one-gun salute from the ramparts, and the parade winds through the entire city. It is headed by the veterans of 1870, in top hat and frock coat, some of them shiny with wear, for a frock coat is bought only once in a lifetime. Decorations and medals gleam on their chests, and they shoulder their umbrellas like rifles.

The marching veterans are followed by horse-drawn cabs carrying disabled veterans, some minus an arm, some minus a leg.

> Mrs. Quiver has a sliver
> In her tongue, in her lung, in her liver . . .

Behind the disabled veterans march the clubs, guilds, and other organizations, each with its own band.

> Come and see, come and see
> The lousy rotten infantry!

and each plays a different march.

And finally the schools, each with a fife and drum corps. In the lead the municipal high school, the yellow flag with the griffin billowing in the breeze, the young men looking sternly ahead—"My father is a pharmacist"—they are not just anybody. They all wear school caps, each class a different color: red, brown, yellow, white, and orange. Some of the teachers are in uniform, they are reserve officers.

On the heels of the high school come the primary-school pupils, *without* caps, of course, and they don't march quite so well in time. Exasperated teachers: "You'll report to me tomorrow after recess!"

Bringing up the rear is the "Wooden Clogs" school from Old Market, something of a raggletaggle; they say the teachers carry a cane up their sleeve.

Piping and drumming, with bands large and small, the parade emerges onto Sedan-Platz, a meadow in Barnstorf Forest. The place is swarming and seething with people. On the platform a much-bemedaled man is making a speech. Korli stands on tiptoe in order to see better, but his view is obstructed by the flags of the artisans.

Then the "Hymn to the Rhine" is sung, and after the great "Hurrah!" the ranks dissolve and the popular festivities begin. People settle down in the grass or go into the tents to drink beer and eat knackwurst.

If here's a pot of beans
And there's a pot of stew,
I'll turn my back to stew and beans,
I'd rather dance with you.

Rising above the busy throng are climbing poles crowned with brightly colored wreaths from which hang sausages, boxes, pocket-knives, and one pocket watch to each pole. The poles are of considerable girth, they are very tall and smooth. The boys who reach the top clutch the pole with one arm and finger the little packages and boxes hanging from the wreath. Naturally everyone wants the watch known to be there every year. With a tug it is pulled off and whish! you slide down, never mind the blisters.

Did Korli ever manage to climb to the top and grab himself a watch? Most of the boys have to give up half way. Once, when he was younger still, he took part in an egg-and-spoon race. Mr. Stoll the watchmaker took Karl's thumb and placed it on the egg: "That's the way to do it, my boy . . ." otherwise the egg would have fallen off after the first four steps. Mr. Stoll the watchmaker with his bowler hat and white Santa Claus beard, yellow under his nose from smoking.

By suppertime the crowds start back into town. Every streetlamp has a gadget spouting gas flames in the shape of Iron Crosses and Imperial crowns. The Blücher Memorial is surrounded by a circle of shallow bowls sending up red and green flames.

A fine drizzle sets in, as happens every Sedan Day, the people of Rostock expect this. The more thoughtful among them say it is the tears of the dead because people no longer care.

12 Yet Another Schoolmate

My name is Wesselhöft and I was born in Rostock. I suppose I'm a bit of a washout. Two wars and twice losing all my savings and finally to leave Rostock—it's not much fun. Of course, I often think of Rostock and of younger days, and of course I can well remember Sedan Day.

The Sedan celebrations were held every year in Barnstorf Park. It was a tremendous affair, what with all the organizations, clubs, and, of course, schools. There were speeches, and people sat about in the grass, and it ended with a huge fireworks display, really spectacular, with bonfires of old barrels, kindling, and burning wood shavings flying through the air, and we, the university and high-school students, marched back into town from Barnstorf carrying torches, and on New Market we threw them all into a pile.

As time went on, it didn't seem quite as impressive anymore, the whole thing. After all, it was the same thing year after year, we got pretty fed up with that "sworn enemy" psychosis.

The speeches were always the same, too, whether it was for Sedan Day, or the Kaiser's birthday, or the Grand Duke's birthday. One or other of the teachers would be sentenced to make the speech, someone whose turn it happened to be and who, as often as not, had no liking for all that toadying. So the result was often somewhat contrived.

It's over seventy years ago now, but I recall a physics teacher once speaking very topically about "protection of the environment," that long ago! He didn't use those words, of course, but he spoke about the conflict between "culture" and "nature."

He had been in the Alps, he said—he touched only briefly on Sedan Day and what it stood for—and on some beautiful rock wall in the Alps he had come upon a huge advertising sign for some brand of coffee, and hadn't liked that one bit.

It was because he pronounced the words "culture" and "nature" rather strangely—"*cul*turre" and "*na*turre"—and, furthermore, emphasized them strongly in order to distinguish them, that I remember the speech so clearly. Perhaps also because for weeks we students took every opportunity to repeat those two words, which had occurred so frequently in the speech.

Our school was a dilapidated old building where more or less everything was in poor shape: heating, ventilation, lighting, desks, yard, toilets, and ink. And our teachers were a bunch of uninspired old fuddy-duddies. The books we inherited from the others were always marked: "Watch for joke!" and of course it promptly came, and we would laugh immoderately.

One of them was called "Popsi," he always wore some crazy get-up. For instance, he would wear an old tuxedo with light-colored pants and a flowered tie. We were always making bets on what he would be wearing the next day.

(The name "Popsi" came about this way: at noon one day, when school was out, his daughter came to the gate and asked: "Has Popsi come out yet?" And presto! from then on that was his name.)

There was one poem I often had to recite in his class because I could put so much drama into it:

> Drusus let his Roman legions
> Through the German forests stray,
> But when the Elbe's banks he reached,
> A woman stopped him on his way . . .

or something like that, I can't remember exactly, he liked hearing that because I could recite it with such feeling.

Yes, the teachers were a bunch of old fuddy-duddies. Quite different from today: they even looked different—the way they walked, the way they stood, they personified the very idea of "teacher," the image of authority. Today when you see a teacher you think: *That's* a teacher? He looks more like a tramp. (Which of course isn't ideal either.)

> Drusus let his Roman legions
> Through the German forests stray . . .

We had to learn this rather odd poem.

Whatever for, I ask you, it has no artistic merit at all, has it? Take Mörike, if you like . . . I don't mean to say that now in my old age I would still read poems by Mörike: "Gently crept the night toward land . . ." or whatever. But I *might* do so if in those days, when we were young, we had learned some such poem at a time when we happened to be in the right mood.

No. No Mörike, not even Goethe, at most Schiller with his "Bell."

We also learned the "Song of the Good Man" by heart, whole generations of schoolchildren had to, a poem so warped in its bias and so inferior in its language.

And those Botany lessons! How much time was wasted on identifying plants, "papilionaceous" and "labiate" plants, and I don't know what all, sterile, dry, utterly lifeless. Instead of going out and enjoying some of those nice flowers!

Year after year, parents had to spend a lot of money on new textbooks, although by the end of the year we hadn't come anywhere near working our way through most of them. For Geography, every student simply had to have the unabridged Diercke, whereas the shorter edition would have done just as well. All that money for expensive compass sets containing so many parts that were never used. A *single* pair of compasses and *one* triangle would have been more than enough.

The Math teacher couldn't grasp the fact that a person couldn't grasp Math. For those he didn't like, he made life intolerable. "Well, Levy? Do tell us!" And then he would taunt him. Was he from Galicia and so on and so forth.

On the other hand this very man could be quite uninhibited.

When he had written something on the blackboard that he didn't like, he would wipe it off with his coat tail.

Mind you, the educational system also had its good points. Perhaps the most important was the immutable order of things. The time-table was valid for the whole year, come what may. I cannot recall the timetable ever having been changed. Even the extremely rare illness of a teacher was regarded as quite astonishing, and it was taken for granted that there would be a substitute. It was virtually unknown for a class to be canceled, and don't forget there were six or seven periods a day!

Naturally there were good teachers too. There was Mr. Lehmann, for instance, who had a very nice way of acquainting us with his-torical subjects: not merely the "War of Succession" or the "Treaty of Xanten," no rigid learning by heart of German, French, and English kings. No, he would ad-lib about how the Reich came into being and how the French destroyed Heidelberg as well as Worms and Speyer out of sheer wantonness. How we hung on his words! Sometimes he would bring along pictures to illustrate his theme. Like Emperor Henry IV's humiliation at Canossa, for example. He cut these pictures out of books and magazines and stuck them onto cardboard. I can still see the picture of the opening of the Kaiser Wilhelm Canal. Quite something, any way you look at it!

He also encouraged us to start collections of our own, and I can still remember using Mother's embroidery scissors to cut up all her *Ladies' Journals*, castles and churches, and what a walloping I got.

For a while I also went to school with Karl Kempowski. He was transferred to us from a parallel class, preceded by a reputation for being rather cheeky and lazy. The teachers tended to hold up their hands in despair.

And then that strange thing: when he was with us he almost reached the head of the class. They must've read the riot act to him at home.

I'd recognize him on the spot if I met him today as a schoolboy. He wore rather thick glasses, they were quite noticeable, and he had a deep voice.

I didn't like him all that much, he was a bit of a showoff, gold cufflinks . . . After vacation we used to ask each other: "Where did you go?"

"We went to Bad *Oeynhausen,"* he would say. That was something very special. "We went to Bad Oeynhausen." The likes of us stayed with our grandparents in the country, and young *Mr.* Kempowski stayed at a spa. "We go there every year." Oh well.

One day I even went to his house, I don't know how or why. I had tea there, with him and his mother. He had a pretty sister. And then there was also a gentleman in a wheelchair, he didn't join us at table. It must have been his grandfather. I've no idea how I came to be there. Perhaps because of my stamp collection. Even as a schoolboy I had a pretty impressive collection. (I had to leave it behind over there when I escaped in 1952.)

I remember his mother showing me her books upstairs, I don't know why. Would I come upstairs with her, she said: and wasn't it nice to have a library? And then she gave me a book by Wildenbruch, I had it till I moved to Darmstadt, in 1957. *Children's Tears* it was called. She was very distinguished-looking.

It just occurs to me: strangely enough, in 1921, at our class reunion, to which pretty well everyone came who could possibly make it, Karl Kempowski didn't show up. Young Mr. Kempowski, you see, was above such things.

1912: gone are the days when Karl plays "Tipple-Tapple" with his friend Erex on the street, or "Abo, Beebo," a ball game that goes according to the alphabet:

> Abo
> Beebo
> Ceedy-Reedy
> Dead-as-Doornails
> Eggs-for-Breakfast
> Flags'n'Banners
> Grit-Your-Teeth!

A ball game where you must take care the ball doesn't fall into Mrs. Jesse's garden, for she sits there all day long, fuming.

Gone are the days when Korli plays "Abo, Beebo" and swaps patriotic picture cards from Stollwerck chocolate bars for the album: "Heroes of the Spirit and the Sword."

> When does the child get
> Stollwerck Chocolate?
> When he gets up early
> and says his morning prayers.

Stollwerck's German Alpine Chocolate: "Won't make you thirsty!" Cards showing Arminius mounted on his rearing horse and urging his warriors on against the Romans, Frederick the Great who looked upon his princely calling as a sublime and sacred trust, and Goethe holding a book and gazing at a skull, that man over whom creative Nature scattered the entire cornucopia of her most glorious gifts.

Heroes of the spirit and the sword.

. . .

Now stamps are being swapped: England, France, and the German colonies: eighty pfennigs crimson-and-black on pink (SMS *Hohen-zollern* at full speed). At the office his father collects the stamps from his correspondence in a large envelope: pretty good, what mounts up there.

Nothing could be cozier than when Karl and Erex sit in the dining room with tweezers and magnifying glass: Does the German eagle have a large or a small coat of arms on its chest? Is the denomination in kreuzers or pfennigs? Are the stamps notched, perforated, or cut? Or

DFUTSCHES REICH,

has the E not been clearly printed on the brown three-pfennig stamp (too funny for words, when you think of it!)?

The edges of the stamps have to be intact: if the serration isn't perfect, it does make a difference.

When Giesi comes into the dining room with the napkins and the knife rests and wants to set the table—Giesi from Parchim who is no longer the least bit anemic—she is sometimes allowed to look through the magnifying glass to see whether the coat of arms is large or small, and the two of them look together through the glass, and finally faces get slapped and sting agreeably for a while, and from the dumbwaiter shaft comes the cook's voice: "What's going on?"

Needless to say, Erex is in love with the daughter of the house, who unfortunately never even looks at the stamps. The small, agile, plumpish Silbi already has friends whom she meets at the brand-new water tower built in the style of a Gothic tower.

Karl finds it a nuisance for Erex to be in love with Silbi. "How's your sister?" he is always being asked, and in addition to Erex there are others seeking Karl's company for a chance to be with her.

Up in the attic there is an old laundry mangle: Erex winds a clothesline around the rollers and ties a trapeze to it that he can sit on, then he swings himself out of the attic window and Karl has to lower him, and all of a sudden he appears outside Silbi's window, and she gets the scare of her life.

The linden trees in front of the house have grown taller, and the vine has crept up as far as the overhanging gable. 1912: it is a fine, hot summer, the sap oozes from the linden trees, and the long vacation is twice prolonged.

Korli goes swimming and plays tennis: "Five four! Change ends!"
A snapshot has been preserved, Karl Kempowski with his friend Erex, his friend standing, tennis racquet over his shoulder, Karl astride a chair, his arms along the back, his shirt sleeves casually pushed up, his belt containing a little pocket for coins to give the ball boys.
After the match they sit on the terrace of the Casino, jiggle their legs, and drink fizzy lemonade: watching the world go by.

Once, when Karl has just decided that his white flannel trousers won't "do" anymore, a group of demonstrating workers trudges past, including children and women, hungry, ragged.
Karl adjusts his trouser crease, he is puzzled, who are these people and what are they doing? Are they poor people? People who say: "Look at them batting around white balls!" when they pass the tennis court? People who drink vino and eat tripe?
The poor, as far as one knows, live down by the docks or in the Old Town: two rooms and a kitchen or even worse. In buildings where the people take pride in keeping the staircase waxed and as clean as a whistle: a potted plant on every landing. But as wretchedly poor as these people here, clenching their fists and spitting through the wire fence—as poor as these people here, that they're not, those people down by the docks. These are really in rags. Scum, or some such thing? Rabble?

That's something he's never seen before.

Plückhahn the porter, small and wizened, now there's someone "poor." Father Kempowski picked him up at Central Station, he was wearing his red cap with PORTER on it, groaning under the weight of a trunk. Now he is given a hot meal in the basement kitchen every Tuesday. He's a "widow," he tells the maids, and they think he's sweet and call him "Gramps." He never leaves without a packet of sandwiches, and he always gets a schnapps.

Or Chu-Ching, there's another one who's "poor," an old woman reeking of fish, with Mongolian features and greasy hair, who, if you can believe the maids, has never washed in her life. Chu-Ching comes every Thursday and sits in the coal cellar to drink her soup. (The maids won't have her in the kitchen.) When you walk past her, she gives a start and moves aside, although you have no intention of going where she is sitting.

Those are all "poor people," quiet and mannerly. But that bunch marching past the tennis court, so devoid of discipline or decency, so worked up.

Presumably the result of systematic subversion. It must be the Socialists we have to thank for it, those traitorous bastards.

Karl has only ever met one Socialist, broad-brimmed black hat, inverness, and all. When he shows up on the horizon, people say: "There goes that pinko." He is an editor of one of the newspapers.

These people want to overthrow the existing order, turn everything upside down, extraordinary that they should be permitted. By comparison Woltersen, the Liberal, seems quite acceptable.

Tennis and sailing, the Grand-Ducal Mecklenburg Yacht Club: the young gentlemen are allowed to sail the *Gaudeamus*, Consul Viehbrock's seventy-five-square-meter cruising yacht. The cabin, cavernous and dim, is comfortably furnished. The sunlight dappling the water outside is reflected in bright rings on the mahogany lockers. You put your feet up and help yourself to some soda water from a siphon.

They sail to Warnemünde and to Heiligendamm, the seaside resort of His Royal Highness. They stroll past the villas between forest and sea, past the grand-ducal country estates, and look to see whether "he" is there, and for the hundredth time Erex mentions that as a child he played here on the beach with two little boys, two ordinary little boys who turned out to be princes. They had been quite ordinary, like real people, and yet they were princes. Without a shadow of a doubt.

"Do you know that those were real princes?" he was asked afterward by his mother.

Far along toward the end of the beach, where nobody ever comes, they swim in the nude. Erex is a contortionist, he lies on his back in the water and arches his spine so that only his pecker sticks out of the water.

It is a great event when battleships, "dreadnoughts," lie anchored in the roads. Sightseers go out in launches to look at them. The battleship *Schleswig-Holstein*, for instance, a monster with three funnels and huge guns that sometimes rise and swivel: sailors are scrubbing the deck.

The Imperial Navy now has seventeen battleships—the young men count them off on their fingers—plus armored cruisers and any number of ships-of-the-line. Not bad for a start.

There are other diversions as well. At the race course a pilot is about to demonstrate his skill. Those contraptions that "fly"—or in those days just hop—are called "aeroplanes." Karl and Erex ride out on their bicycles to the race course where they see one of those windy machines that are heavier than air, as is always said, indeed considerably heavier. Half Rostock finds its way out to the race course. People make coffee and play bowls, whiling away the time before the demonstration with all kinds of "tomfoolery."

The police hold back the crowds so that only those in front can watch the aviator taking his place and testing his levers. In his reclining device he is not so much sitting as lying. There is no protection from the wind, he hangs right out in the open. The sputtering roar increases, and to the accompaniment of prolonged hurrahs and waving caps the biplane takes off, rises a bit, and heads inland. It flies over empty fields where no one can get hurt except the pilot.

"Proudly it waves, the Black-White-and-Red," the band of the "Ninetieth" belts out, and the gentlemen salute.

Then everyone waits for its return.

> I do declare. I do declare
> I think I see a bird up there.

Little boys shouting: "That's him!" But it's never anything, just single birds. Finally it happens, a small buzzing dot, and the airplane actually approaches, growing larger and larger, then descends toward the meadow to the accompaniment of general rejoicing, and bumps to a stop.

Another spectacular event is the visit of the Kaiser. Whole areas of the city are cordoned off, and blue-uniformed policemen with spiked helmets and swords maintain order and security even where there is not a soul in sight.

Karl mounts his bicycle and rides to Friedrich-Franz-Station. As he rounds the corner he can already hear the hoofbeats of the coach-and-four. It is an open carriage, and the Kaiser is sitting in it, beside him the Grand Duke, the "Graaand Duke" as the people of Rostock say.

Karl stands at the curb waving his hat, and the Kaiser raises his bejeweled right hand and waves back: No doubt about that, fantastic!

The Kaiser can also be seen on the cinematograph screen, flanked by his six sons, on his way to give his New Year's address to the troops in Potsdam. It is all a bit jerky and too fast because in those days the machine was still cranked by hand. The Crown Prince in his fur hat (with the skull and crossbones on the front) and one of his brothers in what looks like an admiral's uniform. The plumes wave in the breeze, and they are all laughing and happy.

· · ·

The first movie to rattle and flicker its way across the screen in Rostock is called *The Faithful Horse*. Next comes *The Chicken with the Golden Eggs*, the very, very first colored movie! The picture is lurid red and yellow, all over: the film is copied onto colored celluloid. Ocean scenes with ships are dark blue and snow scenes are green.

The "flicks": for the princely sum of five pfennigs you sit on a wobbly garden chair. The better seats cost ten pfennigs, and there it's like being in a little restaurant: tables with checkered tablecloths and waiters going around with trays of beer from the bar.

There are usually three persons sitting just below the screen. Their job is to explain the action and lend their voices to the leading characters.

"Now the-ah lips approach each otha and a-kiss in a-red-hot, a-passionate love . . ."

Sounds are supplied, too, barking and kissing. The audience imitates this with much smacking of lips, to such an extent that eventually the whole theater is in an uproar.

When nature scenes are shown, the somewhat overloud orchestration goes into action: it rattles away at "The Mill in the Black Forest" or the overture to *Poet and Peasant*, regardless of what appears on the screen.

There is a smell of wet coats, but when the show is over the boys stay behind to see it all over again.

Karl sees some programs three times, and Erex Woltersen even makes his own films. His father, the "liberal" Professor Woltersen who is so receptive to the new technology, presents him with a crank camera. Ludwig II seated on the terrace—wearing a bowler hat!—that's what he films, with the servants approaching him behind open umbrellas.

Karl, wearing a false beard, plays the part of the misanthropic Bavarian monarch. He covers his face with his hands and rushes down the stairs. "Ludwex the Secondex" they call it, and it's filmed in Rostex, by schoolboys, in 1912.

They raise the necessary money by selling their fathers' empty wine bottles. During vacation they go to Papendorf, where they earn money at the brickworks by pushing carts. Eight hours = two marks and forty-five pfennigs.

In the evenings they show their home-made films, in the canteen. After that, Karl sits down at the piano, and the Czech workers, men and women, dance and drink rose liqueur, five pfennigs a glass.

The young gentlemen wear check suits and starched shirts with gold cufflinks.

14 The Dressmaker

I am only too glad to write to you about my experiences as a house dressmaker; I started to do so once before, but I am a bit shaky these days and my hand doesn't always behave as it should. Besides, I am inclined to ramble, and that has been my chief problem. So today I will try to be brief, or I shall never get it done.

My name is Anna Dierks, I used to live on Lager-Strasse, and half the people of Rostock were among my customers, I don't mind saying that. I came to know all the prominent houses, Mrs. von Öhlschläger, for instance, on Graf-Schack-Strasse, Mrs. Besendiek, the Consul's wife, and of course Mrs. Kempowski—who didn't know *her*? I was always glad to be called in by her, I always liked it there.

"Oh," she would say, "my husband, my husband, if he only knew . . ."

I say: "Madam, it won't be as bad as all that."

Her husband was in a wheelchair, he was a rather repulsive person, grubby and unsavory! And no manners at all. I once heard him grumbling about lunch. "Anna," he said, "that beefsteak was as tough as a sexton's ass." I had never heard the expression, and I hope you won't be shocked, but he really did say it. And loud, too!

Once he said the cake was no good, there was too much flour in it!

Mrs. Kempowski, on the other hand, was always cheerful. She would stand in front of the big mirror and say: "Now make me look beautiful . . . It's a pity I'm a bit broad in the beam."

"Never mind," I say. "I know how to take care of that problem."

We got along very well, I liked going there, she was never petty, which is more than one could say of some of my other customers. Some of them were really quite outrageous. When I had finished a dress they might say: "By the way, I have another length of material, would you mind cutting it out for me? I can take care of the sewing myself."

There were some for whom you could do nothing right. Sometimes I would have to shorten a dress by a quarter of an inch and then lengthen it again by a quarter of an inch. I would say, "Certainly, Madam," take it home, and bring it back next day without changing a thing, and then suddenly it was right.

Or getting paid, that was another story. For weeks I could wait for my money, oh dear me yes! The more elegant and demanding, the more tight-fisted. Some of my customers never sent for me again because they didn't want to pay me what they owed. I would have to waylay them on the street. Such people are never at home when you call.

At Mrs. Kempowski's, things were not like that. She used even to invite me for a cup of coffee, I actually sat with her in the drawing room chatting about this and that.

The daughter, too, was quite delightful, Silbi she was called. When she was little she used to crawl around on the floor picking up bits of material for her dolls. I asked her: "What's your name?" And the little thing answered: "My name is Sorrow, but only in the theater Butterfly, otherwise I have a different name."

In those days one used to wear a little bustle under the back of the skirt, a *tournure* it was called. And Silbi once fastened two tapes to a doll's pillow and tied it under her skirt.

She was a bit on the plump side, very affectionate and sweet. Later on I made her entire trousseau, and what a trousseau that was, I can tell you! No expense spared. I was also at the wedding. I was there in the church, what a handsome couple they made!

The son, Karl was his name, well—was *he* a cheeky one! I knew him too from the time he was a baby. I made boys' suits also, and when it came to trying on and his mother said, ". . . Get undressed, Korli," he'd run like lightning into the bedroom and hide under the bed. No amount of cajoling or threatening would help.

Karl refused to come out, he'd crawl away into the farthest corner. His mother's patience would end by her sending for brooms from the kitchen, and with these we—Mrs. Kempowski, the housemaid, and I—would poke around under the bed; and that boy actually had the nerve to laugh!

In the end the bed would be pushed out from the wall so that we could catch him, and then of course he would get a *real* hiding.

I had a son myself, such a dear boy. He just loved the harbor and the water and would spend all his time sitting on Schnickmann's Bridge, watching the fishermen.

When he turned fourteen and left school, the question was, what was he going to do? I screwed up my courage and asked Mrs. Kempowski whether my son could be apprenticed to her firm. And Mrs. Kempowski went across to the old man and I can still hear him shouting: "Nonsense! Can't use him!"

There was no getting along with him. Mrs. Kempowski then brought me a large envelope full of stamps for my boy, as a kind of consolation prize.

"Here!" she said. "Can you be patient? I'll try again later."

And what do you know, after a couple of months she suddenly says: "He can come now, send him along to the office."

So she'd managed it, she'd brought the old man around.

My son worked for the company for many years, till 1939 in fact, and then he was killed right away in the war.

He liked working for the firm, even though he often complained about the old man. Sometimes he rode off on his bike at five in the morning, to be the first at the dock and tie up a ship. Mr. Sodemann often praised him. But the old man? Never. He was very unpopular with everyone. Oh I could tell you a thing or two! The way he chased the women!

One day he wanted me to sew on a button for him, here in front.

"Not me," I say. "You'd better ask your wife."

Mrs. Kempowski herself wasn't always cheerful, of course. Many a time she was in tears, and when I asked her she'd say: "Oh, never mind."

Then next day everything would be fine again. Oh, the bustle down there in the kitchen, they'd be running around, and pots would be sizzling and bubbling.

There was always a lot going on at the Kempowskis', you know. Some days I was sent away as soon as I arrived, it wasn't convenient. Some days I sat at the sewing machine in the next room, and then I could hear what they were talking about. One gentleman used to come often, Volkmann was his name, some sort of a professor I believe, he wrote the theater reviews. And when he spoke the others kept quiet. Later on I did some sewing for his wife, too, and she told me that her husband was writing a book: "When that's published, Mrs. Dierks, we'll be on Easy Street."

It was about life after death.

I don't know whether the professor ever finished that book. I would be very much interested and would buy it if only I knew whether it exists. Do you happen to know where I could get it?

15

In 1912 Robert William Kempowski buys an automobile, a four-seater touring car, 1908 model, right-hand steering; gate-type gear shift and hand brake outside on the running board, many highly polished brass fittings, comfortable leather seats, and a horn with a rubber bulb.

The car requires a chauffeur, of course, and when he brings the brand-new car around to the front door for the first time, Mrs. Jesse across the street pulls aside the drapes and pointedly shakes her head: Now she wouldn't be surprised if the same thing didn't happen to them as to Gütschow—that the Kempowskis are over-extending themselves and will have to get out of the villa. In that case would they, like Gütschow, come to her back door and beg her to take one of their thirteen clocks?

She won't be at home then, Mrs. Jesse decides that very instant. No, she won't be at home.

The touring car has a folding roof that stays down even when the weather is really too cold for that. (Cranking the motor requires care, the crank sometimes kicks back.) Scarves and traveling rugs are needed for these trips, and even goggles. Leather caps, too, for ordinary hats get blown off at that speed and, strangely enough, blown forward.

The automobile proves very useful for the many trips to Bad Oeyn-hausen that Mr. Kempowski now has to make, since his insidious disease, which is persistently diagnosed as some form of arthritis, necessitates cures in the "town without steps." There are parks there, and fountains with rising and falling jets, always changing, and a spa orchestra in the pavilion and many benches.

He is treated with thermal baths and massage.

> A baro- and a thermo-
> Journey to Palermo . . .

Father Kempowski in Oeynhausen? He sits in his wheelchair, his cane between his legs, leaning on the crook. His moustache has grown longer, his hair sparser.

"How, in what way?"

Ore from Sweden and coal to Denmark: that's the whole trick. And: invest the profits in buildings. Or perhaps in building a cinema? Out in the working-class district? The cinema, that's where the people should go, it keeps them occupied and they don't get silly ideas. In fact, they should even be given the money to go. I mean it.

The wheelchair attendant is always with him and entertains him in his own way: What so-and-so's doing these days, he says, and: So-and-so's died too.

His companion, a woman who knows how to handle him, is also always with him: "What d'you say, Mr. Kempowski? We're quite a pair, aren't we?" She is Jewish, and very pretty. Sometimes the wheelchair attendant is sent away. (Later, in Rostock, he will supply a detailed report.)

There is always someone with him. He can't stand being alone! He is particularly fond of the little Jewess and calls her his "violet." Every evening he gives her a posy, and the spa orchestra has to play something for her:

> Glow, little glow-worm, fly of fire,
> Glow like an incandescent wire.
> Glow for the female of the specie,
> Turn on the A.C. and the D.C.!

She tucks the blanket around the old gentleman, and the wheelchair attendant spins his yarns about the Franco-Prussian War of 1870, how a wounded Frenchman was lying in a ditch, still moving, and his comrade gave him another poke with his bayonet—"*J* never did that!"—and how a grenade once came flying at him, he could actually see it with his own eyes, and then—bang!—and how the splinter lay beside him, the splinter that ripped open his leg.

"Sir, I fought the war of '70/71!"

"And *J* fought the war of '80/81!"

This joke is repeated many times, many many times.

Father Kempowski tells how as a child he always went barefoot and had to address his mother as "Ma'am," and that once when he was plastered he had smashed a cab window. "This time I'll pay like this" (rubbing thumb and forefinger together), he told the cabbie, "but next time I'll pay like this" (brandishing his cane). His illness, he used to say, was probably the result of having kicked over garbage cans as a young man . . .

"Things like that catch up with you."

The "violet" laughs all night. The nights are so warm and pleasant. The lanterns are lit, and champagne bubbles in the tall, slender glasses. Another three full weeks to go.

"He reigns, her reins, it rains . . ."

Karl sits with them, smoking a cigarillo, rimless pince-nez on his nose. He narrows his eyes, and this turns the many colored lights into streaks; he puts his head on one side and makes the streaks grow longer and longer. Wherever could that little dark-haired person be, he wonders, the one in the cycling skirts? Could she have left already?

That's the kind of wife he'd like to have one day, a self-possessed, outdoor type who never has a headache or gives herself airs.

"Korli, don't gulp down your beer—you must slosh it around in your mouth first."

With his friends Erex Woltersen and Paustian the butcher's son, who have come here for the Sunday, he is engaged in so-called studies. For what little they can glimpse of girls' legs they have a whole gamut of descriptions: "billiard table" or "piano" legs. Later a special category will be added: "medium-thick poles, covering trenches, for the use of," to quote from the sappers' manual, and, later still, "dime-novel legs": first they *can't* get together, then they *do.*

But that's still some way off.

He is glad when Erex comes, and Paustian, the fat butcher's son who already looks like his father.

PAUSTIAN'S "SEVEN TOWER" BRAND SAUSAGE

Erex Woltersen is forever griping about his "old man" because the latter gripes about the Kaiser while at the same time aping him: that's the best part.

Karl is glad when they come, but he is also glad when they leave. Then he sits in the café or goes for a walk. Once in a while the chauffeur lets him drive the car, at night when the old man is asleep. He lends him his leather cap and the goggles and uniform.

"But don't drive too fast, Mr. Kempowski."

Along the highways, restlessly. In the beam of the headlamps, a cat: a self-possessed little wife is his dream. He sees himself sitting in a room, at a round table, under the warm glow of a lamp, and he sees her enter, simple, unpretentious, serious, and totally without airs. She pours him a cup of tea, and it is peaceful and snug.

Anna doesn't go with them to Bad Oeynhausen, she prefers to stay home, where she has absolute authority. Every Thursday she has her "At Home." She smooths down her waist, artists come to call, and students, and they sit in her elegant north-facing salon.

"How are you?"

"I never give it a thought . . ."

"How is your husband?"

"Oh well, you know . . ."

The grandson of the painter Böcklin is studying law at Rostock University, and he talks about his famous grandfather who was always so annoyed at the workers of a nearby factory: they were constantly doing their big business in his garden. And Marshal Ney's great-granddaughter sits there listening to it all.

. . .

Professor Volkmann, who has written a book on street names and is preoccupied with life after death, almost finishes off a pot of coffee by himself and consumes a whole pound cake. He calls Rostock "the metropolis on the banks of the Warnow" and claims to find a tremendous interest in art there as well as profound scholarship.

While he explains that Stein-Strasse is called "Stone Street" because it happened to be the first paved street in the city, Anna embroiders the big tablecloth on which all her more important guests have immortalized themselves in pencil: the grandson of Böcklin, that highly poetic painter of genius, and the great-granddaughter of Marshal Ney. And of course Müller, the tenor from Hamburg, the man with the rolling eyes; he is just crossing the room with a glass of sherry for her.

Army officers rarely attend Mrs. Kempowski's "At Homes." Occasionally Captain Stahnke is there, Herero uprising of 1904: Captain Stahnke, whose "heroic ride" is discussed in every school. "Captain Stahnke's heroic ride." Some important message or other that he had to deliver: now pretty much of a lush, and the same goes for his wife.

Stahnke brings along a young officer of the colonial forces by the name of Schenk. Arthur Schenk. He wears elastic-sided boots and a small but nevertheless well-waxed upturned moustache. He positions himself beside the tall potted palm and asks whether the young lady of the house is present.

Yes, the young lady of the house is present. The young lady is running all over the house, looking first out of one window then out of another, sitting down for a few seconds in the library, opening a book, shutting it again, flushed from her heels to her head. (She had spent six weeks in a finishing school in Holstein, but the people there had really behaved abominably, they had accused her of carrying on a flirtation with the gardener.)

The flush runs throughout her body, and sometimes she laughs hysterically, even when she is all alone, and she deliberately arrives at her mother's "At Home" an hour late, always when everybody is about to leave.

Lieutenant Schenk fixes his monocle in his eye and detaches himself from the potted palm: So that's what she looks like, the young lady of the house. Not nearly as bad as he had expected.

Anna also gives evening parties—just so she's never alone!—and they drink punch and play cards for low stakes.

"Dewdrops shine in the grass of the night . . ." Müller the tenor, accompanied by Strahlenbeck, sings one song after another: "The Clock," for instance, and "Sounding Rhymes." Bulsky the student is no longer invited ever since he had the notion of describing the various types of abscess, their rampant growth, and their suppuration. It was made clear to him that his presence could easily be dispensed with.

Professor Volkmann is asked: "How do you manage to write a whole book—all by hand?" And old Ahlers, who usually sits a little apart from the others, must listen to calculations according to which he has already drunk up a whole shipload of cognac, a claim he wistfully disputes: "Maybe, maybe not . . ."

Later he will be telling the master of the house about all the goings-on here while Kempowski was taking the cure in Oeynhausen, in his quiet, genial way laying the groundwork for right-royal battles.

There are forfeit games too, of course: "What is the penalty for the owner of this forfeit?" Kneel before the stove or polish Mr. Schenk's monocle?

Lieutenant Schenk takes Silbi for a walk, Lieutenant Schenk from German Southwest Africa.

Oh lilala, oh lulala, oh Laila!

Across the Schiller-Platz they go, moths flutter around the gas lamps, and the scent of lilacs is wafted from the gardens. And as they stroll along Silbi wonders whether she wouldn't rather go home and dance? And when she dances she wonders whether she wouldn't rather go upstairs and read? And let the guests ask: "And where is your daughter, my dear?"

Now she is walking along here with Lieutenant Schenk.

The big fountain has been turned off, of course. Typical! Why in the world? Couldn't it be playing now and spraying into the lamplight?

Schenk is telling her about the Herero uprising of 1904 when the outposts were massacred by the blacks.

"They aren't human beings, you know, Miss Silbi . . ."

He had been through all that as a child, when he was ten years old, and he could still remember how the farmers' families floated in their own blood, sprawled and terribly mutilated.

Silbi imagines them lying there, "massacred," and she shudders at the thought, yet she would like to hear more and more about it. Every little detail.

Across the street another couple are strolling along, who could that be? Certainly not a real live lieutenant from German Southwest Africa.

When Karl is fifteen, the family arranges for the young man to receive some manual training. Books are hand-bound: *Jettchen Gebert* in crimson half-binding, and *Henriette Jacoby*, and model ships are built, fishing smacks and caravels, at a studio on Badstüber-Strasse, where the artist mixes his colors with a special bitters that is said to contract all the holes.

> At Cape Misenum stands a princely sight,
> A house with columns, mosaic floors, and busts,
> Accoutrements for feasting and delight . . .

For a while Karl even receives private tuition in literature, upstairs in Anna's charming library with its flowered wallpaper. His tutor's name is Lüders, and because he has studied Sanskrit he calls himself Ludarassa.

. . .

He comes at three in the afternoon: he places his briefcase on the little white table and buries his face in his hands—his eyes, how tired they are again . . . Then he gets up and examines the books on the white shelves, cursorily and shaking his head, and he opens his briefcase and takes out the imperishable basics of German education, bound in red and gold, and taps each book with his finger: "Now *here's* a book . . ."

They read Paul Heyse, and Fontane, and Goethe too: "My heart beat fast, to the stirrup I sprang!" And love is hinted at, and that a man must be prepared to wrench himself away, as a last resort, if, for instance, he realizes that she is not the "right" person—without a qualm he is entitled to listen to that inner voice and wrench himself away, even if her life is ruined by pain and grief and in the end she may have to sell ribbons for a living, like Friederike von Sessenheim. Yes, one is entitled to do that, for the reverse may easily happen too, meaning that *she* might wrench herself away, mightn't she?

All this is discussed by way of innuendo, and it is implied that many a young man has put a bullet through his head as a result of unhappy love.

As for the name "Kempowski," it comes from "Kempa," which is Polish and means *Büschel* in German (bunch), and "ski," which is the equivalent of the German *von*. Hence Karl-Georg von Büschel: he has every right to call himself that if he wants to.

At four o'clock, tea is served, and Anna joins them (she is embroidering some petitpoint, a courtly scene: a troubadour with a harp and in the background a castle), and the two grownups start chatting while Karl fiddles with his pencil.

They talk about Schiller, who, by virtue of the purity and matchless idealism of his whole being and creation, has become the sublime luminary of German literature; and about Nietzsche, whose noble spirit was destroyed by an incurable disease.

> The rooks are screaming
> As they fly with whirring wingbeats toward the town . . .

Ludarassa writes poems himself and he does it for her and can't
stop talking, and when Karl leaves the room they hardly notice.

And then dancing lessons. *"En avant!"* The dancing instructor,
called Frenz, wears patent leather pumps and has a way of tripping
lightly across the room.

"Now then, everyone over here, please!"

Mr. Frenz's dancing school on Friedrich-Franz-Strasse. A delightful spacious room with a parquet floor and a gallery where the
mothers sit with their knitting.

"Chaine anglaise!"

When it comes time to choose partners, the boys slither across to
the girls as fast as they can so they won't get stuck with the daughter of Mr. Krüger, owner of the delicatessen, she's so terribly fat.
(But she's a good dancer.)

They dance quadrilles and the "Kegel," a Mecklenburg dance in
which the whole group forms a chain that is rolled up like a snail:
it looks very pretty from above.

Frenz is bald, and when the boys use the wrong hand in the qua-
drille and get everything mixed up, he pinches them in the back.
(The girls too, of course.)

> Be like the shrinking violet
>   That shelters from the light.
> Be ever steadfast, loyal, and true,
>   Though hidden out of sight.

Korli's partner at the graduation ball is Valentine Becker. When he
asks her to meet him on the Oberwall, she laughs in his face. But
then after all they do go walking for two solid hours through the
Warnow meadows, silently, past the alder bushes.

> Friendship is better than Love,

she writes in his "poetry album"; it is gilt-edged, and he keeps it
under his mattress.

· · ·

In the afternoons you meet your friends "promenading" along Blut-Strasse between five and six, summer or winter. There are so many idlers sauntering past the store windows that there is hardly room for ordinary pedestrians. You sweep off your cap with a downward gesture, that's the fashion. Members of the Obotrite fraternity sweep off their red caps and the Mecklenburgers their green ones. The Vandals and the Redarians, the Balts and the Wingolfites: it is a colorful scene.

From time to time a lieutenant makes his appearance, blue tunic, black trousers. He touches his hand to his cap.

The girls expect caps to be raised and hands to salute, and keep count of how many times these gestures are meant for them. They're here by the merest chance, of course. They walk in twos or threes, their skirts lifted slightly to one side to reveal feet of varying daintiness.

When the shops close their doors—Schlüter's Military Tailors, with epaulets in the window, and Stüdemann's Lending Library— the promenade is over, and the girls hurry home, pursued to their front doors by their admirers.

An annual major event is the Navy Day concert at Mahn & Ohlerich's, the brewery, known as "Em and O" for short. It is invariably a fine evening, it has never been rained out. Karl and Erex find themselves a good spot near the bandstand. It is warm, and mosquitoes dance around the beer glasses. There are also some young ladies present, but they are accompanied by corpulent mothers and fathers with heads like bowling balls.

> You're off your head, my dear, to Berlin you must go,
> Where all the nitwits are, that's where you should go.

In the bandstand, Lentschow, the old white-bearded conductor, with his fusiliers, presents melodies from operas and operettas.

"Waiter, how much longer do we have to sit here?"

When the trumpet solo "Until We Meet Again . . ." resounds through the evening with all its flourishes and coloraturas, the audience is so quiet that no one dares to clear his throat, and the thunderous applause that follows can be heard as far away as the Kröpeliner Gate.

The concert ends with the battle potpourri. From various corners of the garden come bugle calls, battle noises, and cannon shots, produced by musicians hiding behind shrubs and in arbors. Gradually the racket blends into a battle scene with the whole band gradually joining in. Then when the drums roll and the trombones give their all, there is a sudden burst of fireworks. The first rockets hiss through the night and explode with a bang, scattering stars that evoke an *Ah!* from a thousand voices. At the end, entire flowerbeds appear in the sky, and the climax is a dazzling Imperial crown.

Karl and Erex observe the white-trousered gendarmes who are keeping back the curious spectators from the pyrotechnicians. They dream of the cavalry: Swinging your sword down onto the fellows who are shielding their heads with their rifles . . .

> And off the horse on either side
> A half-a-Turk is seen to slide . . .

But—mightn't they thrust their bayonets into the horse's belly and you would tumble off and be trampled on? The soldiers in the first wave are doomed in any case, and they are well aware of that . . .

On reaching home Korli tiptoes up to Giesi's room in the attic. He sits on the edge of her bed and tells her about the battle potpourri. She feels hot under the thick down quilt, and he unbuttons his collar.

16 The Family Friend

Rostock was where I had my first engagement. I had studied in Hamburg, and right after that I was engaged as leading tenor at the fine new Rostock Civic Theater. And not long after my first appearance, I met Anna Kempowski.

Femmes à quarante have their own charm: Anna Kempowski was a darling person, talented and generous to her fingertips. She radiated a great warmth, she was slender and of medium height, and she always had guests in her house.

On Thursday Anna was "at home," in her elegant north room, and there we all used to meet, Professor Volkmann, and Stahnke from German Southwest Africa, Mrs. Öhlschläger, and that little minx, what was her name . . . we'd meet at five, for tea, in her beautiful home, it was all very relaxed and amusing, a pleasant crowd.

You were always welcome at Anna Kempowski's, the whole town knew that. And it was a pleasure to go there.

As you were ushered in by the maid in her black dress, Anna would come toward you like a bright vision. She was so gentle, so enthusiastic, she would make you sit down beside her right away: "Now do tell me, how are you? Have you any worries? Can I help you in any way?" And then she would push the cake toward you or pour your tea with her own hands (a gesture I have adored ever since).

She could tell from your expression what mood you were in, a botched rehearsal, the intrigues of one's dear colleagues: she would soothe you and had a way of talking you out of your black mood. The other guests would stand aside, regardless of who they were—

and there were all kinds of people there. Rostock had a university, writers and scientists of every persuasion—all these guests would stand aside, and for a while you were the undisputed central figure, until you had regained your composure.

How often she used to do me little favors, either social or very practical ones: on coming home from the theater I would sometimes find a letter with a kind message and more often than not with something crisp inside, a small or sometimes even a large bank note. Yes, I am not ashamed: in those days, artists like myself had a hard time making ends meet and one had to go very carefully and was dependent on fortune and favor.

It was quite something, I must say, to be patronized like that by a society lady. Later, in Berlin, I had a similar experience, although, of course, the wealth and corresponding luxury there were much greater. In Berlin, too, one used to be invited—I recall one evening at the home of the Danish ambassador, but that was really more of a nuisance—by that time such things were no longer as necessary as in frosty old Rostock, which in winter was really the boondocks, and one tended to take it for granted: established artists—and in Berlin that's what I was—frequently receive such invitations, and one accepts that kind of thing as no more than one's due.

Goebbels incidentally—but that's another story, I suppose.

It is so depressing for a young artist to get into a cab after the performance and be driven "home." I mean: what a contrast. Only a few minutes ago, bright lights from all sides, people in full evening dress, waves of applause, and the artist the center of attention, and then: groping one's way up the narrow staircase, tiptoeing past the landlady's door—"Is that you, Mr. Müller?"—Oh God, now she's going to open her door . . .

Dreary, windy Rostock, Number 8, Kleine-Wasser-Strasse, I can still see it, a sagging old building with a landlady who hadn't really wanted to rent a room to "stage folk" as she put it. Twenty marks a month including breakfast. (Once when I had crept upstairs with a girl, there were *two* eggs and *four* rolls on the breakfast tray next morning.)

During the first few years I used to always go to the Stage Door

restaurant after the performance. There I would sit at the round
table with my colleagues, under paper lanterns and fake grapes,
drinking my wine, each of us laying it on thicker than the next, and
everyone kept telling the same stories, and one listened patiently because one dreaded going "home" to the dismal room from which
there was no escape.

So when I met Anna Kempowski, things changed, I saw her sitting in the stage box and knew: you'll be taken care of—that wonderful house and the sophisticated atmosphere . . . That's what
an artist needs. The Rostock Civic Theater wasn't large, how many
seats would it have had? Five hundred perhaps? Nor was it the best
opera in its class, but Rostock produced good average work, the
management was imaginative, and often the seemingly impossible
was made possible. Just to think that the entire *Ring* was performed in Rostock!

The number of colleagues who used Rostock as a jumping-off
place for a great career!

No, I had a wonderful time, and the fact that it was so wonderful
I owe in no small part to Anna Kempowski. After the premieres—
and this was taken for granted—we would all drive to Stephan-
Strasse, and there we celebrated, and how! There was always a
long table, with lighted candles, set for twenty or thirty guests, it
made not the slightest difference in that house. Plates were changed
and glasses refilled: the kind of life they led in those days wouldn't
be possible today. No one could afford it. A cook and so-and-so
many maids, and everything always tiptop!

After supper we would all go over into the salons, and the guests
would sing or recite.

Year after year a dove descends from Heaven . . .

Strahlenbeck at the piano—he later went to Mannheim—and then
we'd sing duets, and the guests stood or sat around us.

Incidentally, the piano in that house had a transposing keyboard,
very practical if a singer could no longer reach the high notes, then
the pianist would simply shift the keyboard a half-tone lower. (I
have never seen anything like it since.)

. . .

Silbi was just a young thing in those days, a charming child, temperamental and very uninhibited: I can still see myself in the garden, my God! The smell of lilac and honeysuckle . . . She was standing on the steps, the steps of the veranda, slightly above me, and I with my height had put my arm around her waist and was singing softly to her, when she suddenly threw her arms around my neck, a red-hot little bundle . . . The next thing was, she even came to my dressing room, but I wouldn't go for that, Anna wouldn't have understood.

A most unusual family.

The son, "Korli" as he was called, kept rather more in the background. I really don't remember him that well. When he was a little boy he once crawled under the table during a big dinner party and untied the shoelaces of all the guests, which naturally caused a lot of merriment. A little North German boy, pale and unprepossessing. Then later on strangely shy: always in the background. Was it his father's illness, I wonder, did he worry about it? Who knows? Might he have thought he had a germ of it in himself?

Not everyone is able to accept a situation like that so easily: one's father permanently confined to a wheelchair. That *must* have affected him, his father forever needing help, bring me this, bring me that . . . and always someone to undress him.

When we were having a party, Karl would stand around in the doorway, and he seemed almost to be shaking his head a little. Never joined in the dancing either, later when he was older, when we were having a good time, when we did a polonaise through the whole house, over tables and chairs . . . He never once joined us.

One day I saw him in town, he must have been fourteen or so, and he actually raised his hat, as solemn as a churchwarden! One was almost tempted to grab him by the shoulders and say: What the hell's the matter with you anyway?

It must have been his father, his father's illness. The deterioration and the feebleness. Perhaps also a growing desire for dignity in a home overflowing with entertainment.

· · ·

I recall Robert William Kempowski usually sitting in a corner, with a hot-water bottle on his lap. An original, if you like, and in spite of his illness fantastically active, but—how shall I put it—a bit vulgar somehow. Strong language and flippancy, both direct and indirect. Enjoyed behaving like an *enfant terrible*. He liked to offer chewing tobacco to the ladies, for example, wouldn't they care to try? he'd ask them. And then of course he insisted on speaking only dialect! And in *those* circles!

It was embarrassing, too, when he felt himself called upon to entertain us! Then he would pick up some dog-eared old volume and read aloud from it, haltingly and with amateurish emphasis. Someone like Fritz Reuter, that boring old dialect writer. Or, worse still, he would recite poems from his schooldays—to us, professional actors! A cobbler should stick to his lasts, as they say. Really, it was almost an insult!

And then there were times when he would send for his violin and play folk tunes for us. His friend, a lame duck if ever there was one—Ludwig Ahlers, his name was—sometimes actually egged him on, and the two of them would get a kick out of our agonized expressions.

And the stinginess of the man! A thrift that bordered on avarice: "businesslike," he used to call it, he was being "businesslike."

How often he let our tongues hang out for champagne, he simply refused to come across with it.

I remember one occasion, at dinner—we were having roast pork with crackling—when he took a knife and cut off the *entire* crackling for himself; it happened so fast that all we could do was gape.

Most of the time, of course, he wasn't there, thank heavens, he was in Bad Oeynhausen taking the cure. When he was in Rostock he would usually gather up his magazines around nine o'clock and have himself put to bed: there was a general sigh of relief all around. Out came the champagne, and the corks popped, and the younger women could move more freely, for when he managed to grab one of them, old Mr. Kempowski, God knew where his hands would land.

Many, many times we would drink the whole night away, just to show! And in the morning the whole lot of us would go upstairs to the old man's room and wake him up with glasses and bottles in our hands.

I never had any trouble with Mr. Kempowski—mind you, I usually kept out of his way. He had a way of looking at me through his pince-nez, "fixing" me and sniffing audibly—thinking, I suppose, that he could embarrass me because I happened to be coming in from the garden with his wife.

But of course I also knew—what *everyone* knew—that he had something going with that little minx, what was her name, and that he couldn't say anything, *because* of that.

When you saw husband and wife together, the old man in a suit that always seemed much too big for him and Anna a handsome figure (although showing some signs of age in her face)—not very tall but well built and always beautifully dressed, with fantastic jewelry—you simply couldn't fathom what kept the couple together.

I've no idea what she saw in her husband, a man who had arrived from Königsberg with nothing but a briefcase under his arm. On the other hand, when you see the photos taken of him as a younger man, maybe you can understand it after all: that vitality, and that sensuality going straight to the heart of the matter. They say she courted him herself, as a young girl, Strahlenbeck once told me that, and of course a girl should never do that. She would stand looking out the window when he was on his way to his office across the street—in those days he was still a junior clerk—and she used to stuff little notes in his overcoat pocket.

Yes, the marriage lasted. Strange. Mind you, he was a very shrewd man and extremely smart. When she was on the warpath, he would withdraw. Avoid her.

Many a time I'd come to her late at night, in all weathers, through the service entrance, which was left open for me, and then we would have supper together, in her charming sitting room, with the lights turned low. Always the choicest delicacies. The old man upstairs must have been listening, but what could he do?

Anna looked after him devotedly, it can't be said often enough. She led a life of sacrifice: "No, first I must go to my husband

. . ." How often she was heard to say that. Although—perhaps one should touch on that here—I mean, she was no angel in the conventional sense, her own past had not been without episode. And the fact that she nursed him so selflessly—there were some quite repulsive aspects to his disease, he had hemorrhoids as well, and they would burst—may have been largely a self-imposed penance. She once indicated, I'm not sure whether I should mention it, she once indicated that it was *she* who had . . . that *she* was unwittingly the one who had infected him. How else is it to be explained that during all those years she . . . After all, she was a wealthy woman, she could have left him. But no! In spite of all her esthetic refinements, to put the old man to bed every night and sponge him down with lukewarm water? Without a word of complaint?

That it was *she* who had infected *him*—to be quite frank, she even told me that once herself, and appropriately enough under rather piquant circumstances.

Oh, those wonderful years in Rostock. Then, right after the war, I went to Berlin, plunged right into the twenties, and we lost touch.

17

In 1913 the Kempowskis travel to the Baltic, to Graal. Oeynhausen, Berlin . . . all well and good, but it's time for the whole family to do something together again.

Graal lies between Rostock and Stralsund on the Baltic coast—"with a sandy beach and excellent surf," according to the prospectus. It is a small seaside resort with only a few hotels and pensions. Five marks a day, all inclusive.

The Kempowskis have wardrobe trunks, which the two porters, Fritz and Friederich, rope onto their backs and stagger up the stairs with. They are like regular closets, these huge monsters: on one side hang the dresses, and the other side is fitted with drawers for underwear and jewelry. The proprietor ushers them personally to their rooms and opens the windows, while Fritz and Friederich accept their tips, baring heads.

Father Kempowski is already installed in an armchair, he is in pain, nerve pain, and he is all sore down below again, and he has to pass water, urgently. It doesn't suit him at all, here on the second floor, he would much rather be at ground level, he feels imprisoned here—where is the bell, he wants to know, otherwise he'll feel imprisoned.

After a commode has been brought and he has been seated on it, and Anna has washed and powdered his behind, he begins to feel much better.

What's on the menu today, he'd like to know.

Pension "Waldperle," Pearl of the Forest: meals are taken at a large, common table in the glassed-in veranda—table d'hôte. Honey-colored flypapers hang from the ceiling, with flies stuck to them, some of them still moving their legs or wings.

When a new guest arrives, a new face—stumbling over the door-step, of course, and hence tripping forward into the attentive circle —the proprietor shows him to his place and introduces him to the other guests.

"The napkins are here on the right."

When the Kempowskis show up for the first time, with maid and wheelchair attendant, whispers are exchanged: Who can this person be? . . . can't walk properly? . . . jerks his legs so queerly? . . . supported on either side? The two females, on the other hand, mother and daughter, the woman still definitely a handsome figure and the daughter a cuddly little thing, a pretty face and a nice plump little figure. (Besides: they arrive by car, and that tells you a thing or two.)

Karl, the pale-faced youth, arouses no immediate interest.

When the guests are all seated, the waiters start serving. Sometimes they begin at the lower end of the table, sometimes at the upper end, and sometimes in the middle. No one is to say that he is always the last to be served.

> . . . They all ran after the farmer's wife
> Who cut off their tails with a carving knife.

Table d'hôte—some of the guests don't care much for this, eating at a long common table, they would rather be at separate tables, whereas others are very much in favor because it enables them to meet people with whom they can discuss the weather or politics.

Every day the guests dine as if it were a wedding. Father Kempowski tucks his napkin into his collar and plants knife and fork upright in front of him: "Ain't ye got a few lingonberries for me?"

He'd like some cranberries, that's what he's used to, after all they grow right outside the door here!

But of course he can have cranberries—why, they grow right outside the door here!

. . .

There is bouillon with egg drop and tiny dumplings, piping hot, a fish course, a meat course with vegetables, a salad, compôte, and dessert. Every wish is catered to, and the proprietor looks through the serving hatch and is pleased: he actually loses money on the food, but he makes it up elsewhere . . .

Father Kempowski strokes his moustache, and such is his appetite that his forefingers scratch inside both ears at once, and he says: "Gimmie some of those taties . . .," he really goes for those little new potatoes, they soak up the gravy so nicely.

Mother Kempowski can't resist, and Silbi heaps so much onto her plate that one can only wonder in amazement: Wherever is the girl going to put all those spareribs? She certainly doesn't show it, does she?

The dashing gentleman from Berlin sitting across from her, with dueling scars on his cheek, keeps shaking his head and finally makes the following pronouncement: "Man should practice moderation!" and pointedly serves himself a very small portion.

"Don't you like it?" he is asked, with a full mouth.

Ludden Lücht, the waiter, has noticed that the young lady enjoys her food, and serves her the biggest plaice he has. When Silbi has finished the plaice she reads the motto on her plate:

> Let them tell the tale—
> I've eaten a whole whale.

Karl has just turned fifteen. At table he blossoms: he has perfect manners and is adept at polite conversation. Do they have regular outdoor concerts here, he asks, he'd be interested to hear, can anybody tell him? The elderly ladies ask him about train connections or what the weather will be like tomorrow, what does he think? The young gentleman is so well brought up and makes such a good impression—a bit pale and unprepossessing, mind you, but he always holds the door open so nicely and he does play the piano beautifully!

"Not a bit like the young people of today!"

"Does the man have a lot of hands?" asks a little girl with a ribbon in her hair when once again after dinner he rattles off

Sinding's "Rustle of Spring"; and Karl closes the piano and lifts up the little miss: "Well now—and who do we have here?" and puts her on his shoulder: Giddy-up! Giddy-up! And he teaches her to play a little tune with one finger.

After the midday meal the guests retire. Father Kempowski is put to bed; he has bought himself the book *Quo Vadis?* in Rostock, and he reads a couple of pages. He tears a strip in the last page and folds it over as a bookmark. And then he goes to sleep: How good it feels to be clean *down below*. And the cool bed, it really feels very good.

His wife sits on the balcony, indignant at the racket coming up from the hotel kitchen. A sun umbrella has been put up for her, and she is reading the letter from Müller the tenor that she found waiting for her. And her face relaxes, for the letter says he misses her very much and that the little Linz person was atrocious again.

Through the half-closed bedroom door she can hear her husband's snores, and now she comes to that somehow elegant turn of phrase, at the bottom, in the P.S., and at last she has time to analyze it and decide whether it really means what she so joyfully thought it meant at first reading, which had of necessity been very hurried. So nothing has changed, she needn't worry.

In the reflection of the glass-paneled bedroom door, she looks at herself sitting there under the white umbrella, the dainty white lace collar and the wistful eyes.

Behind her the tips of the pine trees move slightly. Perhaps it would be a good idea to lie down for a bit after all.

Silbi roams around restlessly. First she goes upstairs to her room, pulling herself up by the banisters, of course she can't sleep now, in this heat, so downstairs again, into the lounge, where there's nobody, where only the flies are buzzing. Should she look through the dog-eared magazines, or should she stroll for the hundredth time along the two or three streets, past the hotels and pensions where the sound of snoring comes from every window?

She is furious and bad-tempered, and she eats one toffee after another. They are real English toffees, when she was little they used to be called "dentist's delights."

She would much rather have stayed at home and gone to Warnemünde every afternoon. That lovely beach promenade and all those elegant cafés! And now she's stuck in this neck of the woods!

Most of the furniture in Karl's room is painted white. On a white table stands a white vase containing a flower, and under the wardrobe are his boots and shoes, side by side according to height, with the bootjack at the end.

A leather writing case lies on his table—"Correspondence"—gilt-embossed and with lots of little pockets inside.

"Dear Erex, What a shame you're not here now, there is/are plenty to look at here!"

He keeps letters in it, a precious one from Valentine Becker written before she moved to Dresden with her parents, and photos, tickets, stamps.

Karl pushes the table under the window; beyond the treetops sparkles the sea: he reads Valentine Becker's only letter again, for the umpteenth time. No, they yield nothing more, those lines, they have been explored in every direction: only on the envelope, at the point where the stamp has slipped a bit, is there still a shiny place: Valentine Becker moistened the stamp herself, with her own tongue.

In a locked compartment of the writing case Karl even keeps some verses.

> The sun descends, the heavens darken,
> A song within my soul I hearken:
> > 'Tis vanished!
> Oh vanished are my youth and dreams,
> And Life is duty-bound, it seems.

Such are his poems at age fifteen, and he has to take care that his sister doesn't find out, she's always poking her nose into everything: he can just about imagine her derisive laughter.

. . .

He has to be even more careful with his sketch for a tragedy: it is about a mother who ignores her son and prefers his sister. Holding a glass of wine she wafts across the stage (that's how he has written it down), and she laughs in his face: "You? You were only an accident! . . ." (That had actually happened to him.) And the son leaves the room only to hear the laughter and banter of a depraved society.

He is not entirely satisfied with his work. He stands by the window looking down on the maids who are scouring wooden tubs. At this moment Friederich the bootboy emerges and slaps their bottoms.

Perhaps it's time to get a new pen and pencil set or better paper? Perhaps writing would come a little easier then?

After a week one feels quite at home here.

Graal is surrounded by forest. To get to the beach, one must first walk for a quarter of an hour through the forest along narrow, springy paths that are slippery with old pine needles. Pine trees sway like masts against the sky and the scurrying clouds. There is a smell of stinkhorns, the mushrooms that grow under the wild raspberries.

With a pocketknife one can carve a boat out of bark, bore a little hole in it, and stick in a twig for a mast. It is left to the imagination to fill the boat with people sitting in the little cabin, around the table, their calloused hands on their knees, looking at each other, these people, solemn, with none of that easygoing frivolity.

Every morning, when Fritz and Friederich are cleaning the long row of shoes down in the yard, before the painters have set up their easels beside the storm-tossed pine trees along the beach, Karl swims in the still silent sea, and Stribold comes with him. The water seems quiet and smooth enough to walk on, and the beach is deserted. Seagulls pick their way about and run away from the tiny waves.

With quiet rhythmic strokes Karl swims far out, parting the smooth surface, a wedge forming behind him that gets wider and wider and finally fades away. When he has swum out far enough, he turns on his back and plays "dead," with minimal movements and cradled in coolness. The gray morning sky and the distant edge of the forest like a straight line. Stillness all around, only Stribold back there on the towel, whimpering.

After his swim Karl dresses carefully, and under his jacket he flexes his muscles, yes, they are already a little harder. In the afternoon he'll go for another swim, far out where nobody can see him, that's what he plans to do.

Silbi is not so keen on swimming. She sits in the café eating apple turnovers. She is surrounded by a number of gentlemen looking on. They wear white suits with black pin stripes, and straw hats secured to their lapels with a black ribbon because of the wind. Perhaps they could slip away to Rostock, to the Barberina, the gentlemen have carriages at their disposal, they have only to snap their fingers, and one of them even has an automobile, he's from Africa, Mr. "von" Schenk, as he is known, he's among them too.

"How about it? Wouldn't you like to slip away to Rostock?" says Schenk, placing one foot on a chair.

While Anna Kempowski is writing long letters, Father Kempowski has himself wheeled along the promenade. "Don't hold it against me, I'm from Reval." The wheelchair is secured, and the attendant sits down on a bench provided by the Society for the Improvement of Local Amenities, they read the papers from top to bottom, and then the girls strolling by are surveyed and assessed, the cane with the two lenses attached coming in handy.

"Look at that one!"

And strange jokes are cracked.

In the morning various young women in charge of girls' classes pass by,

> To journey is the miller's joy,
> To journey is the miller's joy,
> To jour—hur—ney!

They practice marching in time, the girls shouldering little canes.
They are dressed in sailor blouses and navy-blue pleated skirts.

"He reigns, her reins, it rains . . ."

As they approach, the wheelchair attendant stops telling jokes and
Father Kempowski stops twiddling his moustache. He raises his
hand in salute to his navy-blue peaked cap. So help me! There are
some cute little dollies among them!

He doesn't want to miss a thing, that Mr. Kempowski, he must
always have his "perspective," as he puts it. The young lady, for
example, who at about a quarter to twelve regularly rides by on
her bicycle, a tennis racquet strapped to the carrier: that little
bottom is really admirable. How annoying that Karl, that good-for-
nothing, never has anything to report. Not once. What does he do
all day? Where does he hang around?

Karl? Karl is an expert at swinging his walking stick. He wears a
check suit and spats over his shoes. Every day he goes to the
tourist bureau where the names of arriving spa guests are publicly
displayed. Through his pince-nez he studies the list very carefully,
nor is he the only one to do so.

One day Karl is taken out by a fisherman who rows his boat with
one oar. And out at sea he slides his net into the water, where it is
held up by cork floats. Slowly the fisherman rows in a circle, dragging the net behind him. When he pulls it in, Karl is amazed at all
that is picked out of it. Gasping for air, the fish lie in the bottom
of the boat, slapping their tails with waning strength. The plaice
positively flutter: never yet has any of them regained its freedom,
except for the baby plaice, they are thrown back, they aren't worth
bothering about.

In the evening Karl stands on the pier, his dog beside him, Stribold,
bought at the fair for thirty pfennigs.
"Dear Erex, The evenings are fabulous! You stand on the pier

and let the fair sex file past you!" He watches the sun gradually sinking into the sea: you could swear it was jerking! Not until it has disappeared does it all become truly beautiful, the whole sky blood red, just like in the picture "Sodom and Gomorrah," where the artist painted the sky exactly like this.

Beside the life buoy, which hangs in a glass-fronted case, and a little box containing a hammer for smashing the glass, stands a gentleman with upswept hair; he is also watching the sunset.

> Keep sun in your heart
> Come rain or snow . . .

He is a poet who has a cottage here in Graal. He carries his *Simplicissimus* magazine visibly in his coat pocket. Karl knows who he is, he has observed him before. Once he even saw this man pulling out a little brown notebook and jotting down something in his own hand!

Perhaps, why not? Perhaps one could go up to him one day and show him some of one's own work? Perhaps he'll give one a long, serious look, and nod wordlessly, or say: "I have been waiting so long for this moment, for someone to come . . ."

Perhaps they are of incredible value, the lines one commits to paper every evening?

But perhaps this man will give a whinnying laugh and say: "Don't bother me, sir!" That would be less pleasant. "Surely you must be aware that I cannot be disturbed." *That* would certainly be less pleasant.

In any case, why not a cautious greeting? A hint of a nod that could also be interpreted as a nervous twitch—that will show whether or not he would care to be approached. And why not buy a copy of *Simplicissimus* and carry it visibly in one's pocket: "Ah, you too?"

"Compasión," now Karl is smoking these things himself: there is a picture of a woman on the lid, cutting up bread for hungry children.

When he drinks beer, he does so in great gulps.

·   ·   ·

A slender blonde with her hair parted in the middle appears one evening on the pier, Grethe de Bonsac from Hamburg; father: import and export wholesale (that's what it said on the visitors' list) : she has come to see whether the fishermen catch anything. Taking the fish off the hook must be terrible.

When the red float disappears beneath the surface, that means a bite.

Part Two

The poor? There have always been people, of course, who were unable to cope with life. They were what you might call failures.   K. F.

Poverty was something that really didn't strike us in those days, perhaps because one simply didn't notice such phenomena in one's youth, or turned one's back on them.   L. P.

In our village the poor were somehow taken care of, one way or another. Mind you, there were some old women who had little enough to eat and were poorly housed, but their poverty was really not all that conspicuous.   M. M.

Tenement houses for the poor were all built alike: one room at the front, then a windowless room where they slept, and the kitchen at the back. That front room was used only on special occasions.

Typical of those people was their determination to keep the staircase as clean as a whistle.
    S. T.

The local poor lived in the almshouse. As children we used to take them their dinner on Sundays, exactly the same as we had ourselves, a roast hare or a roast of venison. They would say: "Oh my, what nice things you've brought . . . !"

They would make that meal last several days.

The essential part was the gravy.   K. S.

For as long as I can remember, a man used to work in our garden and was paid precisely one mark a day. That's what he lived on.

That wasn't right.   C. J.

I was born in 1903, and my upbringing was very patriotic.

"Ever victorious . . . !"

that was us, the "privileged," and

"Boiled potatoes every day!"

that was the others; we were well aware of that.

G. F.

Our skates were buckled on by old men for two pfennigs.   T. J.

Alcoholism was rampant among the poor.

S. K.

To our left was a street of single houses where professors lived, and to the right was a street where the "guttersnipes" lived. Since my father was in trade, I wasn't classy enough for the children of the professors, whereas for the "guttersnipes" I was *too* classy. I was always in a dilemma, which way was I to turn?   R. S.

My playmates were the children of an artisan's family in the neighborhood, although they couldn't always play with us since they had to help their father. He produced china doll heads that were set out to dry on shelves, were then painted by the children, and finally taken to the factory to be fired.   A. C.

We were plagued every day by tramps. Generally they begged for anything we could spare, but often they also asked for something to eat because they were genuinely hungry. I would watch them as they ate and be glad when they enjoyed it. For me those were poor people who deserved our pity. Our maids did not always share my opinion.   s. o.

We had one maid called Katharina, a regular factotum of whom we were all extremely fond. When one day she asked for an increase in wages, maybe twenty-six marks instead of twenty-five, my father was furious. "The unions are ruining us!" he shouted.   G. F.

18

Hamburg 1902: Wilhelm de Bonsac has his office on Grosse Bleichen
—importing English wool, exporting German textiles—and lives in
the suburb of Wandsbek, although Wandsbek is in Prussia and the
money earned in Hamburg should really be spent in Hamburg, as
Hans and Bertram, his two brothers, point out.

"Don't you agree, Willi?"

And they look at each other and shake their heads.

Number 7a, Bären-Strasse: a big house with Wilhelminian timbered
gables. From the round attic window a flag is hung out on the
Kaiser's birthday, black-white-and-red, the good old German flag.

In the hall stands the family clock, 1885, a wedding present from
Uncle Bertram, with the carved coat of arms of the de Bonsac family:
goblet and grapes.

Bonum bono—the good to the good.

De Bonsac, a Huguenot family ennobled in the sixteenth century.
As a cupbearer, their ancestor had, according to the family papers,
been able to distinguish quickly between good and bad wine. This
story is repeated over and over again, and the family believes it can
detect the French element in their blood: so sensitive and overbred—
superb.

Of even greater importance than the house, which was built with
the profits of a single year (1902, when every Japanese insisted on

wearing a navy-blue suit), is the big garden, for Wilhelm de Bonsac is a passionately keen gardener, he has a "green thumb" as his brothers say, flowers and vegetables, everything thrives as if in Paradise. In the opinion of a neighbor who sometimes comes to look, much of it is fit for an exhibition. A lily with thirty-three blooms, would you believe it?

And the fruit! On the sunny side of the house, morello cherries; and on the lawn, apple trees of every variety, grafts have been procured far away.

Under the fruit trees long tubes have been sunk into the lawn for fertilizing, sunk into the "drip ring" because that is where the fine hair roots are. At the far end of the garden stands a barrel containing blood and guts from the butcher, seething and stinking and actually forming bubbles. When it is ready and the weather looks like rain, Mr. de Bonsac strides to the back and scoops blood into the watering can. Add water, stir well, and then carry it to the fruit trees and pour it into the tubes. Oh that will do the fine hair roots so much good, how greedily they will suck up the nutriment! It will reach the trunk and the branches and from there every single fruit.

If the rain fails to materialize, the stench is, to be sure, considerable, and Wilhelm is a little shamefaced, there being no lack of reproaches. (The neighbor slams the veranda door, also the windows, one after another.)

The harvest is predictably good. Plums, apples, pears: one year the Louise-bonne yields seven hundredweight of pears. The fruit is all carried down into the cellar and laid out on homemade boards: it has to be turned every few days because of the blemishes it would otherwise acquire. The rest is packed into chip baskets, covered with sacking, and given away to the brothers, to Hans and Bertram.

"I say, Willi, what marvelous fruit you have!"

Hans, who has an English wife, and Bertram, handsome Bertram, whose marriage has been blessed with six equally handsome daughters.

Apples, pears, and plums are served for dessert, on fruit plates similarly painted with apples, pears, and plums, artistically combined with other fruit: with exotic pomegranates, melons, and grapes (as explained on the underside of the plates). "What superb fruit!"

There are apples, pears, and morello cherries. And those wonderful heart cherries! In springtime a great cloud of glorious blossoms! A thousand humming bees collecting all the riches of spring without a moment's rest.

He who rests, rusts.

Yes, one can learn a lot from these industrious insects, and one does.

At ripening time, pieces of string are knotted together and strung between house and tree. At the top of the cherry tree a rattling can is tied to a branch, and from his bed Wilhelm de Bonsac rattles this can to scare away the starlings: Those pests! They peck at every single cherry!

With each passing day, Mr. de Bonsac rattles his can at night more furiously because with each passing day the starlings fly off more lazily and eventually are not even bothered when Mr. de Bonsac appears at the window in his nightshirt, clapping his hands and shouting curses. (That's not the way it was meant, that those pests, like the lilies of the field—they sow not, neither do they reap yet the heavenly Father feedeth them—should gorge themselves! In their good-for-nothing way!)

"Oh Willi!"

If they would at least eat up the cherries, those starlings, but all they do is peck at them! There was really no need to refuse good old Bertram when he turned up with ladders and the intention of climbing into the tree with his family to gorge themselves to their heart's content.

No, they no longer fly away, those starlings, despite frantic rattling and cursing; all they do now is twitch their wings. And even that is mere courtesy.

Instead, nightshirted figures now also appear in the windows of the neighboring houses, and they shake their fists—but not at the starlings.

. . .

Beside the blood barrel lies the compost heap, a very important object. Every drop of dishwater and every vegetable leaf is carried there. The heap is divided in two and shoveled from right to left and then from left to right. It is mixed with soil and lime, and with phosphorus, and the large lumps have to be broken up with the fingers.

The neighbor looks over the fence and shakes his head. Now what does all that mean? But one day he also starts a similar compost heap and also carries every vegetable leaf to the back of his garden, and the pulp from squeezed red currants, as well as withered leaves and sawdust, and his mouth waters when he looks at his beautiful pile.

Oh yes, the garden. The gooseberries and the currants, the beans and the radishes. Lovely, the way it all grows. For breakfast, home-made strawberry jam, on the table spread with a white cloth, under the birch tree planted by oneself! There's nothing like it! In the cellar the jars stand side by side, each with its own label, *when* it was bottled and *how*, that's something you can't buy anywhere.

"Willi, you're a lucky fellow to have all this!" say the brothers as they give him a wooden rake for the fallen leaves.

Yes, it had been a good idea to move out here to Wandsbek. So nice for the children, too! Hertha, Richard, Grethe, and Lotti, what a healthy, natural environment for them to grow up in! Always in intimate contact with growth and decay!

Obviously they're not allowed to run wild in the garden like Hottentots, that's quite obvious and they realize that: all that trouble Father has gone to . . . They can pick some of the red currants if they like, but certainly no strawberries!

"D'you hear that, children?"

The path leading past the strawberries is called the "path of temptation," and there are harsh words for anyone who succumbs.

Young as they are, each child has his or her own plot. They grow radishes, which their mother buys from them, sorrel, and spinach.

These plots are at the far end of the garden, and before any seeds are sown Father inscribes each child's initial in the soil and then sows cress in it, something he remembers from his own childhood: an $\mathcal{H}$, an $\mathcal{R}$, a $\mathcal{G}$, and an $\mathcal{L}$. Amazing how quickly the cress grows: what a charming idea!

And how easy it is to tell who is looking after his plot properly!

"Look, children," says Uncle Bertram when he comes with his family on Sundays. "There's a good example to follow!"

And out of his pocket he takes four candles and gives one to each of the industrious children, and to his own children, who are standing there silently biting their nails, he says that they will also be given candles if they do as they are told.

As soon as the garden is in good shape, some pigeons are acquired, glorious creatures, so single-minded and faithful. And the gentle sound of their cooing! The neighbor has some too, they always fly so prettily in circles.

Of course, Mr. de Bonsac builds the dovecot himself, in the cellar, rhythmically swinging his hammer: dum-dedum . . . For in the cellar he has a regular little carpenter shop, with bench and vise and drills hanging on the wall, arranged according to size like organ pipes, with various planes and saws and a glue pot that gives off a great stench. The building of the dovecot is a major undertaking, and the curses when he hits his thumb can be heard throughout the house.

The pigeons arrive in a basket, and the children stand on tiptoe and look under the cloth cover to see the pretty birds. They are picked up with both hands together and placed in the new dovecot, where they flutter around foolishly, dropping a lot of feathers from their plumage, and one wonders whether they should really be fluttering like that?

For a certain period of time they must not be let out of the brand-new dovecot, such was the neighbor's advice—but how can one possibly wait that long? The poor creatures! Birds? Locked up?

The dovecot is opened and—whoosh!—they are all back at the place where they were bought!

Nor does Willi have any better luck with chickens. They are stolen by thieves. A pool of blood and a cock's head bear witness to the nocturnal struggle. Wilhelm is beside himself with rage. He works himself up to such a pitch that his wife must admonish him: "Willi! That's blasphemy!"

There is nothing to be done about the thieves. Wandsbek is still Prussian, and when a gendarme shows up the thieves escape through a few gardens to where the Free City of Hamburg begins—the border can be seen from the change in paving of Hammer-Strasse—and beyond that point the gendarme may not go.

But when thieves steal all the silver—the forks, spoons, and knives, all polished and neatly packed in velvet-lined boxes, including even the magnificent centerpiece—and put it all into the best tablecloth (hand-embroidered by Martha de Bonsac herself) as if into a sack, and then deposit their excrement on the dining table, a dog is acquired: his name is Axel Pfeffer, and he is a schnauzer.

He listens attentively when he is told: "Bite thieves, right? Will you do that? Always go bitey-bitey if thieves come?" He listens attentively, and his hair bristles: Oh yes, he'll bitey-bitey the thieves, they can be sure of that, and growling ferociously he hurls himself onto the rug lying between dining room and living room and shakes it around his ears.

He takes his duties seriously, very seriously. He runs through the whole house like a policeman in case there should be anyone hiding there, anywhere. At night too, trot-trot-trot, through the whole house. He stops at every door and listens: downstairs on the main floor, where the only sound is the ticking of the grandfather clock, upstairs where the parents are snoring, hand in hand, at Richard the son's door, and those of the three rosy-cheeked daughters: Hertha, Grethe, and Lotti, and on the top floor outside that of the maids, Lisbeth and Lene, of whom one sleeps on her left side and the other on her right.

Trot-trot-trot: it is reassuring to lie in bed and hear the dog making his rounds; one stretches luxuriously, such a good boy . . . Let the thieves come! It would be really interesting if they did come; one might actually *wish* for them to come . . .

Part of the butcher's offal, the sinews and guts, destined for the fruit trees, is now set aside so that Axel Pfeffer can have a good chow-chow; he stands with his legs apart, that's how strong he is. A fine dog, a strong dog. It is a pleasure to groom an animal like that.

In the bathroom there is a bench; when Axel is shown his brush he jumps on the bench and lies down on his side. And when Mistress says: "There, now other side!" he turns over—whoops!— and closes his eyes.

"I say, Wilhelm, what a magnificent creature!" is what his two brothers say. And Bertram allows his six daughters to stroke the dog, which they do very cautiously and which Axel puts up with in silent meditation and finally with a yawn.

Bertram de Bonsac explains to his children how many different breeds of dog there are, and that afterward one has to wash one's hands, with soap and nail brush, because otherwise one might get worms.

The kennel is also homemade, with mighty hammer blows, as a companion piece to the dovecot: roofing paper on top, and a glance out of the window to see whether the dog actually goes inside, into his kennel. Yes, the neighbor has also seen that the dog actually uses his kennel, that he "accepts" it, as one might say, and from the window he congratulates Mr. de Bonsac on his achievement, with eloquent gestures.

Every day that God has granted, the whole family assembles for morning prayers. Father in his black suit, Martha, the mother, rather stout, Richard in his sailor suit, and the three daughters, small, smaller, smallest, all with braids, short, shorter, shortest. Lisbeth and Lene, the two maids, join the family although they are not actually obliged to: one of them tall and slim, the other short and fat.

> As on drooping herb and flower
> Falls the soft refreshing dew,
> Let Thy Spirit's grace and power . . .

Father sits in his chair surrounded by his bevy of children, and Mother pedals the harmonium. Lisbeth and Lene with clasped hands: Lisbeth the pretty one who can sing so well—sometimes a bit too loud, and she doesn't react to a gentle shake of the head—and Lene with the little humpback: she is a trifle obstinate, but no one can peel oranges like she can: the peel as an unbroken spiral or made to look like a water lily, the sections of fruit fanning out.

> The hen parades her chicks so soft,
> The stork has built his home aloft . . .

Oh, that's their very favorite song! It has fifteen verses, and not one is omitted. They always sing it and enjoy singing it.

Then come the prayers themselves, the "unabridged version" as the prayer book calls it on page 42, with numerous readings alternating with countless prayers. The "unabridged version" of the reading is chosen so as not to stint the Lord, so as to offer thanks for all the beauty and goodness one has received from Him, one still receives, and will continue to receive.

Hence much space is devoted to thanking. Thanking for the wonderful night, for instance, in which the Devil's cunning has not "gained dominion" over us, at which point everyone looks at little Richard, and prayers are said for practically everything that is not nailed down.

When Hertha is still quite little, she keeps shouting: "Amen, amen, amen!"—a story that is told over and over again with an indulgent smile: "Amen, amen, amen . . ." It is no use sending her out of the room, she promptly comes back in through the dining room.

Before meals, grace is said:

> O Lord, bless this food to our use.
> And us to Thy service.   Amen.

But only before the main meals: at the fully extended table spread
with a starched tablecloth, in the mornings when the canary,
touched by the sun, sings his first song, when the warm rolls lie in
the basket, the excellent honey and that marvelous red-currant jelly;
or at noon when the golden, piping hot broth is steaming in the soup
plates . . .

In the afternoons, when coffee is taken on the veranda, grace is not
said. There has to be a letup at some point, or it will get stale.

Otherwise:

> For what we are about to receive
> may the Lord make us truly thankful.   Amen.

Indeed: Amen! It's true. Shouldn't one be grateful for this superb
sausage, for instance, or for the fragrant farm butter? A vase of mar-
guerites and phlox stands in the center of the table, sharp-scented:
click! blossom petals fall onto the table.

During the meal Hans and Bertram are discussed, Hans with his
English wife, who is very, very nice, mind you, but, how to put it,
somehow foreign. Don't you agree? And: doesn't *want* any children? What is one to make of that?
    Bertram on the other hand with his six children, and all girls—
funny somehow, but nice too, somehow, charming and all taking
after their mother, that quiet, gracious lady whose eyebrows meet in
the middle in such an odd delightful way.

> From His bounty He hath endowed us with grace . . .

Six daughters, always so strangely quiet, at most occasionally whispering but who, despite severe admonishments, bite their nails, incessantly.

Then the conversation turns to the stock exchange, whom one has
met there—"*Attention aux enfants!*"—and Father keeps an eye on
the children. Here good old-fashioned custom prevails, together with
Biblical austerity: butter *or* jam, that is the rule. When the children

spread jam on top of the butter, Father raises an eyebrow and says: "My child, you can afford that when you earn your *own* money." Butter *and* jam? Such extravagance . . .

It is finally suggested that they spread one half of the roll with butter and the other half with jam, then they can put the two halves together and get exactly the same effect.

"See, children? Isn't that a wonderful idea?"

And never more than two pieces of cake. And when the children say: "Oh dear, we're still *so* hungry!" the answer is: "If you're *hungry* you can go into the kitchen and eat some bread and butter!" And it is said severely. And the hand comes down on the table: No more than two pieces of cake. That's it. After all, cake isn't intended to satisfy hunger; and at dinner one has to finish what's on one's plate.

"Sit up straight!"

When the children simply can't eat any more and stare disconsolately at their plates, it does sometimes happen that Father will say in a stern voice: "You *can't* finish it? Really? Well, let me have it," and he will gobble it up himself.

When he has finished, he cleans his plate with his knife by systematically revolving the plate, which is then as clean as if it had been licked.

"I *can't* eat any more," one has to say, under no circumstances may one say: "I don't care for any more" or "I don't *want* any more."

"Don't care was made to care, don't want was hung . . ." that's what is said then.

There is no mercy. One simply has to like *everything*.

It is different if, mute and pale, one collapses in front of one's plate and manages to look pathetic.

Now tell me what's the matter . . .

someone says.

You're eating nowt?
You're drinking nowt?
Don't tell me you are sick?

That's what they say, and the child's forehead is pressed against a cheek. The child doesn't seem to have a fever, but one must be careful with a growing child; looks like death warmed over.

Maybe they should get some cod-liver oil again, that yellow stuff that's so nourishing? Or an afternoon nap with curtains drawn and a cold compress on the tummy?

"How about that, eh? Shall we be sensible?"

19 The Aunt

I was born in England, and at Christmas 1903—seventy years ago!—
I came to Germany for the first time, as a young bride, I can remember it as if it were yesterday. It was my first visit abroad. My fiancé,
Hans de Bonsac, met me at the boat, which in those days meant a
bold defiance of all prevailing custom, for traveling by train to
Hamburg with one's fiancé was regarded as highly unsuitable. So
it had to remain a deep dark secret, otherwise my reputation would
have been lost forever. Hans was very impertinent, you know, he
loved to provoke his brothers. Taking a taxi, for instance: You
couldn't do that! That was much too expensive! Or going to a café.
But he did it anyway. "But Hans! All that money!"

I can remember as if it were yesterday, the first time I met my
brother-in-law and his wife Martha and Willi de Bonsac on Bären-
Strasse in Wandsbek. Three little creatures came running toward
me: Hertha, Richard, and Gretchen de Bonsac. (Lotti was still in
her highchair, her face smeared with jam.) The little girls wore
tartan dresses with puff sleeves and had flaxen braids reaching almost to their knees. The boy bowed deeply, and the girls made a
so-called German curtsey by first bouncing up in the air, which
seemed terribly funny to me. Actually it was sweet, but so totally
different from English children.

Martha de Bonsac was quite plump in those days and expressed
a wish to lose weight. My innate courtesy prompted me to assure
her: "But you're not all that fat!" which caused a great deal of sup-
pressed merriment.

In those days, as was the fashion, Willi wore a big black beard
and in his black frock coat he looked to me as if he could be my

grandfather, although he was still a young man: in England beards had long since gone out of fashion. He filled me with enormous respect and awe. I found it quite impossible to address this lofty being as "Willi," so for many weeks I got no further than "Mr. de Bonsac" and the German "Du." I had no difficulty over the latter since I had not the slightest feeling for this distinction: on the contrary, I used the "Du" on the most inappropriate occasions.

The atmosphere I entered was totally strange to me; I came into a genuine, typically German family circle, a circle that belonged to a past generation and that today no longer exists. It was part of the old Germany and radiated a childlike simplicity and kindness, combined with a deeply religious attitude, which, although I did not share it, I found warmly satisfying.

Every morning the family would assemble for prayers. My brother-in-law would read a chapter from the Bible amid an atmosphere of general devotion, interrupted by little Lotti sitting in her highchair and every now and again hurling one of her wooden blocks across the room. That produced a mighty clatter, which gave her tremendous pleasure.

The grownups behaved as if nothing had happened.

My brother-in-law Willi was in the truest sense of the words a good man and aroused in me both respect and love. I have rarely known anyone of such childlike and devout faith, and his whole life served to confirm this. Often he would show me his beautiful garden with all the lovely flowers, or his heated aquariums, where air somehow bubbled through the water. Marcopodes and all that kind of thing. To please me he would feed them, give them worms. He'd lay the worms on a board and cut them into little pieces, and they'd keep on wriggling, and the fish would go crazy.

Hans was always provoking his brothers, for fun but also in earnest. Oh, what fights there were! "My dear Hans," they would say then, as if he were a child, and they would smile at each other behind his back, which made him furious.

What I never really understood was that Willi and his brother Bertram didn't support my husband in any way when he started his own business. They sat in a warm nest, and they could have easily afforded to let him have some of their customers. Those were difficult years.

There is a lot I could tell you about the family, fine, honorable people, but it would take far too long now. At the time I had the feeling of entering another world, an old-fashioned world but a good one where one could not help but feel at ease. Everything was so totally different from our modern world of today, a world that certainly has its advantages but nevertheless is far, far removed from those earlier days and their atmosphere.

On summer evenings one sits on the terrace, when the children are mercifully and finally all in bed, something that is becoming harder and harder to achieve because they are getting older and have an intercessor in Uncle Hans: "Come on, Willi, let them stay up for another five minutes . . ." In Uncle Hans, who has no children of his own, not one, and who permits himself many a liberty without —strangely enough—it having done him any harm so far. It remains to be seen how he will end up, this at heart so gentle, kind, and generous man.

No, it can't be permitted, five minutes, what next? They have to go to bed, and early, in order not to become neurasthenic or scrofulous; in order for the grownups to be given a rest, the longed-for rest after the strenuous exertions of the day. And lively Uncle Hans can most certainly not be allowed to say "good night" to the children:

> This little pig went to market,
> This little pig stayed home . . .

For he loves that kind of fun:

> This little pig cried Wee-wee-wee-wee
> All the way home . . .

And he tickles the children, which, of course, only serves to excite them even more. Instead of soothing them, telling them a fairy story or singing them a song! That's what happens when one has no children of one's own, one sees it all too rosily: Children, one thinks, children must always be merry and romping about.

Children who won't hear
Get boxed on the ear.

A pillow fight? What next? Such things can't be tolerated.

When the children are finally in bed, everything seems that much more enjoyable. One sits on the white garden bench, hand in hand, inhaling deeply. The birch tree—"Just look at it, Martha dear"— how graceful it is: a virginal tree, a tree like a young girl . . . The rock garden needs weeding again (where in the world do all those weeds come from?), and the shrubs need to be divided, next year . . .

A wave to the neighbor, who is also sitting out on his terrace, and more deep, joyous breaths, the "grateful evening mild," how lovely it is.

After half an hour the pocket watch is pulled out, the heavy gold one, the lid is sprung open: Now we've sat here long enough, "Haven't we, Martha dear? Come along, Martha dear . . ."

Now for a turn in the garden, if for no other reason than that the neighbor has gone into his house to fetch his French horn, which is somewhat less to one's taste. On the first occasion one had said a little too loudly: "How beautiful that was!" Now one's stuck with it.

The paths are called "pretzel paths," they are laid out in figures of eight and bordered with privet. Here one can wander about, always in a circle, now this way around and now that, one can stroll about with a pensive expression. All the goodness, all the beauty in the world, this glorious blossom for instance, isn't it wonderful? Holding it carefully in one's hand one says: "Isn't it won-der-ful, Martha dear? Isn't it? Hm? And one should always be kind to everyone, shouldn't one, Martha dear? Hm?"

Only when one meets someone are they too narrow, those paths, and one person has to step back, for to walk on the grass is really not "done" either.

The lilac arbor, at the far end on the right, although luxuriantly covered hasn't really turned out a success. One stops in front of it, perplexed. It is drafty, according to the brothers; besides, Axel Pfeffer always does his business in there, this otherwise so splendid a creature.

During the day Lene the maid sometimes sits in the lilac arbor, when there are peas to be shelled or red currants to be stripped. The children with their tight braids sit with her, helping her or making daisy chains.

> Up in the tree sits a wise old owl,
> Ruffling and puffling . . .

She knows strange poems, that little humpbacked Lene does:

> There came a riffle-raffle stick
> And stepped upon the owl's flat foot.

They make her say it over and over again. Really, very strange poems:

> Peee—says the ol' owl,
> Can't I sit and ruffle and puffle
> My riffle-raffle-ruffles?

Poems that, to tell the truth, one doesn't quite understand.

There is a family called Brettvogel, with seventeen children, living on Hammer-Strasse. And who is it who can rattle off all the names? Lene. A little hunchback, true, and a bit obstinate, but Lene has her good points too, you can't deny that, at least she knows all seventeen names of the Brettvogel family.

The girls practice "ball school" against the house wall. Head, arm, chest, stomach, knee . . . The ball is no ordinary ball, it is brightly painted, with flowers on it. The neighbor watches, he has no children, and then he tries it himself, ball school, but quickly gives up and runs after the ball, the confounded thing.

It's a different story with Lisbeth. She's not going to be done out of that. Ball school, that's right up her alley. She comes running out from the kitchen, between peeling the potatoes and stirring the soup.

Head, arm, chest, stomach, knee . . . a hundred and fifty times and
more, from behind her back and under her leg.

"Lies*beeth!*" someone calls. "Where *are* you?"

"Lies*beeth!*" as Father de Bonsac always says, and now and again,
when he gets the chance, he puts his arm around her waist.

("Come now, Wilhelm," his two brothers say then.)

That beautiful garden. Next to the lilac arbor there is a swing,
Grethe's favorite place, where one can daydream to one's heart's
content: about all the things that are going to happen, and how
glorious it's all going to be—Life—and what a dear good girl she's
determined to be, those are her daydreams, and she hardly swings
at all, and she has drawn one leg up beneath her. What a dear good
girl she's determined to be . . .

But also a madcap sometimes, when the occasion offers. Why
not? Suddenly run like the wind, for instance? Or later, when she's
grown up, steal away to the soldiers? Like Johanna Stegen? And
hand the cartridges to the soldiers . . .

When Grethe has such thoughts, she starts swinging in earnest.
And it'll be the Devil's own fault if she doesn't reach that branch
at the top of the pear tree with her foot . . .

Down below, Lene the maid is hanging out the wash, underpants
and bloomers, in order of size; she takes the clothespins out of her
apron pocket and reaches up high so you can see the damp patches
under her arms.

In the neighbor's garden you can see the wooden screen that he
has put up himself, but not what's happening behind it, no matter
how high you swing. You have caught a glimpse of the two lawn
chairs on the far side. And of husband and wife sometimes going
in there carrying cushions.

Sometimes the children play fire engine. Brother Richard is the
horse and is fed brown bread and sugar out of their hands, that's
the chief point of this game. (It's nice to have a brother, not so
dull as at Uncle Bertram's with his six daughters, who never do
anything but stand around and don't know how to play properly.)
Richard is harnessed to the little cart with pieces of string, and the

girls get in with whips in their hands. Then they pretend the alarm is sounded, and they tear around the privet paths, past the house and onto the street, scattering the passers-by. Once the shaft got caught between the neighbor's legs and, his coat flapping, he fell on top of them with much cursing and snorting.

"It was bound to happen."

A scratch or a cut, and off one goes to Mother, holding the bleeding finger aloft, and Mother opens her medicine chest, which contains boracic acid solution, bicarbonate of soda, iodine, arnica, and gutta percha, takes out some sticking plaster, blows on the finger, and sticks the plaster on it.

> Three days of rain
> Three days of snow
> And all the pain
> Away will go.

In the case of serious accident one is sometimes given a tiny lozenge to suck, or is allowed to lie in Mother's bed, which is credited with special healing powers.

The boys in the neighborhood are working-class boys, fun to play with, although they often use bad language and are not very clean. They wipe their noses on their sleeves . . .

Karl Meier asks the girls what they want to be when they grow up. "Needlework teacher!"

He brings them a pile of string saying: "If you can untangle this, *then* you're capable of becoming needlework teachers!"

In the horse apples on the street he shows them the nice kernels of corn they still contain, round and shiny and undigested. They pick out these kernels and eat them. They really do.

When the boys are there, Mother finds something to do in the garden: "Children, children! Calm down, will you? And *don't* run onto the strawberry beds again, d'you hear?"

But the boys are just too boisterous. They swing as if they were going to fly right over the top, they're just too wild!

Richard is no trouble, he has a quiet nature. Richard loves to ride up and down the figure-of-eight garden paths on his hobbyhorse, blowing his trumpet and looking left and right. He wears a helmet and carries a sword over his shoulder.

> If you want to join the Army
> You must first possess a gun . . .

Horse and rider are one: Giddy-up! he says, and snorts as well. At the back of the hobbyhorse are two little wheels that draw wavy lines on the raked path.

"Richard! Get off that path, it's just been raked!"

And not on the lawn either, of course, it's about to be mowed again by Josten, the white-haired handyman who lights the stoves in winter, shovels snow when necessary, and cleans the shoes, which he does with shoe polish, and then spits on it: a man for whom a special moustache cup is kept in the kitchen cupboard.

> A moustache glorifies a man.
> So care for it as best you can.

So Richard is not allowed to ride on the lawn either, he'd better do it back there around the blood barrel. No objection to that. "But not too fast!"

Richard is sometimes given a beating. Not because he crawls around the living room on all fours and keeps lifting one leg, observed by Axel Pfeffer who cocks his head to one side—no, but because he pretends to be Struwwelpeter: "I'll go out and you'll stay here" and puts Grethe's little thumb between the blades of the big dressmaking scissors, or because he puts a cut-glass bowl on his head like a helmet and can't get it off again.

"That's enough! Now you'll be sorry!"

First the bowl has to be wiggled off his head, which requires pressing his ears to his head with two cold knives; then he has to stand at attention and gets his cheeks slapped, left and right. Aunt Minna's lovely bowl! Which she glances at every Sunday! If that were to get broken! Doesn't bear thinking about . . .

From spinking comes spunking and from spunking comes a spanking.

The list of his silly pranks is a long one.

One Sunday morning he puts on his father's gloves and pretends to be Mr. Lempel the teacher, just when Father is about to go to church! Looks everywhere for his gloves, and Richard has them on: "I'm the king of the castle, and you're the dirty rascal!"

And then does the cane go to work! Into the study he is bidden, where the portrait of Bismarck hangs over the desk, the one that looks so much like Uncle Bertram. And while Father swings the cane rhythmically and deliberately, Richard can have a good look at the African things standing and lying about all over the room, for his father has been to Africa, indeed he has, in 1884, to Cameroon, where he had to be carried ashore because there was no dock for the ship.

After the chastisement, which often turns out to be slightly excessive, father and son kneel down together and pray to the Savior and weep and embrace.

Each child receives twenty pfennigs pocket money a week, and strict accounts have to be kept. "Balance," they have to learn what that is, and "carry forward": "This side is for Income, my child; over the top you write 'Income'; and *this* side is for 'Expenses' . . ." And always take care that you don't spend *more* money than you receive.

One third must always be left over, and Hertha is severely rebuked once for buying a bag of plums. "We have *such* lovely fruit ourselves, whatever were you thinking of, child?"

It isn't sound business practice.

The girls play for hours with dolls, in summer in the lilac arbor, in winter indoors. They have a dolls' corner with a dolls' washstand and dolls' bed, and all the dolls together make up a family: the doll father is called Mr. Schröder, he has a sailor cap glued onto his head. In his back there is a mechanism that can be wound up:

> Early to bed
> And early to rise,
> Makes a man healthy
> Wealthy and wise.

Mr. Schröder spends most of his time sitting on a wicker chair, that is to say, he sprawls since he can't bend his legs. Or sometimes he sits at the dolls' piano, which looks just like a real piano only it has chimes instead of real strings. The doll mother, that is to say Mrs. Schröder, who has long flaxen curls and glacier-blue eyes, supplies him with food, a plate of tiny lozenges, and a crust of bread representing a cutlet.

The doll mother is called Luise Schröder: she owns a copious wardrobe hung on clotheshangers in the wardrobe.

For a good child

There are five children in the Schröder family, they are constantly being put to bed and dressed and undressed. Sometimes they are scolded or laid across the knee and smacked with a dolls' carpet beater.

"Children! Do calm down!!"

Hertha and Grethe converse like mothers, in an undertone so as not to disturb the real mother who is having her afternoon nap down below. They are inseparable.

"What shall we cook today? Pork and beans?"

There is a cooking stove in the dolls' corner, but nothing is cooked there, it's too dangerous, and Lene, the humpbacked maid, is watching, she blabs. The curtains might catch fire, you see, or the rug. A little water, dyed with tissue paper, is all the cooking amounts to. A cloth lies within reach, to prevent spots on the polished floor.

Doll father, doll mother, doll children. Not forgetting the doll "Mary": the big doll "Mary." She was given to them by Uncle

Hans and stands in the cupboard, and they are only allowed to play with her on Sundays, when she is a "visitor." "Mary Gold" from England, "British born," something very special. She can open and shut her eyes, and when you bend her forward she says "Daddy!"

On Sundays they play with the big doll house: it is a spacious house with a grandfather clock in the hall. It has a timbered gable with a round attic window from which a flag could be hung on the Kaiser's birthday, if the dolls had a Kaiser and the girls had a flag. All the doors can be properly opened and shut, and there is a library with wooden books glued to the shelves. In the doll-house attic there is some real broken doll furniture, and in the cellar there are barrels. And next to the doll house there is a stable with real hay in the manger.

Uncle Bertram goes down on one knee and looks through his spectacles. If only they could have had something like this when they were young, as beautiful as this. When *they* were young they had an almost Spartan upbringing . . . a whip and a top—"at the very most!" says Uncle Bertram waspishly, and he dusts around the doll house a bit with his handkerchief. He tells his daughters that it's not at all a good thing, an extravagant toy like that, you can play just as well with an empty cotton reel.

"Can't you?"

And he hasn't seen them play with the tin merry-go-round for such a long time, and you can wind it up so nicely. He gave them that, remember? Why do they seem to have lost all interest in it?

Uncle Hans is quite different, although he does tease them about having permanent Christmas in the doll house because there's always a Christmas tree in it, glued to the floor.

And where is the W.C., he'd like to know.

And do they have a harmonium in there and hold morning prayers, he'd like to know that too.

Uncle Hans owns an opera cape and laughs smugly: "My rich

brothers . . ." he likes to say. He sometimes goes to a café, and once he is said to have actually been to a cabaret, and he a Hamburg merchant! His English wife uses safety pins to fasten her blouse, as her sisters-in-law report to each other, shaking their heads: "Poor Hans . . ." She's been in Germany three years now, and she still massacres the language.

"I'm sure she does it on purpose . . ."

When St. Michael's Church burns down, watched by the whole family from the roof, Uncle Hans brings the children a ball of molten glass, pulling it from his trouser pocket.

"Oh! It's still warm!" say the children, provoking roars of laughter. How funny they are, these children! And how charming they look, with their braids and their little starched white dresses!

He has a soft spot for the children, has Uncle Hans. He brings them putty, window putty, a big lump of it, and shapes it into all kinds of witches, devils, and ghosts, one more scarifying than the next so that they usually don't remain very long on the buffet. One morning they happen to have all fallen over and so are promptly thrown away.

Sometimes Hans de Bonsac takes the two older girls for a walk, one on either side, and tells them stories for which he has prepared himself in advance—about Gustav Nachtigal, for instance, who discovered the countries of Barken and Wadei and acquired Togo and Cameroon for the German Empire. And he demonstrates what the savages look like, and the way they eat human flesh! Sometimes *still* eat human flesh—here, little girls' cheeks, they must taste best of all . . . Or he tells them about the cholera epidemic of 1892, when there were no more coffins to be had. So many dead. That's right! He saw them lying there on the street. He tells them about a time when little eels are said to have come out of the tap.

These walks are with the girls, the boy Richard has his turn another time.

·   ·   ·

On one occasion he takes them to Ahlers' monkey theater, where trained monkeys and dogs perform entire dramas, with the dogs always hopping about on their hind legs as they push carts and carry away on a stretcher a dog dressed up as a criminal whom they have shot to death with great aplomb. He goes with the *older* girls, Lotti is too small of course.

21 Richard

Yes, you're right, my name is de Bonsac, so I do know the family whose history you are poking around in so persistently; I know it very well indeed. I was born in 1893 in Hamburg, and Hertha, Grethe, and Lotti de Bonsac are my sisters.

I was the only person of my generation to bear that name—Richard August Wilhelm de Bonsac is my full name—and this always gave me a sort of special position in the family. My father's two brothers either had no children at all or only daughters.

At table I sat beside my father, and when I was confirmed I was given the de Bonsac signet ring that I still wear: goblet and grapes.

The grandfather clock was also handed down to me.

It is a strange feeling to be the last male offspring of such an old family. I remember as if it were yesterday that many a time on my way to school among all the other kids I would mutter to myself: "You're the last now, you're the last now . . ." And I made up my mind to work very hard at school, although I'm afraid I didn't live up to that resolution.

From time to time my father would call me into his study and appeal to me in his own way. He would show me the big family Bible with all the names of our ancestors. "Emanuel de Bonsac, Heinrich de Bonsac, Kaspar de Bonsac," with slight variations in spelling, "Bonsacius" was one and, humorously, even "Bonesack." This Bible, which dated from the early eighteenth century, possibly even from the late seventeenth, bore impressive witness to the unbroken line of Huguenot pastors.

It was a large Bible, with embossed lettering and brass clasps, the capitals richly ornamented.

When I sat beside my father, listening to him, he would stroke the pages of that Bible with his broad, slightly trembling hands: "Look, my boy . . . you must always remember: we are not just anybody. Understand, my boy?" And then he would give me a graphic description of the flight of our French ancestors, at night by ship, with dimmed lights, and how the boatman deliberately delays the departure and the women weep and the men urge the boatman to cast off for the love of Christ! And they give him money and so on and so forth.

"Feet in the Fire," no doubt you know that ballad? That's what I'm always reminded of when I think about my Huguenot ancestors.

He used to tell me about Kaspar de Bonsac, the notary who took part in the Napoleonic War of 1813, and about Emanuel de Bonsac, the doctor in Ritzebüttel who operated on himself and used to fall asleep on his horse while riding at night across the moors. About Captain Becker, the pilot, who owned a monkey. And about the wives, the brave wives, bearing one stillborn child after another. Have you ever looked at a baptismal record? "Anonymous, died two days after birth." Children without so much as a name!

The way people found each other, how different it must have been in those days from today! First the carefree circulating in society, then the hesitation and the realization: Yes, *you* were made for *me*, and *I* for *you!* Not that trembling passion that sends the blood coursing through your veins, but rather the certainty based more on reason: Yes. Who or what drove me to attend that function at which I met my dear wife?

The joys of love and the sorrows of love, oh, I could tell you a lot, such a lot, and not only about the de Bonsacs. But young people don't want to hear that. Young people think it's "old hat."

They think: today, right now, if only love is consummated everything will be fine. No! That's only the beginning of suffering, that daily testing, not simply to throw in the sponge and clear out, but to stick it out, year after year. That's what etches the lines in your face . . .

22

Every year the de Bonsacs go to Süderhaff. Summer after summer. Süderhaff is a little place north of Flensburg consisting of a beach hotel with a coffee garden and seven houses lined up along the dune path right by the sea. Each house has its own garden and steps going down to the beach. Pastor Kregel stays in the first, and the de Bonsacs with their children in the last, the one with a flag pole in front of it flying the red flag of Hamburg. The house is small, five rooms and a kitchen, built of wood, surrounded by elderberry bushes. Tiny windows with shutters outside, painted green.

In the little rooms, sticky flypapers hang from the ceiling, and on the windowsills stand mauve "pans," glass bowls of "curds." You eat curds with black bread and sugar; very refreshing.

In front of the house a little garden with geometrically laid-out paths. It is kept scrupulously neat, this is the father's responsibility.

"I have planted a copper beech in the center of the lawn," he writes in the guest book. "I expect it to be regularly watered."

Every year the de Bonsacs go to Süderhaff: "Isn't it marvelous, children?" Every year in the summer.

Big hampers are packed for the journey, woven of willow branches and the top is covered with oilcloth to keep out the rain. The day before departure they are picked up by Josten the handyman and taken to the station on a handcart, along with the bundle of umbrellas, spades, rakes, and fishing rods.

Another wonderful summer to look forward to! How nice we are all going to be to each other, and how grateful for being allowed the experience! Not like the Brettvogel family with their seventeen children where, although Kaiser Wilhelm is godfather to one of them, Jack Spratt rules in the kitchen. Their place smells of herring, and the children sleep two to a bed!

The children play on the beach, bare-legged like the village children. But an eye is always kept on them from the house, to make sure they don't go too near the water or sit in the wet sand, which is harmful for this, that, or the other.

There are flat stones on the beach that can be made to skip over the water, and shells, washed smooth by the sea. Richard is an expert at making castles, he builds them right out into the waves, using seaweed and bits of flotsam.

"Splendid!" says Pastor Kregel. "I must say, you've made a really splendid job of it."

Inside it is a pond with a fish swimming around and around. And stuck into the top is a flag, and when the castle is submerged by the waves they salute.

Meanwhile the girls bake little cakes of damp sand, sprinkle them with "sugar sand," and sell them to each other for shells.

Bathing is a somewhat elaborate procedure, embarked upon only on the third day. They undress in a bath hut and in full regalia walk down the canvas-covered steps into the water, striped knee-length cotton swimsuits and ruffled bathing caps. Mother goes in first, she has the children passed to her one by one and dips them once, twice, three times, and they scream blue murder.

"Marvelous! Isn't it?" calls Father from the beach. "Isn't it glo-rious? Isn't it?"

Watch in hand, he checks to make sure that the children don't stay in the water too long.

"Children, are you tingling yet?"

A pleasant tingling is supposed to occur, according to the manual, and *when* it occurs it is time to leave the water.

. . .

Lisbeth, the maid who has been brought along from Hamburg, receives them on the beach and rubs them down with a towel. It feels as if one's skin is being scraped off.

"Lovely! Isn't it?" says Father, squaring his shoulders. "Glorious!"

He is the last to go in. Headfirst he dives into the black water, and the children, now warmly wrapped in woolly garments, still shuddering from their last sobs, watch him do all those things. He even swims under water; they wonder where he'll bob up again.

In the late afternoon, when there is no one else on the beach, the fishermen's children bathe, naked as the day they were born. They run straight into the sea, without any preliminaries. The little Hamburg girls stand behind the dunes and look on. They are wearing white dresses, and the fisher boys down below are brown.

Behind the house the ground rises steeply into the forest, and in the forest there is a meadow, a snake meadow which the children are told to stay away from. Snakes lie around there in thick coils, mating.

"Don't you *dare* go onto that meadow!" they are told.

Beyond the meadow is a stand of massive blue-gray beech trees. This is where Pastor Kregel holds his service on Sundays. He looks like Saint Boniface, with his white hair blowing in the wind.

> So take me by my two hands
> And lead me on
> Until I reach those blessèd lands,
> Forever on.

His daughters sing hymns that, to their ears, breathe a deep, exultant love for Jesus, and Pastor Kregel runs his fingers through his beard as if through a harp.

"What Does Christ Mean to You?" is the title of a talk he gives one weekday, commendably enough. "He doesn't have to do it, does he?" Thus Father de Bonsac to his wife, and he greatly admires the dedication of this man.

At times Pastor Kregel can also be whimsical. He is so enthusiastic about Süderhaff that he rewrites popular songs in order to sing the praises of this hamlet.

> From Greenland's icy mountains,
> From India's coral strand,
> 'Tis Süderhaff that reigns supreme
> With all her golden sand!

The fishermen don't attend his services, they go to church in Hardborg where once a month there is even a sermon in Danish. If you climb up one of the beech trees you can see the green spire. The bells can be heard too.

Smaller bells hang from a tree in front of the house of a retired ship's captain. They are made of glass and hang from the branches, and when there is a breeze they tinkle against each other like fairy bells. The captain has hung them up himself so that he can hear a storm approaching. Then he fastens all the windows and doors.

Another kind of music is produced by the organ grinder who from time to time comes strolling along the beach. He won't be given any money, he knows that, just coffee and bread.

He carries his barrel organ on his back, it is inlaid with mother-of-pearl, and to play it he stands it on a stick. The children hop and turn, but they agree that the music is really rather "awful," not as pretty as in Hamburg, where there are also quite different organs and much more up-to-date tunes.

> Come and dance, come and sing.
> Fairest in the land!
> Be my queen, be my king.
> And hold me by the hand!

The man drinks the coffee and puts the bread in his pocket. "For my children," he says.

"D'you really have children?"

"Yes." He indicates with his fingers: "Three."

So they bring him a second piece of bread and a third. In return he feels along the side of his barrel organ where there is a worn brass button, under a leather strap; when he presses it, out comes a new tune.

It is Lisbeth whom they ask for the bread, not their mother. Mother believes that this kind of scrounging should not be encouraged, honest work behooves a man, and of that there is more than enough to be found.

When he is out of sight, the children play barrel-organ man, and they also play at being very, very poor; but after ten minutes Richard has had enough. "That's it!" He finds it too dull to be poor. Straddling his spade he rides along the beach, then he does some more work on his castle (who wouldn't want to defy the waves?), digs trenches, and dams the receding water. He isn't alone, boys from the other houses help him. They decorate the tower with a patchwork of flags.

One day a man with a straw hat and a Vandyke beard appears and asks permission to photograph the children. Mother gets out a comb and smooths down their hair and straightens her daughters' dresses. Meanwhile the man crawls under his black cloth, and: Click! out comes the birdie in front.

A week later the parents hold the photos in their hands, and in Hamburg they are stuck into an album: three little girls with legs askew and a boy in a sailor suit.

Most evenings Pastor Kregel drops in for a while: "Am I intruding?" Bare-headed, his hair blowing in the wind even if there is no wind. "Thiss exquisitt peace!"

They sit in the cobblestoned front yard, inhaling deeply and watching the seagulls fly back and forth over the glittering water, big and little gulls whose names one intends to look up, some day.

They watch the sun too, of course, when the time comes for it gradually to sink below the horizon.

"That sun . . . just like Life—oh how quickly it has gone! . . ."

And then their neighbor in Wandsbek is discussed, and his habit of apparently exposing himself *naked* to the sun behind his wooden screen! One has not actually *seen* it, although one has watched very, very carefully, but it is a known fact. He works for the post office, and he exposes himself to the sun without a stitch on, mother-naked, and in the company of his wife. Shameless.

Symptoms of moral decay, that's what they are, quite beyond comprehension.

It occurs to Wilhelm at this moment that *he* has *never* seen his wife naked, not once. The very thought seems sinful to him.

Symptoms of moral decay. Just like those young men who roam the countryside with flowing hair and no tie. How awful to think one's own children might ever behave like that. All the effort one has put into their upbringing, and irresponsible people like that can bring it all to nought.

What possible good can come from that?

When the evening mists rise from the sea toward the house, they decide to go indoors. They sit in the crooked parlor, on the sofa, waiting awhile before lighting the kerosene lamp.

The children in their little bedroom under the thick down quilts and enveloped in the smell of the pans of curd, can hear the pastor reciting a psalm in the next room. They should have fallen asleep long ago, but they can't because it is so stuffy and because mosquitoes are whining over their beds.

Here in Süderhaff five more minutes aren't granted either: "No! You heard me! Tomorrow is another day!" And reading is forbidden because of their eyesight, they might ruin it and then have to wear very, very expensive glasses.

"Have you any idea how much such glasses cost?"

If they are lucky they are read to, and then for just fifteen minutes: *Holidays in Süderhaff* by Elise Averdieck. And sometimes there is a square of chocolate. Fancy chocolates are not permitted, they are for ladies of the demimonde who lounge on silken sofas and reek of perfume. There is one little square of chocolate for each child, Reichert's Family Chocolate with an Imperial standard on the wrapper. And then the children are inspected for signs of prickly heat, and if they show any they are told: "In a day or two it'll all be gone." And "Good night" they are told, and "Sleep well." And each child gets a kiss on the forehead.

"Tomorrow we'll pick some leaves from the walnut tree, that'll keep the mosquitoes away!"

When their mother has left the room they show each other the square of chocolate on their tongues: "D'you still have some?" they whisper, and when it is all gone they finally fall asleep, barely nudged in their sleep by occasional bursts of laughter from the grownups.

In Süderhaff their mother looks after the household herself, she is quite heavy in the hips and when she bends down she creaks. "Lisbeth! Be sure and sweep under the beds!" (A hairpin thrown underneath, to check whether she really does.)

Only one of the two maids is taken along every year: Lisbeth, the prettier one who has such a nice voice and such a ready laugh. Lene stays behind in Wandsbek; she has a little hump. Peee, says the ol' owl. It is her job to see that nothing is stolen in Wandsbek.

In the morning Lisbeth likes looking out of the window; she gets up especially early to do so, lights the fire, and looks out of the window.

> How happily I now awake
> From blessèd sleep the whole night long!
> I will be good for Jesus' sake
> And thank Him with a joyful song!

The sky, arching over the sea, rose red with delicate streaks of mist, and the sea reflects it all! Over there the red is deepening, that's where the sun must appear. Lisbeth can't stand here for very long because the porridge is already bubbling. She has to go in and set the table for "all those hungry mouths."

When Lisbeth has a bit of free time in the afternoon, and this does happen every now and again, she makes little gnomes' houses for the children using moss, bits of bark, leaves and twigs. Then Father himself sometimes comes to have a look, with his narrow head, ennobled in the sixteenth century.

"I must say, Lisbeth, it's just beautiful."

And it wouldn't have taken much for the man to get down on his knees and lend a hand: gnomes' houses made of moss.

Father de Bonsac with his Edward VII beard. There he stands up on the dune, looking far out to sea, his eyes following the ships sailing to distant lands. His left hand points toward the horizon even when no one is present to be shown anything. He has been "out there" himself, you see, in Africa, in 1884, something he will never forget.

Every morning he rows out into the bay, flexing his muscles more than necessary and inhaling deeply. That's still the good old air, you can't get enough of it. Sometimes he takes along one of the Kregel girls: Hella, the tall blonde one, and she inhales deeply too: you won't find air as good as this anywhere else.

When he stays away a little too long one day having landed on Ox Island where there are wild swans and sat there with Hella, the pastor's tall blonde daughter, Kregel drops in at noon and has a long serious talk with him.

"Those who play with fire will get burned": this is the text for his Sunday sermon, and woman is sinful "by nature."

> Life's thorny path I dread
> Alone to tread.
> Where Thou dost walk and stand,
> Oh take me by the hand!

Pastor Kregel with his expansive gestures, they must revere the Word, now and forevermore, with no thought of reward.

It is glorious in Süderhaff, it really is. There are magnificent walks, to the "Waldhaus," for example, on the High Shore, an inn where the children are given a glass of warm milk. There is an old clock standing in this inn, and on its face ships keep sinking and reappearing. The inn has a wide balcony from where you can look far out over the sea.

One day Father de Bonsac takes his son to Düppel, where the Germans won such glorious victories under Papa Wrangel. After all, a

German boy must see the place where the people of Schleswig-Holstein had their true fatherland restored to them, and where the invading Danes were finally forced to keep to their own country!

Richard must see the earthworks raised by the soldiers but now overgrown with grass. A veteran with two medals on his chest tells them about it and shows them his leg, which looks like the stick the organ grinder used to fasten his barrel organ to.

Every morning Grethe walks to the village with her father to fetch the milk. She is allowed to carry the pitcher, Grethe and no one else.

"You're my little helper."

They walk along by the bay and collect pink shells, a tall man and a little girl.

"Look at these, my child . . ."

They lie in a row like coins on his broad, clean hand: "And look at this one—isn't it beautiful too? God's glorious creation!" And he lifts the little girl from rock to rock. When he lifts her across she feels as if she were flying. She feels so light, and those strong arms . . . She'd like to fly like that forever, her whole life long.

On the way home Father carries the pitcher of milk, it's really a bit too heavy for such a small child. Besides, it mustn't be shaken: he tells her the story of the frog in the milk—that one must never give up, keep on kicking, kicking, kicking until one can feel the ground under one's feet again.

The tall man thinks about the sun, and what it must feel like to offer oneself up completely to the sun. To become one with its rays? To receive life from it? Strength and well-being?

Sometimes he carries the little girl piggyback: Ride-a-cock horse! Then she nestles her head against his brown neck, the rhomboid creases in it are white, and she thinks her own thoughts . . .

Sometimes—not very often!—they stop at a bench and she may sit on her father's knees and be held in his strong arms, oh and to be cradled back and forth . . . And they listen to the songs the Kregel girls are singing as they sit on that wall over there.

> I know not just what is this yearning,
> The sadness filling my heart . . .

You can listen to that for hours, and you look at Father's fine broad hands and let yourself be enfolded and feel utterly safe . . .

The children are not allowed onto the new landing stage: "Don't you *dare* go on the landing stage!" Of course little Grethe with the long braids *does* run onto it and falls into the water, and the water penetrates her clothes and her long frilly drawers and makes them all heavy. For a moment she seems about to float, supported by her skirt that has blown up like a bell, then she sinks until she reaches the bottom.

> O land of dreams,
> Shining afar!

Down there with open eyes she sees mute jellyfish in a forest of seaweed that she parts with her hands. Where is the merman with all his mermaids?

Suddenly her father's big legs come stalking along, she clings to them and is hauled up into broad daylight.

23 Sister Lotti

Although I am the youngest I can still clearly remember Süderhaff, and Pastor Kregel with his daughters who always sang so nicely, and our dear parents.

I can also clearly remember our grandparents.

Once a week we all went to Ritter-Strasse. At that time they were already quite elderly but regarded as the "eternal bridal couple," and they usually sat hand in hand, something that always impressed me very much. Grandfather with his snow-white beard, and Grandmother, "little Marie" as she was called, in a voluminous dress with countless rustling ruffles, a velvet ribbon around her neck and a little lace square on her head. After her husband died she always carried around a picture of him, wherever she was: "My Wilhelm" she would say, and when she sat down she would set it up so that she could see it.

"Wednesdays" was our name for these visits, it was always Wednesday when we met, every week. Father and his brothers went there from the office, and the wives came with their children from their homes. Vociferous greetings were exchanged, as if one had not met for years, and the noise was horrendous because everyone spoke at once. Cousins of my parents also came, a great-uncle with a stiff leg, Aunt Luise from Doberan, who wasn't very clean— "Come along, Luischen," she was told when she arrived in Hamburg, "let's have a good wash first . . ."—and they all talked at the top of their voices so that we children sometimes jumped around under the tables and barked without anybody noticing.

It was a spacious house, our grandparents' home, with a comfortable drawing room full of green furniture and a dining room

with a big table. The house stood among huge trees, a chestnut tree
and a copper beech with a swing hanging from it.

Dinner was always beautifully served, soup, a roast: twenty-four
persons at table was a mere nothing in that house; china, crystal,
cutlery, everything was in ample supply, nothing had to be borrowed, as was the case in many another Hamburg family. In the
center of the table, instead of a flower arrangement, stood a *plat de
ménages*—an expression unknown in France, incidentally—a silver
cruet stand with four cut-glass bottles for mustard, vinegar, and oil.
What the fourth bottle was for I never did find out, it was always
empty.

When everyone had settled down at the big table, arranged their
stomachs, and planted their feet—I can still see the buffet with
the cut-glass dishes of compôte—and when the first wave of talk
had subsided the patriarch would clear his throat and we would all
sing:

O worship ye the power of love . . .

It was sung with extraordinary intensity and a shrill savoring of the
higher notes, deep breaths being drawn in first in order to belt them
out, those higher notes, and then there were prayers, long prayers—
by the patriarch—and then we were all very contrite, and we children were not allowed to make a sound: they went on for a long
time, those prayers, quite a long time.

It was a magnificent sight, all those relatives at this richly laid
table, in a quiet, sober—but absolutely Protestant—atmosphere, so
united and contented.

Prayers were followed by a moment of devout silence, and then
they all fell to! Gracious me, how they gor . . . yes indeed, I
almost said: gorged themselves! With the same fervor with which
all the aunts and uncles sang and prayed, so they ate: rapidly,
voluptuously, and in great quantity. Really greedily, one must say,
interspersed with groans of "Oah!" and barely disguised belches:
huge napkins, almost as big as small tablecloths, tucked into their
collars.

My grandmother's eyes would dart about to make sure everything was all right. She had a little bell beside her, and sometimes
when the conversation revived and became louder and louder she
would tinkle the bell and call out: "I'd like to say something too!"

Grandfather always had a goblet with a twisted stem; he always
drank half a bottle of wine with his dinner. Held back his white
beard with one hand and drank in long drafts.

After dinner we children had to go around the table and shake
hands, curtsey, and kiss him and all the uncles and aunts. My sister
Grethe once refused, she didn't like Uncle Bertram and refused to
shake hands with him; it caused a sensation. She simply said "No!";
nothing would persuade her, she threw herself on the floor and no
doubt got a beating.

When we came to Grandfather he would stroke our heads and
say: "Well, my little gal?" Sometimes he asked us to recite verses
from the hymn book he had set us to learn by heart, "O Lord direct
us in Thy paths," for instance, that's one I remember. Or the
explanations of the Ten Commandments, and he would be deeply
hurt if we didn't know them. And although we girls were normally
rather giggly, at these quizzes we were pretty much subdued, for
Grandfather had very strict notions. Indeed, he imposed all manner
of duties upon himself, too.

He had made a list of the poor in his parish—the poorest of the
poor, for there were a great many who were poor—and he visited
them like a pastor his flock, each in turn. And when he saw that
there was no more coal, he would order some from the merchant
for his own account. He also had firewood delivered to them, he
would even chop it himself.

Uncle Bertram imitated him a bit, always wore black with the
expression of an undertaker. He also occupied himself with the
poor, but probably confined himself to pious sayings, for he was
most reluctant to part with his money.

Actually he was quite handsome, Uncle Bertram, he had a white
streak in his hair and wore a top hat when he went off to the stock
exchange. He looked very handsome and dapper, which was somewhat in contrast to his rather narrow mental outlook. One Christmas
I even saw him with a white bow on his top hat! And on one occa-

sion someone saw him trotting, I don't know who told me that. He was late and wanted to save the thirty-pfennig fine for arriving late at the exchange. Uncle Hans was more generous. He would sometimes come across with a five- or ten-pfennig piece.

After supper everybody moved to the green drawing room—Uncle Bertram was later to inherit the furniture. The women sat on the sofa, knitting or crocheting away, while the men stood about or sat in armchairs and discussed finance or politics. Unfortunately, being the youngest I was seldom present, for I was usually taken home earlier with my cousins. But I still clearly remember sitting on a footstool and enjoying the company.

Sometimes someone would read aloud, from Fritz Reuter or from the life of Perthes the bookseller and all his experiences under Napoleon—in Hamburg you can still see a memorial stone:

> Here lie the remains
> of 1,138 citizens of Hamburg . . .

The French did behave quite ruthlessly in Hamburg.

The only one who smoked was Uncle Hans—who else!—and when everyone had settled down nicely he would stick a cigarette in his long bamboo holder and hold it over the hot air from the kerosene lamp. When it was alight, he would take his first deep pull on it and with a highly characteristic click of the tongue puff out the smoke at a steep upward angle, past the brown tips of his moustache. Sophisticated Uncle Hans, the *grand seigneur*.

The kerosene lamp was a very distinctive one, it later stood on our veranda; it was made of majolica, with a bulging body. The wide lampshade was made of red silk, and that filled the whole room with a cozy, deep-red twilight.

Incidentally, harmony did not always reign on those Wednesdays. Sometimes there were even quite violent arguments. In those days Uncle Hans was still a Liberal and would make fun of the Kaiser. Oh my, did that arouse a storm! I still remember the "leap of the *Panther*": "What business do we have sticking our noses into

Morocco anyway!" cried Uncle Hans, and his brothers shouted: "No, Hans, that's not it at all!"

Sometimes the women would also start quarreling. Aunt Minna with her bushy eyebrows. I can still remember their harsh words when Aunt Madeleine—she was "British born"—turned up for the fourth or fifth time in a new silk blouse. Her sisters-in-law really went for her! In the end Uncle Hans got up and took his wife by the hand and left with her, she was sobbing with rage.

The Christian patriarch then smoothed everything out, and the following Wednesday everyone gathered together again in harmony.

Yes, those were the "Wednesdays," unforgettable, and a source of support for us children. We felt so secure, all eating and chatting together.

I often look back on it, very often.

24

In fall, life withdraws into the house. The tall standard roses are wrapped up and their stems bent down to the ground, and the veranda is closed. Felt mats are hung in front of the windows to keep out drafts.

When the children are in bed, Mother reads them a fairy tale, by Bechstein perhaps, the one about the Land of Cockaigne: they love that, the tale where roast pigeons fly straight into people's mouths. Then the children say their prayers, and then they are told: "There now, children, sleep well!"

She goes downstairs to inspect the kitchen to see that everything is tidy and locked up, and she listens to make sure that the maids are in their bedrooms and haven't gone off "to mail a letter," she knows all about that, all their little tricks.

Then Axel Pfeffer is given his din-din! One can hear him at it, and finally Martha sits down at the piano and plays Fiebig's "Autumn Leaves." She always starts with that, regardless of the season. Don't imagine it's beyond her: to play the piano. When Brahms was in Hamburg in 1889 she actually played something for him, as a young woman, and Brahms was quite delighted!

Wilhelm slowly lowers the book he happens to be reading, one finger placed between the pages, his narrow head leaning on his left hand: the house with the won-der-ful garden, and the children so healthy! Dear Martha, how she plays! And how handsome she looks, a bit on the stout side but so full of character. What a blessing they found each other, and the thought that they might not have is enough to bring tears to one's eyes.

"Oh, do play that piece again, what's it called, where the tune rises so nicely at the end . . ."

Amazing, the way her fingers land on the right keys, dear Martha, down there in the bass, without even looking!

> One, two, three,
> Dicke-docke-dee!
> Dicke-docke play the fife,
> The miller's lost his pretty wife,
> Searched the land for her in vain,
> I fear she'll ne'er come back again . . .

After the third verse, nothing can keep Wilhelm in his chair; swiftly, purposefully, he strides to the study: he comes back with the *Book of Arias*, clearing his throat as he does so, the *Book of Arias* "for the middle voice." He opens it at page 45 and waits for dear Martha to finish playing that wonderful piece, with a slight smile until she has *finally* finished it, and places the book before her—"Martha, my love? Hm? My dear?"—and sings:

> The fields are all mown,
> The stubble winds waft,
> High up in the sky
> My kite is aloft . . .

Then Axel Pfeffer comes into the room, highly satisfied with his excellent din-din; he thrusts his nose through the crack in the door and flops down beside the piano, his head resting on his paws, his ears pricked, and the whites of his eyes showing.

> This one I love,
> That one I kiss,
> And the other I'll marry someday . . .

When the brothers are there they always insist on hearing this particular song, and they click their tongues in the manner of connoisseurs—"Music, isn't it won-der-ful? Isn't it? Don't you agree?"

Brother Hans with his long bamboo cigarette holder, blowing the smoke diagonally upward, and Bertram, dear Bertram, whose tears come so easily, "family tears," quite automatically. If someone says "The *poor* fellow," for instance, the tears come quite automatically, no matter who is meant.

Daughter Grethe is meanwhile lying in her little bed sobbing, her whole body shaking: the singing stirs her childish soul to the depths. Down the long corridor it all sounds so melancholy. *Weltschmerz* it's called, and perhaps the child should be taken to the doctor: so frail and so highly strung, and always imagining things!

She is a real father's girl. Oh, how proud she is of him! His narrow head with the noble beard, and the way he always carried her piggyback in Süderhaff—she won't forget that so easily: from rock to rock. Herself and no one else! A real father's girl!

A somewhat difficult father's girl: when she is put to bed she is at first very good. As good as gold, she doesn't call out and she doesn't whine, but she keeps herself awake, she is waiting for her father, for him to go into his study and fetch the *Book of Arias.* And no matter how softly he treads, she always hears him. And *when* she hears him, she keeps calling for him until he comes and with a sigh lifts her out of bed.

> O gentle Jesu mild,
> Enfold this little child
> Within Thy wings so warm.
> If Satan comes to take me
> Let angels not forsake me.
> Keep safe this child from harm.

That's what he sings, and the clock ticks on, and his hands are so big that her little bottom disappears in them.

When he has finished singing, he lays her back in her bed, smooths down her nightgown, tucks in the quilt behind her neck, and says,

"God bless you . . . ," lays his big hand on her head: "And now bury your nose in your pillow and fall asleep quickly."

And she tries burying her nose in her pillow, but then she can't breathe at all! And for a long time she wonders:

> . . . If *say, Dan,* comes to take me,
> Let angels not forsake me . . .

Whatever can that mean? Who is Dan and why would he want to do that?

> If *say, Dan,* comes to take me . . .

It is an eternal mystery to her.

Grethe has strange notions about her father's occupation. She thinks: Whatever does he do? Always going into town? She imagines him sitting in a comfortable chair, with many sacks of gold in front of him, and he stirs the gold so that it won't get moldy.

Gold: every Saturday Martha says: "Willi, don't forget the household money!" And although she says that *every* Saturday, he invariably feels as if he had never heard it before, as if it came from distant worlds, this strange demand, and he wonders if that was really what he heard, "household money," and finally goes through all his many jacket pockets for his notebook, breathing heavily: ". . . Where on earth did I put it now?" and makes a note of it and says: "What? How much? *Fifty* marks?"

In the evening he brings it home, the household money, *fifty* marks, in gold ten-mark pieces. He counts out the coins to her, laying them in a row. His big hands caress it, all that lovely money, and he says: "Isn't it beautiful, Martha dear? Isn't it simply beautiful? Don't you agree? Hm?"

And now take good care how you spend it: baloney sausage for the maids, and why shouldn't they eat herring twice a week, why shouldn't they now? Is there any objection? Herring is highly nutritious, isn't it? And head cheese? Head cheese can also be very nutritious, can't it?

And Martha looks at the gold coins and pushes them around this way and that and then pops them one after another into her purse: Gone! Put aside a bit again this week, even if it's only one mark fifty, for her husband at Christmas, without his noticing, so that he'll say: "But Martha dearest, how can you do it?" and "Marrrtha" he says in his astonishment.

Yes, head cheese and, yes, herring, that's what she'll buy, dear, stoutish Martha, and a five-mark raise for the maids, which seems to be in the air now, five marks more a month—she'll have to give a lot more thought to that. Lisbeth and Lene, that's something you can't decide at a moment's notice.

When it is time to go shopping for the now fast-growing children, Father de Bonsac goes "into town," as one says—once in spring and once in fall, he insists on that—with his three daughters. Into good old Hamburg, so deeply and warmly loved. To be sure, the grimly handsome medieval buildings such as the Cathedral, still depicted on Suhr's engravings, have been torn down, as have the city gates, even the windmill at Lombards' Bridge. And whatever was left standing was taken care of by the great fire of 1842, which even Elise Averdieck has described.

In the city the modern era has arrived. Out in Wandsbek the horse-drawn trams are still driving around, but in Hamburg they have been abolished, and even the steam tram has been done away with, the "flat iron" as it was called. In the city they already have electric streetcars. They move around on their own, all on their own, and they also stop on their own, too.

"Just look at that now, children! Isn't that a miracle?" And then when you think of the horse-drawn trams, how awful, those poor creatures.

> One old nag can't pull it,
> The other nag is lame . . .

And no shaft, those old things, and when the driver doesn't put the brake on in time the car rolls into their hind legs!

And then those fantastic "Hedags"! Red, battery-driven taxis! They just glide along . . . In Rothenburgsort there is a place where the batteries can be plugged in and recharged: simply a miracle. (Gasoline taxis are not permitted, they stink.)

One doesn't use those Hedags, of course, they are far too expensive. But one does ride the brand-new subway, as a treat and for no particular reason other than to demonstrate this miracle to the children. Bertram, when he hears about it, is highly critical of such extravagance, and even Minna, his hirsute wife, shakes her head.

Aeroplanes, too, are to be seen over Hamburg, miserable wire contraptions. Necks are craned to follow these apparatuses, and heads are shaken. Aeroplanes? Really, that's like tempting God. Threatening fingers point to the sky. Can that ever work? Driving around in the air? Is the Almighty going to put up with *that*?

So Father accompanies his "womenfolk," as he calls them, on their shopping expeditions.

They walk along Mönckeberg-Strasse, which has been cut like a swath through the demolished medieval quarter, the finest and proudest buildings imaginable, then across City Hall Square, around the brand-new equestrian statue of Kaiser Wilhelm, beneath whose horse's tail the merchants gather—"about eleven under the tail": trees grow on City Hall Square, fine tall trees.

They walk on to the Heuberg, to the corner of Grosse Bleichen: where all the shops are so conveniently close—Hartmann's Ladies' Underwear, Ewers' Toy Shop, then C. Boysen's Bookstore, and around the corner Axin Fashions.

"*That's* what I call a fine bit of stuff," says Father de Bonsac, feeling it with his broad thumb. "*That's* what I call a fine bit of stuff, child, it'll wear for years!"

They stand by themselves, those materials, they're such splendid quality.

.   .   .

Once there is a row about a coat, navy blue with a red collar. It is too showy and too vulgar, says Father. And then: shoes with patent-leather toes.

"No, child, they're not for you—how do we know how they'll wear!"

"Wonderfully!" says the saleswoman. "They'll wear wonderfully! And if they get soiled, just put a drop of milk on a rag and rub the patent-leather toes, and they'll be like new!"

With a grumble Father gives in: "New-fangled stuff! Patent-leather shoes! Milk! Have it your own way!"

And then the bargaining! ("Oh, Willi!"): "Surely that's not your final price?" he says. "You can't be serious!" Everyone knows the profits on ready-to-wear! The lovely gold pieces in his purse, he feels sorry for them. And when he spends them, one feels sorry for *him*.

After shopping, there is an educational side trip to the battle panorama, a circular building in which, against a backdrop painted on the walls, stand real cannons defended by wax soldiers and attacked by wax cavalrymen on stuffed horses. Here the girls feel quite scared, but Father de Bonsac draws himself up and says that this is all part of life, doing battle and they should have a good look to see how fantastically realistic the whole thing is. Over there, for instance, that soldier whose head is just being parted from his body: isn't that mar-vel-ous?

Christmas is always most beautiful. Above all, the children mustn't know, of course, that a Christmas tree is being bought, Father does that secretly. They are sent away when the tree arrives.

"Now mind you bring it at exactly the right time!"

They are sent off to Grandmother's, on Ritter-Strasse; there they can go skating on the tennis courts.

> O Christmas tree, O Christmas tree,
> With faithful leaves unchanging;
> Not only green in summer's heat,

But also winter's snow and sleet,
O Christmas tree, O Christmas tree,
With faithful leaves unchanging.

Josten the handyman brings it, it's over eleven feet tall and reaches right up to the ceiling, and it costs twenty marks. *Corriger la fortune*—where branches are missing, they are inserted, with a drill and carpenter's glue. Josten holds it steady and reiterates his admiration at Mr. de Bonsac's skill, which is one reason why he always receives a handsome gift of money.

When Josten has left, Mr. de Bonsac starts to decorate the tree, in front and also behind, although the tree stands against the wall.

First the glass spike is stuck on, at the very top, looking like a grenadier guard's helmet, then come all the glass birds from the Erzgebirge, and bells and baubles to which threads were attached weeks ago, then the candles, the apples, and the chocolate rings, from each of which last year a small piece was actually bitten out— needless to say, with no clue as to the culprit.

The base of the tree is draped with a green cloth, and this green cloth is covered with moss, collected by the children in Süderhaff, and with bark and fir cones.

Then the Bavarian Nativity scene is set up. It has been ordered over the years, every year a new piece, one year a shepherd and another a sheep, very systematically and very secretly. Here the knowledge acquired at the battle panorama is applied. The drafty stable, artistically humble, is built into the patches of moss, with Mary—after Botticelli—bending lovingly over the manger and bearded Joseph in the background: faithful, steadfast, rocklike. The donkey looks in from outside, and the ox lies massively on the ground, and there is even a dog: it is placed with its back to the manger, facing the sheep, who lift their heads as if about to sing "Glory to God in the highest."

The tree's lowest branches are hung with wax angels, they hover over the manger next to the stars and the chocolate rings: heavenly hosts, waxen heavenly hosts. They mustn't be hung over a candle or their legs will bend, become misshapen, and drip. They were bought at Cordes, on the Jungfernstieg, and after Christmas they will be packed in cotton batting and put away in the attic.

Lisbeth the maid insists on helping to set up the Nativity scene, although she is so urgently needed in the kitchen to help prepare dinner. A little more moss here, and another fir cone there. And maybe a pond made of glass? A bit of broken glass should be easy enough to find?

"Oh no, Liesbeeth," says Father de Bonsac, chasing out the dog who has pushed open the door (he is just about to take a camel out of the box at the same moment she happens to pick it up, and they each pull at it, he from the front and she from the back) : "Oh no, Liesbeeth! Not a glass pond! The very idea!"

She is sent to Vieht's the druggist for some snow powder and some red gelatin leaves for the candles.

Sometimes Lisbeth places a sheep off to one side, *behind* the base of the tree, it has gone astray . . . As soon as she is in the kitchen, of course, Father de Bonsac puts it back among the others.

At five o'clock the children come home; by this time their ages are ten, twelve, fifteen, and seventeen. The cab that the family permits itself for this special occasion waits at the door; they get in and drive to church where Pastor Kregel stands in the pulpit and speaks about symptoms of moral decay such as the Child in the manger could never have dreamed of. They are so appalling, these symptoms of moral decay, that one is at a loss for words. The other day, for instance—ah, what was he about to say? Now it's slipped his mind! Oh well, never mind, at any rate Joseph and Mary certainly had a hard time of it.

After singing all the familiar carols, very loud and dragging, they leave the church to the sound of the organ, past Pastor Kregel, who nods to each and even shakes hands with some, still puzzling over what it was he had meant to say. To himself he wonders whether next year he might take a chance on letting his young colleague Eisenberg preach the Christmas sermon.

The organ music, with the Christmas light from the church, falls out onto the snow. Over there stands the cab with the cabbie sitting on the box, a frozen drop hanging from his nose. Marvelous: in they get and arrange themselves, making the cab sway this way and that, then off they go.

At home they sit down to an artificially extended coffee hour: "Your cheeks are just glowing, children!"

The oval table is covered with the Christmas cloth and set with the best china ordered from Thuringia. The table is decorated with gingerbread cookies and gaily decorated shortbread rings and with lighted candles held up by small, flat wooden angels, not too many lighted candles for it would never do to spoil the anticipation of the abundant joy, the dazzling lights, in store. That joy in all its abundance will burst forth behind those sliding doors, a silent reverential joy.

The sliding doors to the dining room are closed, a rare but expected sight. "Your cheeks are glowing!" the children are told, and they have to be calmed down, tuned into the reverent experience so as to be enveloped by the intimacy of the evening.

When the children have eaten enough fruitcake and gingerbread, which today have been not only urged but pressed upon them, the two maids are asked in, Lisbeth and Lene, and endless prayers are said, in their *most* extended form—"Amen, amen, amen!"

St. Luke's Gospel, which they have just heard in church, is read, about all the world being taxed, and that this taxing was first made when Cyrenius was governor of Syria, and the old and sick are remembered. Which brings tears to Father's eyes, the family tears, so that prayers are interrupted, but it can't be helped.

> What will Santa Claus bring for Otto?
> A little whip and a game of Lotto
> Are what Santa Claus will bring for Otto . . .

Mother plays this on the piano, and the children patiently sing along.

. . .

The last song is called: "The Christmas Tree Is the Finest Tree," to which Lisbeth knows the alto part. The song has twelve verses, or at least so it seems to the children. At about the tenth verse Lene also tries to join in with this simple, really quite logical alto part, and this prompts Lisbeth to increase her volume—and while they are shouting away Father goes into the Christmas room and lights the candles; for this he has a long brass apparatus, a tube containing a waxed thread that is pushed up. One more candle here, and one more candle there, and then at last, at last, he tinkles the Christmas bell, a brass gnome carrying a little bell on his back, slowly and solemnly opens the sliding doors—first the right, then the left (that bolt needs oiling again, what a nuisance!), until they reveal the whole wondrous affair: Oh, such radiance!

Needless to say, they are not allowed to rush into the room, first they must stand at the door and admire the colorful, glittering tree from whose topmost branches comes the gentle tinkling of tiny bells.

There the children stand, in their white muslin dresses (puff sleevs, frills, and blue taffeta sashes tied at the back in big bows), the boy in a white sailor suit, first having a general look around and casting an eye toward the corner where the presents are, which they can gradually make out more clearly but which they are not allowed to inspect until Father spreads out his arms like Thorwaldsen's Christ and says: "Go ahead, children, go ahead!"

("That sheep, good heavens, what's that sheep doing back there . . .?" The glass pond actually doesn't look bad at all. Must order a few ducks next year from Bavaria, *swimming* ducks. Might as well look up the catalogue today to see whether *swimming* ducks are available.)

Next day the entire family comes for Heligoland soup, the grandparents and the uncles and aunts as well as the six cousins.

> Green is the land,
> Red is the cliff,
> White is the sand:
> Those are the colors
> Of Heligoland.

Red lobster soup, with little white dabs of whipped cream floating on it and sprinkled with parsley.

The grandparents arrive hand in hand, the patriarch in a frock coat with a fitted waist (the lapels piped with silk, and at the back, in his left coat tail, a big white handkerchief), and diminutive Marie in a mountain of skirts with countless folds and pleats, and a little lace square on her head.

Heligoland soup, cheese croquettes with peas, roast beef, and plum pudding flamed with rum.

Uncle Hans has brought along some bits of magic, a ball that sticks out its tongue when squeezed, hopping metal frogs, or a magic lantern, but these he always takes home with him when he leaves.

Uncle Bertram gives the children picture cards with printed mottoes. And then he waspishly asks whether it is really such a good idea to give the children so many presents? A real horse trough for Richard's rocking horse, for example, plus curry comb, grooming brush, pail, sieve, and canister? Boxes for botanical specimens? Humming top? Is that really such a good idea? Is it?

"Don't touch that, children," he says to his pale daughters, who keep close together, "you might break it." And he takes the "Mountain Maneuvers" out of their hands and places it firmly to one side.

The Noah's Ark, on the other hand, he doesn't object to that: it can be opened right up, with all the wild and tame animals, always two by two, with real hay and marzipan meat. No, he doesn't object to that, and he automatically looks around to see whether the Almighty Himself isn't present somewhere.

Then the uncles and aunts are shown what the girls have perpetrated in the way of needlework; it is also shown to the cousins as they stand whispering in a corner, it is practically shoved under their noses. Unaccountably, they are not encouraged to emulate it. They hardly look at it, these six sisters, they barely glance at it.

Incidentally, they no longer bite their nails, their fingers are now painted with ox gall.

. . .

Now it is time to perform on the piano. The grandparents, solemn and full of dignity, sit on special chairs and give their noses a thorough blow before the music starts. "Christmas Tinsel" is the name of the first piece, set for six hands, a musical medley of all the Christmas carols. Grethe sits in the middle, poor little thing, she can just barely play a few notes. She has to play in the middle octave, and Richard and Hertha play on either side and nudge her when she doesn't count properly. Lotti, the youngest, holds a triangle. At certain places she is supposed to hit it. If you miss the place, it doesn't help to hit it a beat later.

Aunt Minna with her heavy eyebrows thinks what a pity it is that her daughters, who all have heavy eyebrows too, aren't the least bit musical, and dignified old Grandfather wonders whether, from a religious point of view, it is really acceptable, that "Christmas Tinsel," whether the occasion isn't actually far, far more serious what with the Savior shedding all His blood . . . And he pulls out his notebook and jots it down. Tomorrow, at church, he'll have a word with Pastor Kregel about it.

Uncle Hans wears a genuine pearl in his cravat, although it is invisible behind his beard. He cuts himself a piece of Lübeck marzipan, and he seriously offends the gathering by continuing to talk in an undertone while the children are hammering away at the piano— by continuing to talk to his English wife, quite loudly too, and even has the nerve to laugh.

"*Must* he?"

He is talking to his wife, who is from England, a country where they don't even have a Christmas tree.

The following day the visits are returned, and Wilhelm eyes his brothers' trees with a connoisseur's expression: "I must say our own tree is the most beautiful!" But of course he only says this on the way home, and only to his wife.

"Our own tree really *is* the most beautiful, Martha, don't you think so? Hm? Don't you agree?"

They walk along arm in arm, and the children walk ahead discussing their hairy cousins, how stuck-up they are. Richard doesn't think so, he doesn't think so at all, he specially likes the second one from the top. She once put on his helmet, a sight he'll never forget. The helmet in the middle and the curls on either side!

He grabs his sisters' braids and holds them like the reins of a troika: Giddy-up! and off goes the wild chase.

25 The Friend

I went to school with Grethe—my name is Thea Markgraf and my maiden name was Westhusen—Grethe was a delightful child! She had such thick hair, you can't imagine! We other girls had two braids, she had three; she wound those three braids into a knot that covered the whole crown of her head.

It was a private school, with no more than sixteen to eighteen pupils. We had charming little desks and proper chairs. Foreign languages were taught either by an Englishwoman or a Frenchwoman. Whenever the class was taken by a male teacher, our homeroom teacher was always present, as a chaperone.

The nicest was the English teacher, we loved her passionately! We kissed the door handle she had touched, and we cut out her signatures from our exercise books and swallowed them.

This English teacher founded an English circle where we had tea and cookies and were only allowed to speak English. How we adored her! I can remember as if it were yesterday when she became engaged. One day she said: "Today I have something very special to tell you—I'm engaged to be married!" And I said: "What? At your age? When you're so old?" I was outraged. She was twenty-nine, and to a child that's old.

I can remember the names of almost all my fellow pupils: Berta Malchow, Susanne Rix, and Grethe Heise. Grethe Heise was a doctor's daughter and a bit namby-pamby. We didn't like her that much. Gertrud Hilfrich had a lisp, and Fernanda Maus died young of TB, and lucky for her, one can say, for her parents—her father had a bookshop—didn't manage to get out of the country in time, they were sent to that camp—what was it called?—and gassed.

I am sure there were other nice girls in that class, but Grethe was my favorite. We were always together, how lovely that was! We were so inseparable that today I simply can't imagine my schooldays without her. We always sat together, we were never separated. Everyone said: "Thete and Grethe must stay together, Grethe has such a good influence on Thete."

We were never, never, never separated.

School was marvelous, we really enjoyed it. The only boring subject was History. "Why should I care about those old stories?" I used to think, and Grethe felt exactly the same. Those old stories about Egyptians and Romans and about wars, the Seven Years' War and the Thirty Years' War, didn't interest us one bit. And then Luther, all that about the Reformation. Only when the History teacher told us about atrocities, I'd listen sometimes. Then I was flabbergasted by all that could happen in the world.

Augeas, cleaning out the Augean stables—I happen to remember that.

Grethe had an indescribable charm. How I loved her! When we were quite little—I remember it so well!—we were told the story of Joseph and how he was pushed into the pit by his brothers, and suddenly Grethe started to cry. The teacher came over and took Grethe on her lap and said: "It'll be all right," and: "He'll get out of there again."

I don't know whether Grethe was very happy at home. Her father once said: "There's no denying that the *first* child is always the favorite." He also once said it gave him a special feeling to hold his *son* in his arms, one's "son and heir." I believe Richard de Bonsac was the sole male descendant far and wide, otherwise it was only girls, and in those days they only counted for half.

Richard was a bit blasé, but the two other sisters were quite nice, Hertha and Lotti, one of them had sort of a flattened face, she looked like a pug.

Her father was a rather strange man, "Martha dear," he used to say to his wife, "Martha dear." He had a Nativity mania: at Christmas he turned a whole room into a Nativity scene—I tell you, it was a spectacle. Animals, shepherds, angels, he set them all up with his own hands, tiny little trees, moss, lakes and streams made of bits of glass, a whole room filled with the most wonderful figures. I can remember a complete caravan, with camels and goats and so on. It stretched across the entire room. (Can you imagine what that would be worth today?) I was allowed to have a look at it. "But don't touch anything! D'you hear?" I was told beforehand. They really put the fear of God into you.

Mr. de Bonsac was also quite eccentric about his garden. There were nets spread under the apple trees so that falling apples wouldn't get bruised. And when he was away on a trip, some kind of special apples were packed with extra special care and were actually sent on to him by express. He was absolutely crazy about his apples.

The first apple to drop had to be sent on to him, come what might.

Her mother, Mrs. de Bonsac, must have been very strict. While Grethe's hair was being combed, she had to recite her vocabularies, and if she didn't know a word she got a rap on the head with the comb.

Must have been an odd woman, inflexible, strict, almost Spartan.

The bedrooms, for instance, were never heated. Grethe told me that sometimes the water in the bowl was frozen.

A Spartan upbringing.

And they were stingy. When I was confirmed they gave me a transparency showing angels blessing a child who was being confirmed. That was quite usual in those days, but one corner of it was slightly chipped, so at some time they must have received it as a gift themselves.

Because we were such friends, the de Bonsac parents finally called on my parents. They wanted to meet the family their daughter was associating with. That's when Mrs. de Bonsac told my mother they had once lived in a building like ours too, in an apartment building, but *they* had had *two* floors.

She actually said that to my mother! Just like that.

My mother was a bit hurt. Mrs. de Bonsac would have done better to say: "We belong to the same church as you do, and we are happy that our daughter is friendly with yours."

·   ·   ·

Grethe was charming. We were always together. We were inseparable. When we went for a walk, we not only walked arm in arm but also held hands. Although we must have had other friends too, we always came back to one another.

Once we had a big party in dirndl dresses, and we danced together, and everyone raved about us because we were so good at it. I was much taller than Grethe and was the male partner. She followed, and I led.

Later, when I once visited her—we'd been married for years—we also walked like that, arm in arm, from old habit. And then we met her husband, and I believe he was jealous. I can't be sure, I just had a feeling. "Is she here again? . . ." or some such thing, he mumbled to himself, I certainly heard that. One can always tell whether one's welcome or not.

I don't have a single bad memory of Grethe, not one. She looked enchanting. She had a little snub nose, of course, but otherwise she looked enchanting.

Once she made a special visit to my mother to ask her how to make a soufflé, whether you have to cook the mass first or whether it cooks in the dish.

In 1913 the de Bonsac family went to the Baltic again, this time, however, not to Süderhaff but to Graal—let's go somewhere else, not always to the same place, a change of air should do us good too. Richard can't go along, he is grooming horses in Celle: he is serving with the Mounted Artillery.

The willow hamper is left at home, the big Africa trunk is taken along, and the three daughters are equipped with sturdy camphor chests.

Graal, on the Baltic, Villa Ida. Every morning sharp at eight, Father comes into the bedroom—just when one was longing for a bit of extra sleep . . .

"Get up! Get up! Get up! It's a glorious day, child!"

He strides to the window, opens it, and takes a deep breath: what wonderful air he is providing for his children here. And the light! And the lovely sunshine . . . "How lucky you are to be here, child!"

What a splendid idea, to come here, to Graal, and to the Villa Ida, for four marks full board! For four marks good sound money, mind you. The food is excellent—salmon in aspic with mayonnaise and tongue in Burgundy sauce—and even the coffee is good. Maybe next year the brothers can be persuaded to come to Graal too? How about a joint vacation and doing everything together?

But then, it's not likely, Hans may go to Egypt with his English wife—it's a mystery where he gets the money from—and Bertram will go to the country. Six daughters? You can't blame him.

.   .   .

Graal is situated on the Baltic coast—"with sandy beach and excellent surf," as it says in the prospectus. To get to the water, which contains 1.138709% salt as well as magnesium chloride, iron oxide, calcium, potassium, sodium, and 0.00004% silica, you first have to walk through the forest, whose trees inhale carbon dioxide and exhale oxygen, as is well known. You carry along a deck chair and the bags containing the bathing things.

"Go on ahead, children!" their mother calls. "I'll take my time!" She finds walking a bit difficult.

The pine trees sway like masts against the clear sky where clouds race along. There is a vile smell from the stinkhorns that grow under the wild raspberries. (You could build dear little gnomes' houses here, here in the woods, with bits of bark and moss, and the next day you could come and see whether they were still there.)

Bathing is begun only on the third day, and even then you are allowed only two or three waves and a "chain" must be formed, for some deep holes are said to be lurking on the bottom, and anybody stepping into one is doomed.

"Children? Are you tingling yet?" they are asked. Tingling is essential, and when you feel it you have to leave the water immediately.

There are no waterweeds here, but there are jellyfish. Little stinging jellyfish with blue and red markings, and big floppy ones that don't feel nice against your legs.

And the bathing suits? They cling to the body—all over! It's almost embarrassing . . .

After their swim the entire family sits booted and spurred on the beach. There is bromide in the water too. Father de Bonsac has adjusted his deck chair and is reading *War and Peace*, bought in Hamburg before he left. He reads about Prince Bolkonski and that he has a carpenter's bench in his study, and about Count Rostov and how he marries off his daughters and loses his fortune.

Martha sits on a camp stool, broad and heavy, and Hertha, Grethe, and Lotti, those by now almost grownup daughters, sit inside the wicker cabana, dressed all in white, their hands in their laps. They are watching the men down by the water who in turn are watching the shrimp fishermen drag the bottom with a special net. The shrimp will be thrown into boiling water, twenty pfennigs a pound.

On the cabana's folding table stands a glass jar:

Mixed Fruit Drops
Made in England

At decent intervals you are allowed to take one. "Don't poke around, child, take from the top!"

The yellow ones taste best.

What a good thing to have gone somewhere else, they say, four marks full board! And that it ought to be possible to entice at least Uncle Bertram to come here to Graal. Oh, wouldn't that be glorious! All getting along with each other and doing everything together!

"Yes, Martha dear? Hm? Wouldn't that be won-der-ful?"

With wide slanting strips of foam, the sea washes up the beach and splashes along the pillars of the pier.

Over there a white paddlewheeler plunges through the waves, a white steamer loaded with excursionists who look across at them and wave. (One should have brought the binoculars after all.) What a pretty sight—*Fürst Blücher* the steamer's called—and what a pretty sight this must be from over there.

Now she ties up at the pier. People get off, with fishing rods and flapping skirts, and other people get on, also with fishing rods and flapping skirts, holding onto their hats with their left hands and children with their right. The brass bell is rung, the paddles are turning again, and the water froths up.

Sometimes a great gray colossus appears on the horizon, with gun turrets and three or even four funnels. Then Father de Bonsac puts down his *War and Peace,* saying: "Look, children—look over there! Isn't that mar-vel-ous? All that might?" And he can imagine the boost given by these monsters to the worldwide enterprises of the German spirit. Those Negroes—what must they think when confronted by something like that? He gets up from his deck chair—albeit with an effort—and exults in the wind blowing through his hair, tousling it as he stands there pointing toward the horizon.

At the shallow water's edge a boy is sailing his little boat: lovely, the way it glides along. Sometimes so fast he can hardly keep up with it: he has to trim the sails and turn the rudder more to the right.

With a groan Martha hoists herself from her camp stool, which tends to sink backward into the sand. She has gained weight again, and her arms bulge out of her sleeves, she looks a bit countrified, the dear soul, as Hans and Bertram murmur to each other in Hamburg, a bit too countrified. But with a heart of gold.

Willi must surely know what a treasure he has.

Laboriously she plods through the sand to feel the towels and see whether they are dry yet.

The boy has stopped sailing his little boat. He has tucked it under his arm and is also watching the fat woman plodding back and forth and feeling the towels. He comes from Saxony, and because she is so fat and having such a hard time plodding through the soft sand he comes closer and sighs: "The human being is a sad machine . . ." This is quoted throughout the entire vacation, and even later on, in Wandsbek. And they add: "Isn't that a scream?" for one does have a sense of humor . . .

Graal on the Baltic, Villa Ida.

Meals are taken at the table d'hôte, a long table with men, women, and children evenly distributed. On Grethe's birthday—it always falls during the vacation, which is why the day is never properly celebrated—the proprietor's wife decorates the table with flowers and brings in a tube cake with a candle in the middle that no one is allowed to blow out.

The guests rise when the young lady, so slender and pretty, comes skipping down the stairs:

For she's a jolly good fellow, she's a jolly good fellow,
And so say all of us!
Happy birthday to you!
Happy birthday to you!
Happy birthday, dear Grethe,
Happy birthday to you!

They are watching for her expression when she sees the cake and the flowers.

At first Grethe has no idea it is all meant for her: Cake? Flowers? And her eyes fill with tears. She pulls the lace-edged handkerchief from her sleeve—eau de Cologne—and presses it to her face . . . "But my poor child!" says the proprietress. "All we wanted was to give you a nice surprise . . ." And after coffee in the lounge the parents are told, What a modest child, no really, one hardly knows what to say.

From her mother she receives a coral necklace, and from her father a shiny, newly minted gold ten-mark piece. The necklace is immediately put away safely again by her mother, and the gold coin by her father into the purse from which he has just reluctantly extracted it, and he examines it to make sure it is in fact one of those wonderful gold coins that are so extremely hard to earn.

Does she realize that this is a lot of money? she is asked. Ten good German marks.

On their return to Wandsbek it is to be taken immediately to the savings bank, for that rainy day when things may not turn out the way one has imagined.

"Who knows what the future holds?"

She is seventeen now. ". . . As I was saying . . .," the gentlemen say as they turn to watch her leaving the pension full of vim and vigor, so trim and dainty. She carries a tennis racquet under her arm, and over there is her bicycle, on which she is about to ride off. "Top-notch family, isn't it? And good blood. Some French in it somewhere."

She rides all along the promenade past buckthorn and sandgrass and elderly gentlemen who follow her with their eyes.

She rides past the architecture of the bathing establishment, a baroque imitation in wood with a clock in the gable topped by a little copper-green cupola, and when she has got up enough speed she lifts both feet off the pedals and weaves from side to side—what a glorious feeling to buzz along like that! Soon she'll start pedaling again, and her Brennabor will be crunching over the gravel.

The three-hundred-meter-long pier was built into the sea by a Mr. von Hoegh, says a plaque; it costs five pfennigs each time. One stands the bicycle against a wall and walks right to the end and leans over the railing, looks into the frightening depths "seething and roaring and hissing," and thinks: "Suppose I fell in? What would my parents say if I fell in? Would they be very sad? Or would they be sadder if one of my sisters fell in?"

There is a shed with a bench on the pier where postcards can be bought and shown around, postcards of the very shed that has these postcards. And it is at this shed that Grethe de Bonsac meets a certain Karl-Georg Kempowski for the first time, on August 15, 1913. He is from Rostock and wears a watch chain across his stomach.

"Here, Stribold," Karl Kempowski says to his dog. " 'Upon this bench of wood let us repose.' "

And these are the words that start off the flirtation, for Grethe is much amused by his broad accent: " '. . . this baanch of wood . . . ,' " so terribly Mecklenburg!

And he is charmed by her sharp s's. "Would you be from Hamburg?" he asks, and in no time they are discussing the Saturday evening "social" and whether there is a chance of seeing each other there?

He speaks with a fierce Mecklenburg accent, this Karl Kempowski, his hair is cut very short and he wears steel-rimmed pince-nez. To the young lady from Hamburg he explains the various navigational markers, such as light buoys and bell buoys, at which she marvels greatly, and he knows all about flag language and that the white flag with a red eye means "yes."

There are seventy-eight thousand such flags, and white with a red eye means "yes."

They go to the shooting gallery where with a few shots Karl sets rattling figures in motion, a bear beating a drum and a father beating his son.

"Would the lady care to take a shot?" the attendant asks.

No, the lady would not care to take a shot.

Then they walk on to the wreck—"Let's hope no one else is there yet!"— small schooner with a broken mast, "the human being is a sad machine," lying around the bend, on her side, and she is filled with sand.

Here they sit for a long time, with the sound of the sea pressing on their ears. Life, the way things happen, and what do you suppose the poor mariner is doing who owned this boat?

Now Karl tells her about his father, it is an opportune moment: that he owns no more and no less than two steamers, and that the white *Fürst Blücher*, the steamer that ties up at the pier once a day, is roughly half the size of one of the vessels his father happens to own.

Next day they meet at the amber exhibit, arranged by the spa administration to provide entertainment in bad weather. Brown amber, as transparent as honey, and yellow amber, also like honey, like opaque honey. (Here they can put their heads closer together and examine everything minutely.) Pieces with objects embedded in them, such as beetles, flies, or mosquitoes, and pieces that have been melted down and made into cigarette holders.

On the wall a large map showing the location of amber deposits and of the amber trading routes of antiquity, the latter in dotted lines.

Grethe decides, when some day she has the money, to buy herself a necklace of unpolished amber, and Karl counts his money to see whether he has enough to buy such a necklace.

. . .

They walk along the promenade, isn't amber lovely, they say, and ivory, isn't ivory lovely, they say that too: natural, none of that artificial stuff, corals, for instance, they're natural too, or precious stones, the way light is refracted in them . . .

Grethe tells him her grandmother owns a tiger claw set with an emerald, it is an opportune moment, and Karl tells her that his grandmother also owns some magnificent jewelry, and that in Rostock, on Stephan-Strasse, that's to say in his home, there is a glass cabinet containing a cup from which Queen Luise is said to have once drunk.

Along the promenade strolls Karl with Grethe de Bonsac, past the buckthorn and the sandgrass, where at a distance Father Kempowski looks through his cane/telescope and signals in vain: He reigns, her reins, it rains . . . Why don't they come over here, dammit it all! "Here on the bench, on either side of me!" Why don't they sit themselves down and tell me a thing or two!

Karl is an expert at swinging his walking stick, one display follows another, and he guides them in precisely the opposite direction: he tells her that once in Berlin, during the Kaiser's Parade, the drum major accidentally dropped his baton, at the very moment—under the eyes of the monarch and all the people of Berlin and all the foreigners—when the idea was to show what the Germans could do: to drop the thing at such a moment! What that means! Just imagine!

And that later the drum major shot himself, because of the disgrace.

In the evening, when Anna Kempowski is already writing to Rostock that she will be home the day after tomorrow because she has migraine and because she can't stand the beds any longer; when Father Kempowski has already drunk his second pint and is wondering whether he shouldn't send for that little Linz woman with her gay laughter—his bum is so sore again; when the de Bonsac parents are wandering around in the forest guided by an expert to hear the stags belling: the two young people are once again standing on the pier. They lean over the railing. Grethe looks into the water: the seaweed, and the way the current makes it wrap itself around the big rocks, that interests her, where is the merman with all his mermaids? And Karl also looks into the water, but in such a way that her head with its tight little curls is outlined against the sky. That's what he wants to see, her head, it looks lovely.

> Rejoice, my heart, and drink thy fill
> Of these days' golden sunshine . . .

Yes, it is also setting this evening, the sun, favoring the young couple with a gigantic Gomorrah sky.

That night Karl moves his bed onto the balcony: that gentle shushing that might come either from the forest or from the sea. Owls skim over him, and from the distant village comes the sound of a hurdy-gurdy:

> You, you, for you I am longing,
> You, you, here in my soul . . .

He stretches and smiles—could she be that strong-minded little person he desires, he wonders, with no migraine and totally without airs? Who will pour him his tea in the evening, at the round table, while the lamp shines down on the table and the newspaper rustles?

She is seventeen, and he, unfortunately, is only fifteen. A pity, really. But doesn't he seem much older?

"You were only an accident . . ." his mother said to his face, and she laughed as she said it. Not that long ago, either.

Next day Karl hires a rowboat, *Irene,* twenty pfennigs an hour.

"The lake is roaring, seeking out its victim," he keeps repeating to Grethe de Bonsac, although the sea happens to be particularly calm that day, and he explains how it's done: rowing. First lean far forward, and then pull the blades sharply through the water: whish! And don't "catch a crab," don't put the oars too deep into the water.

Wouldn't she like to have a try? (Squeezing past each other in the rocking boat, he has planned it all.)

.   .   .

Then he tells her about fishing, drawing in the oars the better to gesticulate. That first an empty net is cast into the water and later pulled out full. Terribly simple, really, and completely logical: first empty and then full.

He starts rowing again, and Grethe trails her hand in the water, saying: How odd, here she is sitting in a boat in Graal with Huguenot blood in her veins: de Bonsac. She is wearing a white lace dress over a white petticoat.

How very, very strange it seems, she says, to be sitting in a boat here in Graal, and she says it over and over again: only the flimsy boards between herself and the deep sea. And she says: "Stra-ange." To be sitting in a boat, in Graal, and to be of French origin, isn't that very, very "stra-ange," completely oblivious of her mother running up and down on the beach, waving her arms and signaling that it is very dangerous to go out in a boat! Doesn't she know that?

The de Bonsac family attends the poetry reading in a body, for you don't see a poet every day. The poet, who lives here, has consented, for a fee, to emerge from his retreat and to recite samples of his work at the Rifle Club, under dented Japanese lanterns and blue-and-white paper garlands. Seated on the platform at a bare table, he opens his book, which everyone has recently been discussing, and turns the pages hesitantly, back and forth, until—that's it!—he quickly decides: This one, this poem, the one he loves best of all, he'll read that now, but first there must be complete silence in the room, *complete* silence. And he waits until the very last member of the audience has settled down and finished clearing his throat.

> Sing me a little song, O mandolin mine!
> But not for today!
> Sing me a song of times that were gay . . .

Father de Bonsac down there with his narrow head, Huguenot through and through, nods in approval: yes, that's right, times that were gay, the good old days, in the family home, gathered around their mother . . . or later, the days when he was courting his dear Martha, so much in love, oh so much in love . . .

No, Father de Bonsac can't do otherwise than nod, although there are passages in the poet's work that *he* would have expressed differently. Yes sir. *Quite* differently, in fact.

Mother sits beside him, also nodding, but more likely in her sleep, the way mothers do: all that fresh air and the rich food.

> Gentle and steadier the rain,
> When shall we see the sun again? . . .

the poet now reads, and his audience listens attentively and in complete silence. Only when the light in the carbide lamps starts to dwindle does someone in the audience call out: "Waiter! More carbide!" And outside the room the waiter throws fresh carbide into the container, and the lamps blaze up again.

"Ah!"

Now the poet (with his upswept hair) reads about lovers, about a pair of lovers who embrace at night on the promenade for a passionate kiss and are suddenly picked out by a ship's searchlight! Thus love is killed by mocking laughter, according to the poet's words.

The de Bonsac girls yearn passionately toward him, one of them more, the other less. But Father de Bonsac clears his throat: one wasn't prepared for anything like *this*. It might have been better to leave the children at home. Passionate kiss? Love?

And the girls are already subsiding, one of them more, the other less; but farther back, probably in the last row, sits young Mr. Kempowski, and he is leaning forward.

How he would love to see that, Grethe's expression at this very moment. *The Daily Round and Sunshine.* He wonders whether she is absorbing what the poet is saying up there, and she seems to him to be very far away.

. . .

Now the reading is over, and the summer guests press forward, holding books to their bosoms, brand-new ones and dog-eared ones, books by the poet that they want him to autograph.

He looks carefully into the face of each person whose book he is about to inscribe, seasoned age or glorious German youth, and will the seed he is sowing take root? That young man there, with the steel-rimmed pince-nez? Hasn't he seen him somewhere before? On the pier, with wind-blown hair? And that young girl, delicate, blonde, her hair parted in the middle?

"Who knows?" he writes in the young man's book, and "Tears!" in hers.

Outside the Rifle Club, on the dark street, under one of the moth-besieged, new gas lamps, Karl finds an opportunity to approach the de Bonsac family. "Grant freedom of thought, sire!" He raises his hat and introduces himself.

"Kay-e-em, pee-o-double-u, ess-kay-i."

First bow, then wait for a hand to be offered: that's how one was taught at Frenz's. Father de Bonsac is uncertain, his red wine is wait-ing, why are they all standing around here?

Hertha and Lotti stand open-mouthed, and Grethe blushes.

Is it really necessary for those two to go dancing Saturday night? Is it really necessary? he asks.

Why not? Why shouldn't they go to the "social"?

It is the mother who tips the scale, it is due to her that the vacil-lating father says: "Yes." For all he cares. Go right ahead. That's the way things are nowadays. A "social." (And he thinks of *War and Peace*, and of Prince Bolkonski, how churlish he always pre-tended to be and yet had such a good heart.) And now he wants his red wine, confound it. Hm?

Later, when Grethe has wound up the golden medallion clock in her room and put it on the bedside table, she stands by the window for a little while. The wind plays with the curtain, which smells dusty.

The sky is still light at this hour, but it is already dark outside, and bats are flitting around the house. Light and dark: here it is both at the same time.

She stands there long enough for the globe of the earth to turn and the moon to rise behind the trees. When the crickets stop chirping, the frogs begin to croak, and when the frogs stop it is not long before the nightingale under those bushes over there actually starts warbling.

And Grethe still stands there, Grethe de Bonsac, and her thoughts keep rolling around in her head like billiard balls: What is it like, this business of having babies? She ponders on this. She knows by now that they are pulled out of one's belly, but how do they get in there? That's a complete mystery to her. Does a kiss have something to do with it? Or does it all get started by a kiss? By a kiss on the mouth, to be more explicit?

One day she'll find out.

What will it be like when one actually *has* one's own children? Certainly one will be very nice to them. When they come running up with a thousand questions one will put everything else aside, one's sewing or knitting or whatever, and will tell them: It's like this and like that. And everything will turn out beautifully, you'll see.

Karl, the skinny youth from Rostock, is really not that much in her thoughts. True, he is in a way in her thoughts, but more on the edge, and really only in a way.

She lies down on her bed and smiles. Margarethe Hedwig Elisabeth de Bonsac, ennobled in the sixteenth century. Why is she smiling? She doesn't know. She kicks off her shoes—in the next room Father, over his *War and Peace,* goes ahem! ahem!—and she stretches out her arms. And just as she is, in dress and stockings (and smiling), she falls asleep, her hands twitching until she is completely at rest.

Unfortunately there are three mosquitoes in the room, whining above her bed. First Grethe stops smiling in her sleep, then her brow furrows, her eyes open, she lights the lamp: how to get rid of those mosquitoes? She considers the problem, then stands on the bed with her slipper and looks around, but she can't see them, those tormentors, because they are hiding in the curtain, silently and secretly.

No, they are out of sight, but instead she suddenly sees herself in her dressing-table mirror, standing on the bed holding a slipper, and *that's* enough to make her laugh again, and she discovers that laughing really looks very attractive.

She closes the window and now does take off her dress, her petticoat, her bodice, and whatever else is revealed. Before crawling under the quilt, she moistens the mosquito bites with spit and blows on them—amazing how quickly they swell, she has sweet blood. Tomorrow she'll have to pick walnut leaves, she decides, and then she falls asleep again.

Years later she will have reason to remember a "social" she once attended in Graal,

> Swing your old woman
> High in the air!

an unexpected crowd, farm folk who had sneaked their way in, and that she had worn the wrong shoes, or this or that. It hadn't been nice at all, quite different from what she had imagined. They had bumped into each other's knees, but it may have been the fault of the music, that village band on the platform, positively antediluvian, the man with the tuba who kept letting out the water from the bottom of his instrument, it was enough to confuse anybody. And: Fancy playing marches! "The Radetzky March" on a dance floor? Really rather the limit.

After that they had walked along the beach, the sea had been calm, the walking stick had been swung, and it had been chilly in the wicker cabana; she had laid his coat over her knees, and he had sat on the sand wall and played with pebbles and been silent for a long time, had sighed intermittently but had mostly been silent.

"Kempowski?" he had said, a very remarkable name—from *Kempa*, Polish for the German *Büschel*, so it should really be

"Mr. von Büschel." Miss de Bonsac and Mr. von Büschel, in other words both aristocratic, if you like.

Then on the way home he tried to give her a kiss, but it landed in the wrong place. She had thought he wanted to look back, and suddenly she had felt his wet mouth on her cheek, like a frog. And his glasses were so cold.

When the de Bonsac family leaves in September, on the "summer bus," a farm cart fitted with benches, Karl stands at the edge of the forest and waves.

Mr. von Büschel is wearing a porkpie hat, and spats over his shoes, not a very becoming outfit.

Grethe hardly dares wave back, for her sisters are already laughing, and her distinguished Huguenot father with the distinguished little beard widens one eye and screws up the other, looking genial and angry at the same time.

Her mother smiles, maybe she has already espied a son-in-law, but Grethe is only seventeen and there is no great hurry.

27 Sister Hertha

I was actually there when my sister Grethe first met Karl Kempowski in Graal. I saw them standing side by side on the pier:
Grethe was wearing a white dress, they stood there gazing into the
water and looked like children.

In the evenings she always told me everything, bringing me "up
to date." She also confessed to me that she didn't really like him.
She made fun of him, of his broad accent, his Mecklenburg dialect,
and she told me that she smoked cigarettes in the evenings sitting
in the cabana, and that he was forever trying to kiss her.

Staying at the seaside seems to encourage love, doesn't it? Is it bore-
dom, or is it the fresh air? In the mornings you doll yourself up and
have eyes only for the boys, wherever you go.

I was terribly in love, too, in those days, in Graal, in 1913; he was
blond and looked like a Friesian, a charming boy! Oh my, was I in
love! We were together every day, and in the evenings we went to
the fishermen's tavern and each had an egg liqueur. What a joke!

Then when I was back in Hamburg I waited and waited for that
boy to show up. Hadn't I given him my address, and hadn't he
promised faithfully? Finally I went to Uncle Hans and told him how
miserable I was, he had a sympathetic ear for that kind of thing,
you know. We sat in a café eating cake, and I bawled my eyes
out: "What am I going to do, what am I going to do?"

Uncle Hans consoled me in his kindly, understanding way. Stirring his coffee he said: "Don't worry, Hertha, he'll show up."

But he never did, and today I must assume that it was my
father's doing. He probably wrote him a letter: "Look here, young
fellow . . . ," for the young man was only an elementary-school

teacher and as such wasn't really eligible for the daughter of a "merchant prince."

I was so much in love that I walked all over Altona, up and down the streets, always hoping to run into him. All I knew was that he lived in Altona and that he was or wanted to be an elementary-school teacher. I kept thinking: maybe, maybe, you'll see him, just by chance, and then everything will be all right.

He almost certainly was killed in the war, for only a year later World War I broke out, and no doubt he volunteered immediately.

Seen from today, I must almost admit that my parents were right in discouraging him. As a young person one thinks that marriage and all that has nothing to do with reason, to love each other is enough.

When, two years later, I met Ferdinand, love may not have been quite as great but it was lasting.

At that time, by the way, my father sent me off to England, he could see how I was suffering. He had a friend in England who sold those garish cottons to Negro women in Africa, he lived in Devonshire. I was there for two months, I had a lovely time, and my new impressions really did help me to get over my great sorrow.

Really it was a great love, it still hurts when I think about it.

With Grethe and Karl, mind you, things were quite different. For Grethe this liaison was only a game, something to pass the time. She was amused by his persistence. The moment she came out of the pension in the morning, all unsuspecting, whoops! there he was, with his broad Mecklenburg accent, an undersized youth, pale and unprepossessing.

At night he would even throw pebbles at her window, could he have thought she would let him up to her room? A childish mentality. She'd come over to me and say: "You must look, Hertha! He's there again!" and we'd stand behind the curtains and giggle.

He used to tell her all kinds of lies, too—that he was in his father's firm and that he was terribly busy, and so on. Yet he was only fifteen, and looked it, what's more. He was still going to school! Although Grethe always made fun of him when she told me about him, and imitated him, the wealth of the Kempowskis, or, should I say, the affluence, must have made a certain impression on her. Karl dressed well, and he always had money in his pocket. No doubt they drank more than egg liqueurs when he took her out.

And he never did give up: in December 1913 Grethe was invited to Rostock, to his sister's wedding.

28

Silbi's wedding takes place in December 1913, and Grethe de Bonsac receives an invitation.

We have the honor to invite
Miss Grethe de Bonsac
to the wedding of our daughter
Sylvia
to Lieutenant Schenk
from German Southwest Africa.

Can one let the dear child travel all alone to complete strangers? In the middle of winter? After much discussion permission is granted. The photos passed around the table play no small part in this: a house of that kind, after all . . .

A charming white silk dress is bought at Brandt's.
   "If anything happens you'll phone us, won't you."
   And at Zeller's on Jungfernstieg, a topaz on a fine chain.

Her heart beating faster, she sets out: she is wearing little fur boots and has a muff to keep her hands warm. It is her first journey all alone.
   "Mind you don't touch the door handle, and be sure to wash your hands!"
   The train goes via Bad Kleinen and Wismar. The fields are covered with snow, and there is a draft from the window.
   "And remember to say 'Thank you,' child!"

Gradually Grethe settles down, and as the train passes through a snowy forest and the white winter sun glides from tree to tree, she is already thinking: "Like an enchanted world." The trees with their white branches. "Like an enchanted world." Isn't it? And: "Filigree," the word occurs to her, and she thinks of the painting "Silence in the Forest" by Böcklin, only that this is a winter forest, that's what she imagines.

In Kröpelin a farmer gets on: "Well, miss? All on your ownsome?" Snow comes in with him, and cold air. He stows away a wooden coop containing chickens on the luggage rack and sits down. Then he proceeds to cut off some pieces of bacon with a pocketknife and stuffs the cubes into his mouth while the chickens up on the luggage rack look down.

"And where would you be heading for? Pierdknüppel?"

(Wiping his nose with the back of his hand.) He has a niece in Pierdknüppel.

That there is an enchanted world outside is something one really can't say to this man.

In Rostock it is snowing. Karl is standing on Platform 3, wearing a coat with a fur collar, a porkpie hat, and black earmuffs; he is standing right under the station clock and has had a hard time getting rid of Plückhahn the porter, who was trying to tell him that it is snowing today.

And Grethe sees him at once, in spite of all the heavy snowflakes: Is he really that short? Not even a little bit broader? A cold gust of wind blows in her face. She remembers him differently.

Outside the station, in the dense snow flurries, stands a row of green horse-drawn cabs with black patent-leather roofs. Karl summons one, he is good at that. (How long is one supposed to wait?) For this he doesn't need Plückhahn the porter, who has thrust himself forward again and wonders who that elegant young miss is.

The cabbie in his black cape, his whip over his shoulder, doesn't bother to get down. His head to one side, he waits for the young couple to clamber in and settle themselves, then he says "Giddy-up!" and the horses move off.

. . .

Would she care for a little tour of the town? They would still be home in plenty of time.

They drive along Kaiser-Wilhelm-Strasse, where the electric streetcar scatters blue sparks: one villa next to the other, the turrets and gables swathed in snow, and Karl knows every owner and loudly reels off their names: Consul Besendiek—timber merchant outside the Petri Gate (what a fire they had at the lumberyard!)—and Ohlerich, an odious competitor, always drunk. And, not to be overlooked: Menz, Paints & Enamels, Wholesale—an excellent freight customer, a pleasure to deal with.

"He has a very nice son, you'll be meeting him; really a fine fellow."

Robert William Kempowski has named both his ships after Consul Besendiek, after him and his wife. Not after himself and his wife: "We know our own names!" And should the firm acquire further ships, which isn't that impossible, they won't be named after one's own family but perhaps after the Menzes, who knows?

Down Richard-Wagner-Strasse they drive, past the new Civic Theater: "Some sturdy Thespians tread those boards, Miss de Bonsac . . . this chicken is fit for a king!" *Die Fledermaus* happens to be playing—maybe, let's see, maybe we'll have a free evening. Grethe de Bonsac will then be seen with Karl-Georg Kempowski in the stage box, and the citizens of Rostock will aim their opera glasses at the couple and ask: "Who can that charming girl be?"

Past Stone Gate, past the oak tree of 1813 and the oak tree of 1870, the leafless branches silhouetted against the gray sky: this is where the gallows used to stand, with room for three, on an artificial mound so that the townspeople could watch the victim jerking.

"This is our City Hall, Miss de Bonsac . . ."

His father, of course, could have been a city councillor long ago, and a consul too, but: "When all's said and done, what would one get out of it? Nothing but trouble." And: "Do we need that?"

There are seven turrets on City Hall, three on the left, three on the right, and one in the middle, a little taller than the others. Simple and unpretentious, not all jumbled up like the Lübeck city hall, a city that, in many respects, Rostock has quite nicely overtaken.

Beside City Hall is Schwibbogen Lane, with two enclosures for slaughtering the animals that have just been bought at the market. (Poultry is bought live.)

There's no slaughtering going on now. Snowflakes whirl around the fountain, and the fishwives in their black straw hats are just packing up.

In order to see St. Mary's Church towering, blue black, behind the gable of the City Pharmacy, Miss de Bonsac should really lean forward a little, across him, and Karl leans back for her. But one can't see the church today anyway, snow is sticking to the windows, besides, one of those big furniture vans of Bohrmann's has just got in the way. "Oh well, tomorrow is another day."

On Stephan-Strasse, Mrs. Kempowski comes sweeping down the stairs, graciousness personified (she has just been slamming doors). The beautiful birchwood furniture and Queen Luise's cup. She looks coldly at the young lady from Hamburg and shakes her hand somewhat perfunctorily.

The dogs jump up and bark.

From the alcove room comes a voice: "What the heck's going on?" That's where the old man is sitting, going through his mail with Sodemann. (Never a moment's peace, and everything sore again down there!) He is sitting in the alcove, his legs wrapped in a blanket, and Sodemann, the fat head clerk—"All I'm saying is . . ."—gets to his feet and bumps into the alcove balustrade, making the palm fronds tremble.

The old gentleman adjusts his pince-nez and stares at the slender guest just entering the room: So that's what she looks like, the new prospect, not bad at all, his son's taste, Import & Export. Hamburg. That dress, I wonder what that material is . . .

Her father sends his regards, says the young lady from Hamburg, and her mother too, she also sends her regards; and thank you for inviting me. And, bless my heart, if she doesn't actually make a kind of curtsey!

. . .

The following morning a maid brings her breakfast in bed, "like in an enchanted world," pushing the door shut with her foot. Sparkling currant jelly, honey, and plum jam. The rolls are wrapped in a napkin. While the butter is melting on the roll, the stove is lighted, and *warm* water is poured into the pitcher on the washstand. The windowpanes are covered with ice to the very top.

"Be faithful unto death . . ." The wedding takes place in ice-cold St. Mary's, admission tickets have had to be issued to prevent too many gawkers crowding into the church, and there is even a brass ensemble in the organ loft. The bridegroom, Schenk, keeps looking over his shoulder to see whether they've really come, the brass ensemble, as they have promised; their trumpeting sounds a bit thin in the vast church, and is much too soft . . .

> . . . doth thee protect
> as thou may'st elect! . . .

Schenk, the bridegroom from German Southwest Africa: there lay the farmers, sprawled in their own blood, a ghastly sight.

Pastor Timm in his Spanish ruff, which the Lübeckers imagine is unique to them, keeps raising his head to reveal the stud fastening the "soufflé collar," as they call it in Rostock.

As he preaches, he gazes up into the white vaulted roof onto which, for some mysterious reason, are stuck blue plaques with golden stars.

After the ceremony, all the carriages drive along beside the harbor. The steamers blow their whistles, and all the sailing ships are dressed with flags, Sodemann had taken care of that: the apprentice made the rounds and distributed a few bottles.

"You can't have something for nothing."

The seamen lean over the railing and nudge one another: "Look at all them carriages!"

There's nothing wrong with old Mr. Kempowski, but: "His old woman, she's no good."

. . .

On Stephan-Strasse the maids are scurrying around in black dresses with starched caps and aprons. Gütschow is said to have been in church, so they tell one another, the bankrupt wine merchant, if that isn't a bad omen!

A footman has also been hired, in livery with a striped waistcoat of black-and-yellow silk; he stands idly in the doorway. No one is going to listen to his orders anyway. A minute ago, under the stairs he was picking his nose with his gloved right hand.

The guests drink sherry to warm up, and look at the gifts: the baskets of flowers and the porcelain figurines, and very soon the sliding doors are opened: "Dinner is served!" And arm in arm they proceed to the richly decorated table: silver bowls overflowing with fruit and a huge candelabra, although the new gas lamps in the ceiling are already functioning.

While the small ensemble, borrowed from the Civic Theater, plays Mendelssohn's "Wedding March" under the refurbished Christmas tree, there is some minor jostling, for no one knows where he is actually supposed to sit: the place cards have turned out a shade too small, all kinds of spectacles must be pulled out of their cases, and names flit through the air. "Over here, Mrs. Warkentin, over here!" As for old Ahlers, he sits in a corner, half offended: isn't anyone going to look after him?

Thirty people have been invited: Müller the tenor, of course, and also the little Linz woman, and they all run around peering.

At last everybody is settled; old Ahlers, too, is shown his seat, and he is already conversing with the lady on his right, presumably about Pernambuco, a place he has once visited. Too idiotic, that he had to get sick just then, near Cape Horn.

You never can tell, can you?

Little jokes are risked, to relax the atmosphere. The first crackers are pulled, although they are not nearly due yet, and Strahlenbeck demonstrates how someone once tucked the tablecloth into his collar mistaking it for his napkin.

Müller ("Mi-mi-mi!") shows how it is possible to sit at table without a chair.

Why? Because he didn't get one. It is now handed to him across the table, by one leg. The little Linz woman laughs at that a bit too heartily. O Linzi, Linzi, watch out! Someone's looking at you with eyes as cold as a snake's.

In the basement kitchen things are at fever pitch, and everyone has to run around the idle hired footman. The dumbwaiter never comes to rest, there's always something more to be sent upstairs.

Is there enough gravy up there? is shouted into the dumbwaiter shaft from below, and the other maids upstairs, in the light of new gas lamps, can't hear, they call out: "Quiet!" into the room behind them, and the guests actually lower their voices.

Caviar on Ice

Champagne Baudelot sec

Consommé

Medallions of Venison with Fresh Mushrooms and Truffles

Château Coufran 1904

Halibut with Sauce Béarnaise

Valwiger 1910

Pâté de Foie Gras in Madeira Aspic

Chablis 1899

Haut-Sauternes 1903

Roast Turkey, Compôte, Salad

Château Léoville-Barton 1904

Asparagus

Sherbet

Cheese Pastries

Schultz Grünlack

Dessert

Baudelot sec

The bridegroom fixes his monocle in his eye the better to study the menu. It is printed on gilt-edged pasteboard. His parents—more's the pity—have been unable to attend—German Southwest Africa, no wonder. Besides, it all happened rather suddenly.

. . .

The soup splashes softly, and after the first toast they all swallow
their wine at the same time, which is clearly audible and provokes
general merriment.

With the venison the "Bridal Chorus" from *Lohengrin* is played,
and with the halibut the "Love Dream After the Ball" by Czibulka.

With the roast turkey they hear the waltz "Life, Love, and
Laughter."

Everything just right.

Father Kempowski looks *from below* through his pince-nez, wondering why they haven't put some lingonberries beside his plate
and whether he can get any more of those taties? Those floury
little bits of potato that absorb the gravy so nicely? At intervals he
looks *from above* through his pince-nez at all the "crazy folk" who
are regaling themselves at his table: Mrs. von Wondring, for instance, who actually still carries a lorgnon, and Mrs. Warkentin
with her big bosom.

Old Ahlers is just saying: "Maybe, maybe not . . ." and looks
around for bread, which appears to be missing on the table. (Even
today he isn't wearing any socks in his army boots!) He doesn't like
to eat anything without bread, that's something he learned in
France.

Now Professor Volkmann taps his glass, waits until everyone has
finished chewing, and says: "I've been to Rome, and I've been to
Athens . . . ," but nowhere has he enjoyed himself as much as in
the Kempowski home. He describes Silbi, the bride, as the soul of
the house, which doesn't go down well with Anna, the bride's
mother, who feels an urge to knock over a glass, she's that angry
again. But when Volkmann goes on to deplore the fact that this
charming bride is about to go off to the bush down there, Anna revives. Mrs. von Wondring says: That's right, it's really a shame
that she's about to go off to the bush. And a very masculine, angular young man also says: Yes, that's right (he has a little scar),
and the other guests chime in: Yes, quite right, it's a shame she's
going off into the bush, and go on eating.

. . .

Grethe de Bonsac thinks of the Negroes who probably even eat human flesh, and thinks she certainly wouldn't do that, go off to the bush. She wouldn't mind having a little more of that Château Léoville-Barton but doesn't know how to go about having her glass refilled. Her table companion Karl Kempowski is otherwise occupied, talking to the little Linz woman, who is in a somewhat giggly mood today.

With the sherbet a large marzipan beehive is put on the table, with plaster bees stuck into it, on wires, and decorated with little pastries, meringue cups, and wafers. "Busy hands are blessed hands" is the message, aimed at the bridal couple.

Karl Kempowski gives his Grethe one of those plaster bees— What is she supposed to do with it? Pin it to her bosom?—Lieutenant Schenk from German Southwest Africa drops his monocle and thinks of the farm that he will now be able to buy down there, the farm on the Okavango. But, who knows, maybe he won't do that at all? Mightn't there be an opportunity here . . . ?

Silbi has eaten too much, yet she breaks off another piece of the beehive. She looks charming, and it's really cute the way she stretches her arms and legs.

"And you intend to go and live among the Negroes?"

We'll see, not for the time being. Look around in Germany first. In Berlin, for instance, she's never been to Berlin.

"Kurfürstendamm," says the masculine young man with the little scar on his angular face—he has fine strong teeth—and that it's really terribly funny: "Kempinski," that there's a restaurant there called "Kempinski." He has a large, angular face, this masculine young man, and a brown skin.

This is the first time Grethe has heard his voice, she has been listening for it quite a while.

Perhaps he will open a branch in Berlin for his father's paints and enamels, he says, but on the other hand he might buy himself a country estate. "What do you think, Mrs. Warkentin?" An estate also has its advantages, hasn't it? "But otherwise we'll all meet one day in Berlin, won't we?"

And glasses are raised: "To Berlin! To Kempinski's!"

When the beehive has been picked to pieces and its ruins lie scattered all over the table, everyone rises. Father Kempowski is led across to his favorite place beside the stove, where old Ahlers is already sitting with his "cog-nack," waiting to whisper in Kempowski's ear who has been saying what.

The wheelchair attendant will stand behind their chairs cracking mysterious jokes, and the guests will think those three men over there are laughing at them, which they are.

Anna is trying to hurry the maids: how long is it supposed to take for them to clear the table, for heaven's sake? Is one supposed to wait forever: "And none of your impertinence, if you please!"

Tomorrow she's going to decimate the crew, she's already made up her mind. Weed out, ruthlessly!

At this moment a cab drives up to the door. Under the streetlamp a woman is seen to get out and trip her way into the house. The assembled guests, who are just clipping their cigars and waiting for the footman, who is nowhere to be found, are not a little surprised when the latecomer enters the room: it is the grandmother from the Home of the Holy Spirit, who once had a birthday on 8.8.1888, the grandmother who isn't quite all there, wearing a wonderful silk dress, very tightly laced, of bluish-gray silk trimmed with black lace. On her head she wears the wreath of golden myrtle from her Golden Wedding, and in a very high, thin voice she says, rapidly and without inflection: "Oh, what lovely people! Oh my, all these ladies and these fine gentlemen, and the rooms so beautiful, those must be brand-new gas lamps . . ."

In front of the bridal couple, who have taken up a position on the sofa, she curtseys deeply, and immediately starts to sing:

> There stands a little man
> In the wood alone,
> He wears a little mantle
> Of velvet brown . . .

She sways as she dances, actually she only sways, but it is a kind of dancing because she uses her arms, waggling her fingers or pointing heavenward . . .

Schenk has not been told, he laughs good-naturedly: perhaps it's some kind of theatrical gag? "Ingenuous old woman," or some such thing? A grotesque performance that suddenly turns into a clever parable? Or the prelude to the presentation of some strange, unusual gift?

Only then does he notice that the other guests are signaling to him: Careful! Not quite right in the head! Off her rocker!

Only then does he understand.

The performance does not last very long. Anna comes up, turns the old woman toward the door, and swiftly pushes her out.

> Say who can the mankin be . . .

In no time at all she is back in the carriage, the door is held shut from outside to prevent her getting out again, and the maids hasten to bring her a few goodies. A few tears are shed, and the incident is soon forgotten.

Almost at once the ensemble start up a waltz, and it seems inconceivable that this wedding could have been celebrated had Gütschow not gone bankrupt: this magnificent house!

> On his hair some brilliantine,
> In his hand the violin . . .

The pieces played by the trio are full of little allusions that no one understands. The guests are merely surprised at the strange grimaces of the violinist, Havemann, as he looks out piggy-eyed over his bow.

The gentlemen swing their ladies, and the maids stand by the dumbwaiter, watching. And downstairs by the dumbwaiter stand the other maids, listening.

. . .

Above the door to the drawing room hangs a sprig of mistletoe, signifying: anyone who stands under it may be kissed. Grethe does not see the sprig and has no idea what is in store for her when the young man with the little scar and sparkling teeth approaches her. She thinks she is dreaming when he takes her in his arms and asks if she knows what is about to happen? If she knows she's about to be kissed? Because of the mistletoe up there?

He is broad-shouldered and his name is August Menz. Paints & Enamels, Wholesale.

He does not kiss her; he takes her by the waist and dances a tango with her, with sixteen different steps, and whispers in her ear what steps she is to do next: Now left, and stop! And now a quick turn—that's it!

The guests stop dancing and watch: What a lovely couple! She's supposed to be of French descent, and he's an amateur aviator! D'you suppose he got that little scar in a crash!?

Karl pulls out his watch and looks on from a distance. "Studying the scene," Erex would have called it. A sad study: Grethe de Bonsac with her delicate features (in Graal it had all been working out so well . . .): there she is, *bonum bono,* dancing with that pain in the neck, Pains & Enamels, Wholesale, turn to the left and turn to the right, stop!

Karl still has one dance with her to his credit. If she were to look his way, he would start toward her, although—he had noticed this in Graal, at the "social"—they are always at odds when dancing together.

He wonders where the little Linz woman could be? "Basically" rather a nice girl?

Silbi and her lieutenant have already left for Berlin when it happens: at the far end of the veranda the big glass pane is smashed, from the outside. The hired footman, who happened to be hiding there, narrowly escaped being hit by the rock.

Gütschow? So the guests assume as they look at the broken glass and pick up the flowerpots. Could it have been Gütschow? Distraught with jealousy? His magnificent house?

The wind blows in a pile of snow from the outside, so the veranda door is closed and the portiere hanging across the door is let down.

Old Ahlers hasn't heard a thing, he is surprised at the sudden quiet "in the office." He has just taken his purse from his trouser pocket to show Mrs. von Wondring the money set aside for his funeral, here in the inner compartment, here it is. She wouldn't have expected that, would she?

The broken glass is swept up, and gradually the conversation gets under way again—"Did you ever" and "Who could have done it?" and late that night, when old Ahlers has already been carried into the library—"Heave ho!"; when Father Kempowski, "early to bed and early to rise," has dropped *Quo Vadis?* and is snoring at the walls; when Anna is showing the tenor from Hamburg the darkroom in the basement (a lengthy and stealthy procedure); when the little Linz woman has long since hurried home in tears, and Professor Volkmann has hung his tail coat (now with all its buttons cut off) over the chair and explains in rather too much detail the meaning of the street name "Erskerne" (and louder than necessary): Karl sits in his room, staring in front of him. Felix Dahn: *A Struggle for Rome.*

> Gently imploring go my songs
> Through the night to you . . .

From below can be heard the whimpering of the violin and the banging of doors, and laughter. "Koarl!" they are calling: "Koarl, where are you?"

Darkness fills the room. Only the snowflakes outside the window, illumined by the gas lamp, are light.

Across the street, at Jesse the veterinarian's, a curtain is pulled aside: How long are they going to carry on at the Kempowskis, all

that racket, it's really a bit much. But one daren't risk saying anything in case the mortgage is canceled.

Karl gets up, opens the door, and listens. Downstairs the real uproar
is starting, glasses and cups are being smashed. A repeat of the
wedding-eve festivities. Every crash is accompanied by "Hooray!"
Here, this vase, let's smash this too, crash! And now someone even
brings in some snow from outside, the signal for total chaos.

Karl goes up to the attic: the old sofa is still there, where he played
sixty-six and smoked cheap cigarettes with his friend Erex. The old
sealskin satchel and the cherry wood once taken in lieu of payment
are still there too.

  In the corner stands the fort, whose towers can be lit from inside.
Its moats can be filled with water or, if you like, champagne: *A
Rainy Day—Tales from the Mountains*. Should he stand inside the
fort surrounded by a moat of champagne . . . ?
  "What changes God's hand hath wrought!"

The wind lifts the tiles and puffs in a little snow, and the snow settles on his forehead. Sooner or later Giesing is bound to come, and
when she does come he is suffused with warmth. And after they
have disappeared into her little room, those two, Karl and Giesing,
the hired footman can relax his immobility. Behind the chimney,
where he's been standing all the time.

On the last day of the year Grethe de Bonsac goes home: *bonum
bono*, good things to the good . . . she has been given a first-class
ticket.
  "Good-by, have a safe journey!"
  It really wouldn't do for this delicate, well-bred creature to travel
third class!
  The doors of this compartment have silk panels, and there are
lace antimacassars on the head rests.
  Grethe is looking forward to traveling in this compartment; no
bacon-eating farmer is going to bother her this time.

.   .   .

Karl looks at his thick watch, Grethe at the dainty little watch she wears on a leather wrist strap and the station clock also indicates: three minutes to go.

"Good-by, have a safe journey!"

"Yes. And thank you very much."

The whole platform is full of steam and snow. The train starts moving, and Rostock with Karl Kempowski on Platform 3 disappears into steam and whirling snowflakes.

Part Three

We were sitting in a café and somebody with the "extra" said: "War has broken out."   M. P.

I was standing on the balcony and heard solemn trumpet signals from the nearby barracks. And then a drummer marched through the streets with an officer, beating his drum, and the officer read out the mobilization orders.

S. S.

The entire population was as if electrified. Work almost came to a standstill, people went out onto the streets, and newspapers published "extras." Many schoolboys volunteered for military service, the higher classes were soon empty. And the teachers, too, were gone.   B. Z.

I was working in Weimar at the telegraph office and had to transmit all the telegrams to the reservists, where and when they were to report. Thousands of telegrams. There was no room for error.   M. W.

It was summertime, and all around us the woods were full of nightingales and the trains were full of singing soldiers. The nightingales and the singing of the soldiers, they sort of blended together. At night. It was an honor, of course, to shed one's blood for the Fatherland.   M. W.

Behind our house ran the railway, where the
freight trains loaded with soldiers came past.
They sat in the doorways dangling their legs.

My father had had some pig-bladder sausages made, and we girls tied notes to them
with our address and threw them to the soldiers.
We were fifteen. And some of them did write
back.   s. r.

And then before long the first death announce-
ment arrived, Mr. Harms, the grocer. I had
seen him just before, in a blue tunic, he never
did get his field-gray one. Mr. Harms was
among the first casualties, and his wife went
about in black with red-rimmed eyes.   p. d.

One had just seen those men, had carried their
rifles, the cheering still rang in one's ears, and
it was hard to grasp that they were now dead.

The greater the victories, the more days off
we had from school.   s. l.

You went off filled with patriotism, and then
you saw all the horror. You came from a shel-
tered home and then you had to listen to the
talk in the trenches, it was enough to turn your
stomach.   b. k.

29

In August 1914, Grethe de Bonsac happens to be in Chemnitz. She has gone there to play tennis at the home of one of her father's business friends, an easygoing scissors manufacturer who has three delightful daughters and a live deer in his garden.

Grethe isn't particularly good at tennis, but she enjoys it: run for dear life and at the last moment get the ball and wallop it to make the fur fly . . .

Tennis is an English game of "fairness," says the manufacturer, that's why you're not allowed to smash the ball here.

"There's no point in serving so that your opponent can't get the ball," he says in his easygoing way.

The breeze blowing across the terrace moves the dark trees under which stand white benches, and the deer kicks out its legs.

"Johann, where are the newspapers?"

The newspapers with their headlines are in the garden; the servant has put them on the round white table where breakfast has been laid: choice of tea, coffee, or chocolate.

MOBILIZATION ORDERED!

JEALOUS FOES FORCE US TO OUR JUST DEFENSE!

THE SWORD HAS BEEN THRUST INTO OUR HAND

The manufacturer is deeply moved by feelings of German nationalism, but he is also annoyed in his easygoing way; Sheffield, what's going to happen to his partner? Will he get away from there in time? And he is very concerned because he doesn't know how he is to get this young girl back to Hamburg, here she comes running up to him without the slightest suspicion of what's happened.

"War?" she says: 'War?"

And then she says that she has always had a sort of premonition and that she has been dreaming of a red sky, in the west, blood red.

In the end the scissors manufacturer drives the pensive girl by car to Berlin, although God knows this very kind man has enough worries of his own. In Berlin the girl just manages to squeeze onto the express train and stand all the way to Hamburg.

On his way home it occurs to him that he wouldn't really mind if his partner didn't get away from there, from Sheffield, it mightn't be such a bad thing. This is what he thinks in his easygoing way, and that the machines will have to be retooled for other products that are now bound to be required, and no doubt in very large quantities.

Every railway station is full of soldiers, singing soldiers, Grethe gets caught up in the frenzy: champagne bottles are hurled against the railway cars, and complete strangers fall weeping into each other's arms:

Deutschland, Deutschland über alles . . .

they sing, their arms around each other's necks, and the quartermasters have a heyday, distributing live ammunition and outfitting the reservists down to the last gaiter button: the mobilization goes off without a hitch.

What almost doesn't come off is the journey home of the de Bonsac parents. The couple got it into their heads, in the summer of 1914 of all times, to have a look at Paris.

Allons enfants de la patrie!

The Eiffel Tower must be seen, now that the children are grown up and one has a little time for oneself. The Eiffel Tower and Versailles, where the glorious German Empire was proclaimed, one has never forgotten the picture of them all standing there, one from each regiment, and all those different uniforms.

Unite, unite, all ye unite!

Versailles and the Tuileries with all those paintings—some of them pinched, no doubt . . .?

In Paris, bugle calls ring out, and marching blue columns swing through the streets. Concealed behind the curtains of the hotel window, the parents watch all this and at the last moment succeed in getting out of the enemy country: they have to travel via Switzerland and finally in Hamburg can embrace the girls, Hertha, Grethe, and Lotti, the grownup daughters, now so beautiful, each more beautiful than the next.

Not the son, Richard—he can't be embraced, he has already left with the Mounted Artillery, moving westward. "Prepare for action forward!" He wants to see the Eiffel Tower, too.

In Rostock, the "Ninetieth" marches off, the officers on horseback and the men with heavy tread. Loyalty in return for loyalty. Can't leave our Austrian brothers in the lurch, now that it's do or die. Let's show the world that Germany keeps her promises.

When soldier lads come marching by,
With flags aflutter-o!
The pretty lasses open wide
Each door and shutter-o!

In every town, soldiers are marching to the railway station, and all the girls stand in the doorways and wave. Others try to keep step with the men, in their tight skirts and little button boots: on the rough cobblestones. Here and there one of them has linked arms with her sweetheart, which perhaps he doesn't care for that much.

Older, stouter women are weeping, wives who have five or six children cluttering up the kitchen. Or they are soldiers' mothers, holding their handkerchiefs to their nose.

The street urchins run ahead, in the time-honored way, so as to be able to salute the flag over and over again, or they hop around the drum major, who today is not putting on a show with his baton.

The left foot, the right foot, the left foot, the right foot,
Just follow the bugle, the rattle of the drums!

How unfailingly the man with the glockenspiel hits the right plates!
The tiny ones up top, the big ones at the bottom. It would be noticeable if he were to hit the wrong ones, that's for sure. And the
man with the big drum? He has to march on the outside right: magnificent, this German march music, no one else has anything like it.

Rather less impressive is Captain Peters, formerly President of the
Regional Court and now mounted on horseback: he's supposed to
lead the whole affair and isn't much of a horseman! At the Hop
Market the column backs up because of the crowds of spectators,
and at that moment his horse gets pushed into the band, in among
the shiny trombones and trumpets: it rears and shies. The captain,
sword in hand, can hardly keep his seat. The shame of it! In the
end he has to dismount, and Lieutenant Kuhlmann takes over the
lead.

Incidentally, the policeman isn't there, the one who, with sword and
waxed moustache, has always led the whole parade on the Kaiser's
birthday.

Karl sits at the window, looking down at the parade winding its
way through the streets. He is just sixteen, and the next day he tries
to enlist as a volunteer. He strides along the streets, thinking of
Timm, the Mecklenburg hussar who was the only one to capture a
French Guard's eagle during the Napoleonic Wars. And he looks
into the face of each man, wondering why he isn't volunteering too,
he wants the German Army to overflow with manpower.

He goes into the barracks, where young men with cardboard boxes
under their arms are just being led off, young men still in mufti,
wearing straw boaters and stiff collars, and the sergeant looks fero-
cious.

"I'll make you lift your feet!" he shouts, and: "Bloody civilians!"

.   .   .

Karl is rejected. "Under age and poor eyesight," he is told. He is sent away with his tail between his legs, a peewee, no better than a runt.

Furious, he rushes home, furious and rebellious, and at home in the basement kitchen Giesing happens to be beating some egg whites. He asks her what she says to that? That they won't have him?

He paces up and down the kitchen, gesticulating; what do they mean, under age? Isn't he fully grown, doesn't he shave twice a week? Is he supposed to sit on his fanny in a classroom when Germany's future is at stake?

> Gird up your loins!
> The tip of my sword is itching!

No, Karl won't give up, he kicks the closet door shut with a crash. They can't get away with that, he says, and takes the train to Schwerin, to the Regional Command, as do many young men in these days, impatient, afraid the war might be over by the time they have reached the mandatory age.

The head of the Regional Command, an elderly captain, emerges from the next room twiddling his moustache. He understands, of course, that young fellows want to volunteer. Back in 1870 he had the same experience, under age! Under age! they told him. And he so badly wanted to hit those Frenchies over the head! (He remembers it as if it were yesterday.) In those days too young, today too old . . . But no, there's nothing he can do. He simply *can't* take this young man here, sixteen years old, that's just too young.

But wait a moment—Kempowski?

"Isn't your father a shipowner? In Rostock?"

He has a feeling he knows him: Kempowski. Surely he's heard that name somewhere? So perhaps one *could* close an eye, Germany's future is at stake, after all . . .

"I don't see why not, young man!" he says, hesitatingly, and whispers with his clerk whether things can't be fixed up somehow, and Karl stands so stiffly at attention that his pince-nez almost falls off his nose.

Things *can* be fixed up somehow, as it turns out, and in the basement kitchen in Rostock Karl grabs hold of Giesing and whirls her around the stove, from which the flames are shooting out. What does she think the captain said to him? he asks her: that Germany needs many young men of his type, that's what the captain said, and had slapped him on the shoulder.

His father also says, "I don't see why not," youth wants to go to war, that's nothing new, but first he must go to the dentist to have his teeth looked at, who knows whether there'll be a dentist at the front! (How lucky to be owning the two steamers now, back and forth they ply between Sweden and Stettin, with long waits for cargo—ore is needed, a lot of ore, and what a good idea to have acquired an automobile, the horses would certainly have been requisitioned!)

Schenk, in his hand-tailored lieutenant's uniform, says: Don't rush things! It's no picnic, being a recruit. He pours himself a glass of red wine and says: Cheers! He is reminded of those starry nights, he says, down there in German Southwest Africa, and how he used to sit astride his horse, keeping a lookout, and there might have been a nigger behind every bush. Karl shouldn't imagine it's all beer and skittles, being a soldier. It also has its dark side. And he thinks of the dead farming folk he saw as a child. And especially of one, who lay there sprawled . . .

He must first go to the dentist, his father says, to Dr. Moral of the triangular head, on Bismarck-Strasse. But he mustn't allow Dr. Moral to send him to Dr. Mandelbaum, the heart specialist, to make sure he can tolerate the drilling, we know all about that trick.

"How's your father?" asks Dr. Moral as he raises the chair with the foot pedal, and then he discovers that Karl has a cavity, but he gives him only a temporary filling: "You'll be back in a month anyway!"

30 A Friend

My name is Georg Schultheiss, Georg, known as "Georgie"; in the summer of 1914 Karl Kempowski and I were out helping with the harvest.

It's a long, long time ago.

When the war broke out, everyone wanted to make himself useful, serve his country, right? Find an outlet for the idealism that inspired us all. It was different from today, when people laugh at you if you as much as mention the word "Fatherland," when it is almost a point of honor to get out of military service.

Qui Deus ferrum genuit
Nos vetuit servire . . .

When the war broke out, we schoolboys went to Alt-Gaartz, a very pretty, typically Mecklenburg estate right by the sea, with a white manor house behind tall trees and an ancient fieldstone church that in the Middle Ages must have served as a fortress against the Danes or the Swedes, who were constantly invading the area and robbing and plundering wherever they could. In Alt-Gaartz we helped bring in the crop, it was still standing, you see, the farmhands all being at the front.

I still remember that work with pleasure. We were young and strong and full of vigor. An enormous, bright yellow field, stretching to the horizon! And cutting that field, just stop and think: seventeen scythes in a row, moving rhythmically: shipp, shipp, shipp . . . It was really something!

Shipp, shipp was the sound it made, and every time the golden corn sank to the ground. Seventeen comrades in a row, tanned by the sun. And above, over the field, the deep blue of the sky with great billowing clouds.

We enjoyed the work, although we were paid only fifty pfennigs a day: that was meant for wear-and-tear on our clothing.

It was a very hot summer, the one of 1914. The estate was right by the water, at noon we always went for a swim, and we always swam in the buff. Erich Woltersen was quite a contortionist, he used to float on his back and arch his spine so that only his stomach stuck out of the water. And then he would try to make only his pecker visible.

We spent all day in the field, and in the evenings we rode the horses into the water. And then we would flirt with the village beauties. One of us had a squeezebox along, and we'd make music and dance under the stars.

We were all friends, a big circle. All came from the same school, all ate from *one* big cauldron (pea soup!), and we were waiting to be sent to the front. We slept in the great hall of the manor house, under the grim portraits of earlier lords of the manor. There were some fine chests and closets there, but not enough beds, they were one short. So two of us were supposed to share a bed, and no one liked the idea. We wouldn't go for that. Next morning the lady of the house comes in and asks: "Well, and how did everyone sleep?"

"Badly," we said, "very badly."

So she had an additional bed slapped together out of rough planks, a "coachman's bed" we called it, and no one wanted to lie in it. We felt that to sleep on a coachman's bed would besmirch our honor. Finally we came to an agreement that whoever slept on it was not to be made fun of, and that whoever did make fun of him would be beaten up by the others.

When we had finished, helping with the harvest, I mean, and were ready to leave, Karl Kempowski put on the chauffeur's uniform, white with gold braid. And he put on a cap and drove us all to the station. Oh, it was glorious! Hitting the curves, and then: Hooray!

Karl couldn't drive at all, I mean he could but he didn't have a driver's license.

At the station we naturally wanted to celebrate our departure, and Karl had to sit at a separate table, after all he was only the "chauffeur." We told the waiter: "Bring the chauffeur a glass of beer!" That took care of class distinctions.

Pretty soon we were sent to the front. I don't think any of us were left behind. I was sent to Romania—actually that was quite a soft job—and Karl Kempowski fought in all the battles in Flanders, Ypres, and so on. He really lay in the shit, and he soon got the Iron Cross, too. He was very proud of it. At that time the Iron Cross was worth a lot, everyone wanted to have one. It was worth risking one's life for it. Besides, it was a beautiful decoration, so simple, after all it had been designed by no less an artist than von Schinkel. "The Iron Cross," it was meant as a program, everyone was supposed to be eligible, regardless of rank or class. "I no longer recognize any parties . . . ," that sort of thing.

Ribbon decorations were not yet that common. The "Pour le mérite" was awarded to airmen when they had shot down so-and-so-many enemy aircraft. It was blue enamel, I believe Göring had one, and Röhm too, I guess.

Yes, I knew Karl Kempowski. I can still see us, seventeen strong young fellows, all in time, shipp, shipp, shipp, mowing into the sun, I see it like in a picture, like in an oil painting. Can you understand that?

31

In April 1915 Karl marches off to war, to the sound of singing and band music, a flower stuck in his rifle, accompanied by onlookers. By this time there aren't many people looking on, but there are enough.

The band plays the "Forward!" march. At the freight yards it wheels smartly around and marches back to barracks: to pick up new recruits, always new, always more. The officers sit on their prancing horses, they are still a bit tense. Each has a newly sharpened sword in his scabbard.

Karl is wearing a spiked leather helmet with field-gray covering. On his back a full pack; hanging from his belt are his bayonet, likewise newly sharpened, a spade, bread bag, flask, and ammunition pouches. Eighty pounds of equipment? That weighs a man down.

"I, Karl-Georg Kempowski, am marching off to war!" is what he thinks. "I'm actually marching off to war, with a rifle over my shoulder and real cartridges in my pouch."

And he is also thinking of Erich Woltersen, Erex, poor fellow, who is not allowed to go, whose father refused permission.

"Not until you've finished high school," he had said.

Karl has taken leave of half of Rostock, he was offered cigars—"I'd be going too if I were just a bit younger"—and port wine. He said good-by to old Ahlers: "Are yer sure yer know what y're doin', me boy?" and to Professor Volkmann—"I've been to Rome, and I've been to Athens . . .," who had a bust of Zeus on his desk and was in the process of hatching a war poem. He was very keen on adding some valid poetry to his prose, he had said.

. . .

Karl had also been to see Mrs. von Wondring, of course: "Aren't you going to finish school first, my boy?" and Sodemann the head clerk: "All I'm saying is . . ."

But not Mr. Lehmann, the teacher who had given him his first paralyzing slap in the face: he had already fallen at the front. In November 1914 at Langemarck, singing, so they say, with his students.

The troop train is made up of branch-line cars, interurban cars, cattle cars, and open freight cars. The soldiers get on: "Here, comrade, there's room in here!"

Sleeping-car to Paris!

And: "Hey, comrade, there's room for you here too! The more the merrier!" Fine thing, if German soldiers couldn't get along with each other!

Fathers wearing pince-nez stand on the platform, saying: "And don't disgrace me!" And mothers with enormous hats on which flowers and fruit have been arranged.

The mothers say: "Take care, my boy, will you? D'you hear?" And their eyes are swollen from long weeping. But the soldiers are laughing. They positively shake with laughter, they haven't had such a good time in a long while.

Just before the train pulls out, Giesing arrives with some flowers and —more important—with a tuck box full of sandwiches. There she stands, looking up, the little person with the firm face. Karl lifts her up and gives her a kiss, prompting laughter and cries of "Bravo!" The tuck box is distributed—mettwurst from Hohen-Sprenz—and then the train pulls out of the station.

> Must I now, must I now
> Leave this pretty little town, pretty little town,
> While you, my love, stay here . . .

Soldiers are leaning out of every window, and they are all waving, even if no one is there to wave to.

The churches sink below the horizon, St. Nicholas's with the big "1 8 8 8" on its roof. St. Mary's, St. James's, and St. Peter's. St. Peter's last of all, the church with the slightly hunched spine, as if in defiance of the wind. The soldiers are still waving, the train winds its way through the countryside: gentle slopes, scattered woods, and fields where farm women are planting potatoes. Along the railway embankment, flocks of goats and kids herded by little children.

Finally the soldiers do sit down and light up cigars or curved pipes with silver lids on the bowls. They are in high spirits, each gabbling louder than the next. About the heroic deeds they're going to perform, and how they're going to show those Frenchies! The main thing is that they get to the front in time. What a ghastly thought, if the others were to drink up all the wine!

> Don't give up! Don't give up!
> Don't give up in storm and stress . . .

They are singing in the next compartment, and everybody joins in: "German singing—no one else has anything like it!"

Where are they being taken, that's the big question. Latrine rumors are rampant: to Flanders or to Alsace? Or maybe somewhere entirely different?

The main thing is to stay together, in this jolly group.

In Hamburg the train makes its first stop, and at Wandsbek Station! The men are allowed to get out: rice in beef broth is being doled out on the platform, sandwiches with coffee or tea. Wonderful! Young girls are serving, exceptionally pretty girls. If one is not mistaken, they seem to be *upper*-class girls, *better*-class, from the lyceum? What d'you think?

The soldiers, who will soon be on their way again, are favored with tender, uncommitted glances . . .

Karl picks up the bouquet given him by Giesing and calls a boy over to him: he tells him to take the flowers to Grethe de Bonsac on Bären-Strasse.

The boy dashes off with, so it seems to Karl, "shining eyes."

. . .

Grethe is surprised to receive flowers. No, the boy doesn't know any name, he only knows: "It was someone from Rostock!"

A little note is tied to the bouquet:

> Oh, that we must part like this,
> Let me have just one more kiss!

And that makes Grethe think not of Karl Kempowski but of August Menz—although he never did kiss her—and of the tango with sixteen different steps, ". . . left . . . and right . . . and—stop!" and as she recalls that wonderful wedding feast a hot wave mounts in her. *Isn't* it nice of him to send her flowers!

"The lake is roaring, seeking out its victim": the soldiers are on their way again, night falls, they shove their packs under their heads and stretch out their legs: on the benches, on the floor, and in the luggage rack. One even hangs his tarpaulin between the hooks. At the first strong jolt of the train the strings rip, and the occupant falls on top of the others, which first provokes curses but then good-natured teasing, for: fine thing, if such little incidents were to lead to quarreling! Out there in the front lines there will be far worse experiences to be coped with.

Next morning limbs are stiff, some of the men tackle their "Kaiser Wilhelm Torte," as indefatigable wags call the army bread, others look for a chance to wash. The train stops at a small station, the engine driver opens a tap and out flows lukewarm water from the boiler, just enough to moisten face and hands and spread the dirt around so that one looks worse than ever.

On the following day it is clear where they are being taken: to Flanders! To teach the Belgians a lesson. Why did they have to defy the Germans? Instead of allowing them to march through without all this shilly-shallying? Typical of those little nations with their exaggerated national pride. Such brainless stupidity. They deserve a rap over the knuckles . . .

Beyond the frontier everything seems very foreign to the soldiers.

Excursion to Paris!

The train travels on the left-hand rails, according to the Belgian system. This is no longer their beautiful Fatherland. In Germany, people had waved to them from every window, here in Flanders the people lower their shutters or turn their backs, pointedly: How strange, aren't we all of the same blood?

The German soldiers don't let it bother them, they sing louder than ever and merrily toast the passing scene.

> Russian sausage, French champagne,
> German blows—let's have it again!

The train is moving much too slowly, they find, and they think of their comrades in the front line who at this very moment might be beginning to waver, struggling to cling to their positions under the whistling bullets but wavering. They can't hold out any longer . . . and at this supremely critical moment the loyal Mecklenburgers will appear on the battlefield, that's what they are thinking, and in impeccable style at that: "Fix bayonets!"—and the enemy is stunned, for suddenly wave upon wave comes storming out of the woods or out of the bushes or wherever, no one has foreseen this, they are stunned, throw away their rifles, and take to their heels!

The train travels over a section of the main line here, of a branch line there.

> Take, O Lord, whate'er I have,
> I freely therewith part,
> As long as Thou wilt deign to save
> My faithful German heart!

On the map this looks like a zigzag. Every section has to be made use of to keep those vast quantities of supplies rolling according to a minutely detailed plan.

"For God's sake, where's that shipment of muzzle-protectors?"

"Patience, patience, it's on its way!"

The little railway stations of Flanders with all their flowers really look very spruce. "Culturre and naturre." One hasn't expected that at all. Almost like in Germany, but then again quite different. The flowers are the result of a competition, the soldiers don't know that, a competition organized by the Belgian Touring Club before the war, the "Gares fleuries."

Belgian railway officials, however, are conspicuous by their absence. Quite inexplicably, they have refused to do duty for the German Army. German railway personnel stand on the platform, raising their hands in salute, and in some ways this is of course much more agreeable than those sour types who begrudge the German armies their victory.

"Franc-tireurs" or "snipers" are said to have actually shot at German soldiers, so the story goes, without uniforms, without being regular combatants, shooting from some attic window, and the women standing at the door, all innocence: "What, from our house? Someone's supposed to have shot from our house?"

Pretty soon the devastation starts, overturned railway cars beside the tracks (never seen the underside of a locomotive before!), burned-out buildings and wooden crosses on little mounds: graves. The singing subsides, it no longer seems appropriate.

The following morning everyone has to get off the train. End of the line. The packs are deposited on a meadow. Numerous troop units have already camped here, as can be seen from the repulsive remains of the field butchery and the overflowing latrines. What a pigsty: "Volunteers step forward!"

Suspiciously the captain has them number off to make sure the "members of his flock" are all present and that one or the other has not gone astray, *inadvertently* gone astray, by mistake that is; for running away or sneaking off is unthinkable. A German soldier taking to his heels?

Then food is distributed: sauerkraut with beans and pork, everyone can have as much as he wants. And in the end everyone *has* to have some more. Fine thing, if the stuff were to rot here! That would be a sin.

. . .

After the meal, "iron rations" of canned vegetables and meat are handed out. In addition each man receives one mark and ninety pfennigs, four cigars, a hymnal, and extra cleats for his boots. Also, a hundred and eighty cartridges, and room has to be found for these in each pack.

While the men are standing around, watching the locomotive being switched and finally steaming off with the empty cars, still with straw on their floors, heading for home, and while they smoke cigarettes and roll up each other's shoulder straps (because of espionage), endless supply columns drive past along the highway. Among the forage wagons there is also artillery, in staggering quantities, guns of a size one has never seen before.

Isn't it amazing what those efficient men in the Ministry of War have acquired and stockpiled? One hardly knows which to admire more, the courage of the assault troops at the front or the ice-cold intelligence of the best brains in the rear. Slapping a map onto the rough table, tapping it with one finger: "Six more batteries over here, and some shock troops through this cut in the forest. And further supplies from over there, in large quantities, in tremendous quantities. The best ammunition and the best provisions—that's the least we can do for our brave men."

Endless supply columns rumble along the road, wagon after wagon, the horses with raised heads and nostrils, panting, sweat-flecked flanks and tense legs on which the muscles show up like cords and knife slashes: whipped to the limits of exertion, they strain and stomp their way along. Their eyes, those great dark eyes, bulge out of their sockets while the braided leather whips of the drivers crack down on backs and rumps. And behind them rumbles and squeaks the heavy load of guns and gun carriages, bouncing and creaking over the potholes.

Prisoners are to be seen, too: English, French, Indian, Zouaves, and Belgians. The English strangely arrogant and impassive, the French cheerfully waving: family men, no mistaking their recent civilian status.

Suddenly German infantry is moving past, straight from the trenches? The fellows look terrible: they have beards and haggard faces. Their uniforms are encrusted with yellow mud. Why should they look so dirty? Not a bit proud and soldierly. So exhausted, on their last legs?

It dawns on the men that things up front must be a bit different from what they imagined (although the French shells, so one has heard, are filled with sawdust . . .).

However, there is not much time for reflection, they are again ordered to fall in; foot wraps still have to be distributed.

During revolver inspection there is an incident. A reservist's weapon goes off, and instantly one of the men in the front rank collapses, without a sound. The bullet has gone through both his thighs. Deplorable as the incident is, there is still cause for laughter: the tallest corporal in the company faints at the sight of the blood.

After the transport commander has made a speech in which he calls the Almighty the threefold great Architect of the globe, Whom one must thank for having chosen His German nation to punish the English, those braggarts!: "We vow, O Lord, to use the filth we have to wade in here to stuff the mouths of those blackguards, scoundrels, and cutthroats so that they won't open them again for centuries!"—after he has made this speech, which is regarded as "rousing," he drives off in an automobile (blue vapor rising in a spiral from the exhaust pipe): new soldiers must be brought, capital material, new ones and more new ones, and that's why he must return to the Fatherland, although he would much, much rather fight in the front line with his loyal Mecklenburgers! It really makes his heart bleed!

The unit waits for a gap in the transport snake, it squeezes in between artillery and ammunition wagons, just as over there among the French, on the other side of the front, at this very moment other, albeit blue, soldiers are probably squeezing into an endless stream, "horizon"-blue soldiers with strange red trousers and curiously buttoned-back greatcoats, a stream that will in turn flow into the enemy positions and peter out there.

> The birds in the forest
> And their merry merry song,
> Some day, oh some day
> We'll be back home again.

Crunch-crunch-crunch is the sound of the soldiers marching along the highway. Marching songs, that's something new for the Belgians, now they do look, and there are some Belgian children—believe it or not—who run alongside, skipping along wearing paper helmets, saluting. The Belgian back there who is beating up his son for saluting should get a punch in the nose, it would serve him right. Instead of being happy about the young people's spirit that transcends all national barriers.

Crunch-crunch-crunch, in time with the ever-repeated, ever-the-same marching songs.

> . . . some day, oh some day
> We'll be back home again . . .

"Stop song!" shouts the captain on his horse, shaking his head. Wasn't there actually someone singing a second voice? "Listen to the column ahead!" These minor thirds are disgusting, so mushy, so thoroughly unmanly.

Soon they are marching through ruined villages: lonely chimneys in the rubble. Dead horses lie beside the road, charred oxen and pigs. In those houses that are still inhabitable the shutters are closed, there are no more Belgian boys wearing paper helmets.

At one point two children run past, girls, aged twelve or thirteen, with ragged skirts and bare feet, carrying a pot of soup: the free hand of one of them is holding up a stick with a white rag tied to it. What's that supposed to mean?

The sun is high in the sky, searing the countryside. They pass deserted farms as well as trenches and barbed-wire entanglements from which the enemy has been dislodged. The entanglements are a hundred feet wide and stretch all the way to the horizon. Marching has become laborious. The road goes uphill, not steeply but very gradually. The pack starts to press, and the field flask is empty. Hour follows upon hour, the trees stand by the wayside, and so do the milestones: better not look at them, or progress will become even more grueling!

Once an enemy airplane comes toward them, flying very low, they can clearly see the man in it, wearing a leather cap and big goggles. He leans over the side. Could that fellow be waving at them?

The soldiers shoot off a salvo of rapid fire. A thousand rifles shooting simultaneously, the noise is indescribable, and the bullets resound through the air like ocean waves.

Two valleys are crossed, two low hills ascended and descended, toward that distant rumble. The soldiers have ceased to absorb impressions, have long ago stopped singing, either of war or of home, either in unison or in thirds.

The sun shines straight into their faces, the road is a single grayish column of dust. Moreover, there are constant commands of "Move over!" Automobiles overtake the column, empty Red Cross vehicles, ammunition trucks, and senior officers, leaving in their wake a cloud of dust that settles in the soldiers' lungs.

One doesn't mind moving aside, but the impatient, arrogant C.O.'s' automobiles don't make themselves popular: horns bray to the accompaniment of foul-mouthed abuse from the drivers. The officers even stand up in their cars and shout at the "clumsy clods," threatening report and discipline.

Farther on, the column shuffles by stuck automobiles, silently gloating.

> Show the world, show the world!
> All united flags unfurled!

Something to be observed with a certain amount of satisfaction.

Karl eventually feels he can't go any farther, although with his good boots, the "narrow-shafters" his father has had made for him, he is much better off than many of the others whose feet are nothing but a mass of sores.

No indeed, this is no picnic.

The exertion is enormous, not a word is spoken, not even by the captain on his horse. One foot is placed before the other, the blood pounds in one's head, and flashes of light shoot through the eyes.

At one point someone staggers from the rank and pitches headlong into the ditch; he is one of the older men. For a while he lies there, his head on his pack, his spiked helmet placed beside him, his tunic collar open. He is given some water, and then he dies. It happens so quietly, as if there were nothing to it: on the field of honor.

Finally evening comes. They march past a house that is still intact, and through the window Karl can see an officer sitting in the soft light of a kerosene lamp, smoking a cigar and reading a book.

Strange, for him to be sitting there so comfortably and reading! Karl is amazed, and suddenly he feels a pang.

"Are you sure you know what you're doing?"

He is reminded of Rostock, of his little room. Felix Dahn: *A Struggle for Rome.* When peace comes, how he is going to enjoy all that. Strange, really, that one didn't at the time.

At last they stop, in the middle of the night. Thousands of shells have torn up the fields here. They are now immediately behind the front. Although the rumbling is still quite distant, there appears to be some rabbit shooting going on close by, to judge by the isolated shots.

The corporal notes down the names and says: "There, now you

can sleep," and goes off leaving the men alone in the pitch-black night. They throw themselves down wherever they happen to be standing and instantly fall asleep, although the rabbit shooting still seems to be going on close by.

Unfortunately, at this moment it starts to rain, lightly but steadily, and before long the soldiers are soaked to the skin.

He reigns, her reins, it rains . . .

Something has to be done if one is to get any rest, that's obvious. So the tarpaulin is unbuckled from the pack: how was it done? How did it work? In the squelching mud the pegs won't hold, again and again the wet tarpaulins splash down onto the men. They roll over in the mud, grope for the torn-out pegs, and curse.

Finally they lie down resignedly: they can't get any wetter than they are.

Karl distinctly feels the mud giving way under him and forming a little hollow. He draws up his limbs and presses them as tightly as possible to his body. He scrunches up his toes. Don't risk a single movement, not one, for each movement releases a terrible feeling of wet and cold and a violent trembling to the very bone. The fact that it can be cold and wet at the front has been repeated often enough by Bobrowski, his father's wheelchair attendant. Karl remembers this now. But *such* wetness? He didn't mention anything about that, and it really is a bit much . . .

That there are soldiers who will poke their bayonet into a wounded enemy is another thing the wheelchair attendant talks about.

How would one go about that, stabbing an enemy to death, one would have to find the heart, one can't simply poke them in the stomach . . .

And how would it look, a man whose guts have gushed out? Would one get to see such a thing?

If Erex could see him, or Grethe, if Grethe de Bonsac could see him now, she'd be amazed. How sorry she would feel that she hadn't been a little kinder and more responsive to him.

. . .

At three in the morning Karl wakes up. He is wide awake. He pulls out his watch, good heavens, only three? Is that possible? Or has his watch stopped?

He is shivering. If he doesn't fall asleep again right away, how is he going to be able to fight? How can a fellow fight if he wakes up at three in the morning?

He feels more and more awake and finally gets up and sits down under a tree. Collar upturned. In the distance, light flares up. It isn't sheet lightning, he can be sure of that.

As he sits there, in his muddy clothes, his collar turned up and the flashes on the horizon, he sees in his mind's eye one of those patriotic pictures, the kind to be found in the *Berliner Illustrirte:* "Lonely Vigil." Yes, he Karl Kempowski is now keeping a lonely vigil for Germany, and soon he'll be fighting, just you wait, you fellows up front!

At six o'clock reveille is sounded, and he realizes that he must have nodded off some time ago. The soldiers clean themselves as best they can (scraping the dirt off with their bayonets), and some of them start little boxing bouts to warm up. Coffee and bread-and-jam are handed out, and spirits revive.

After that they parade before Lieutenant-Colonel Kümmel, known as "Dauntless" because each of his numerous addresses contains the words "call of duty" and "dauntless." The men form an open square around their colonel. The sun shines benignly, and the larks shout in the air.

The regimental commander speaks briefly, clearly, and "bluntly." And, true enough, that word resounds several times, the one that has earned him the name of "Dauntless." And when it does, no one bats an eyelash, for they have been warned that it's best not to tangle with Dauntless.

He proceeds to review the ranks. Why, this is an incredible bunch of filthy bastards! and his adjutant makes a note. Never in his life has he seen such a bunch of filthy bastards! And this is supposed to be the top-notch replacement he has been promised?

"We'll first have to put them through the mill," he says to his adjutant. "This is hopeless, it's an absolute disgrace."

He looks each man straight in the eye.

Can he rely at all on this man here? It makes him wonder, the fellow's appearance. And can he rely on that man over there? he wonders too.

Some of them he asks: "How must laced boots be stowed in the pack?" He insists on knowing. The answer has to be: "The right one on the left, and the left one on the right!" He also has them run through some manual drill: "Present arms!"

At the next parade he does not wish the soldiers to look so rumpled, he tells his adjutant, who makes a note. That mustn't happen again. Never in his life has he run across such a bunch of filthy bastards.

We're not in Russian Poland, after all.

Then he rides off, to a position behind the lines where there is a dugout and telephones for directing the whole operation. Hilltop command? Those times are gone.

At home in Rostock, Anna Kempowski is at this very moment taking all her son's suits out of the wardrobe and giving them away: "He'll be killed anyway," she says, and through the dumbwaiter she shouts down: "What happened to the coffee? Am I supposed to wait forever?"

32

Father de Bonsac cannot understand why suddenly there is no further advance on the Western Front. He is sitting at his desk with *Andree's World Atlas* open in front of him. Everything was going so well! Brussels, Lille, Amiens, Reims . . . and now suddenly nothing?

Falling back, in fact, if one has correctly understood the reports?

He has locked his French art books away in the bookcase, that's not suitable reading material now. All those stained-glass windows. As if we didn't have anything like that in Germany! Stained-glass windows? *En masse!* Loads of them. No, instead of the art books he has brought out his atlas, the heavy world atlas, and stares at the map of the Western war theater: Why don't they get a move on there! Forward, with full German power! And he thinks of the battle panorama in the city where the wax cavalry slashes down at the wax soldiers.

What a good thing they were still able to see France, he and his dear Martha: hors d'oeuvre, so now one has quite a different feeling when Lille or Arras is mentioned, quite a different mental picture.

Qu'est-ce que c'est que ça?

He is terrified that he might have to starve. True, down in the cellar there are all kinds of bottled fruit and vegetables, homemade in prewar days, but the bread now contains potato flour, and butter is already rationed. At first he refused to buy on the black market. But now he does frequently go to Gurtbüttel's grocery store on

Hammer-Strasse, at night, after ten, coming home with rolled oats and flour, sides of bacon or sausages: smoked spare ribs with kale, he loves that, or smoked eel.

Up in the attic, where the Africa trunks and the camphor chests used to stand, his boy's rocking horse and the cartons containing the Nativity figures from Bavaria, he has knocked together a latticed partition, and that's where he keeps the cardboard drums of rolled oats, semolina, and flour under lock and key, for in the partition is a door with a heavy padlock, and the slats of the partition are so close together that no hand can reach through. At regular intervals he stirs and digs over his stocks to prevent them getting wormy, and crumbles the lumps with his fingers. And while he is stirring and shoveling and crumbling, his mouth waters. No, they'll have to wait till next week before he hands out anything again, he is adamant, Martha can plead and beg as much as she likes: Tuesday of next week. Or Wednesday. We'll see. And when he does, he weighs it out on the scales and hands it to his wife as if it were gold dust.

"Be careful with it, Martha dear? Nice and thrifty, hm? My dear?"

One day the word gets out: Inspectors are on the prowl! They are already at the market square in Wandsbek.

So, puffing and groaning, he carries all the supplies to his office. But however unobstrusively he stows them away, his brother Bertram sees it, and says: "But my dear Willi! What can you be thinking of?" And an unspoken reproach lies in his clear blue eyes: doesn't it occur to Willi that he also has children, six daughters, each more delicate than the other, six daughters who would also enjoy having flour, semolina, and rolled oats? And have *nothing* to satisfy their hunger? Or *very little*, anyway?

Germany is mentioned on this occasion, and the Savior, too, who sacrificed Himself for mankind.

So Wilhelm de Bonsac carries everything home again, no less puffing and groaning, and now deeply worried into the bargain. First,

because of the inspections, and second, because of his Christian conscience. Oughtn't he to share the necessities of life with his brother
Bertram and Bertram's family? That is the question here. But, so
he argues: six children? Why six, come to think of it? *He* doesn't
have six, does he? No. And: if a man does have six, it's up to him
to look after them.

Just as *he* looks after *his* children. After all, it isn't exactly easy
for him to traipse all the way to Gurtbüttel's and inquire after his
wife, how she is and so on and so forth, nobody does as much for
him. And: why doesn't good old Bertram ever go to that devil-may-
care Hans? In that house there is a permanent smell of fried eggs,
and that Englishwoman there wears an expression as if butter
wouldn't melt in her mouth.

And how about those lovely pears, year after year, he hardly ever
received any thanks for those either. Always happy to take, and yet,
come to think of it, never anything in return, a real "sponger," as
they say.

Might have offered a hand, too, at the time dear Martha was
so ill . . .

Or Richard. If only *once* they could have shared the anxiety felt
for Richard—Mounted Artillery!—scarcely a word, just a: "How's
everything?" and quite perfunctory at that.

No.

The garden, too, has undergone some changes. The beds of lily-of-
the-valley and chrysanthemums have been dug over, as have the
beds with the cress hearts *H, R, G,* and *L:* now kohlrabi and carrots
are being grown there; borage, too, which normally one really didn't
care for. "Winter asparagus," as it is now called, with an aromatic
flavor reminiscent of prehistoric times when the wind still whistled
across the heath and the mammoth and aurochs stomped across the
steppes.

The apples from the garden are peeled and sliced, and the slices are
threaded and dried, upstairs on the bedroom balcony; the balcony
door is kept locked, and from time to time one goes upstairs and,

sucking one's teeth, looks to make sure they are still there. The apple slices are intended for the winter when there might be nothing else. The skins are boiled to make apple soup, which tastes so good that one seriously considers having it in peacetime, too.

The Louise-bonne pears are no longer being sold, nor are they being given away, they are all eaten at home now; every day each person gets one. They are stored in the cellar, on the homemade wooden racks next to the jars from prewar days. One's mouth waters as one turns them over and examines them for bruises or bad spots. He does this personally, Wilhelm de Bonsac, all alone, he is not above that, this merchant prince, for there is no one to help him anyway. He has to do everything himself, stirring the rolled oats, flour, and semolina in the attic, threading the apple slices, and turning over the pears. It's enough to make one despair.

But satisfying, too.

Serious consideration is given to whether the paths should be dug up for growing vegetables, and calculations are made as to the possible yield of kohlrabi and Brussels sprouts. Or whether one should obtain some tomato plants, *solanum Lycopersicum*, those new fruits of which it is not yet certain whether or not they are poisonous, but the neighbor has now been planting them for the third year and he always holds them up to the light as he picks them: what wonderful fruit he is picking!

They have to be peeled, sliced with onions, then eaten on bread; like meat, like beefsteak tartare, that's what they taste like, at least according to the enthusiastic neighbor, and he asks Mr. de Bonsac, with all his lilies, whether he wouldn't like to taste one of these fruits of the sun?

No, snaps Mr. de Bonsac, for that so-called gentleman with his seemingly harmless wife has long been known as a follower of the nudist cult, in other words of some disgusting practice that involves taking off his clothes and lying naked in the sun!

No.

Or rather: yes.

He wouldn't mind a taste, a small basket wouldn't be refused, but as for planting them, first wait and see how they turn out. (It is said that in Italy there are whole fields of them.) Perhaps after all they are more poisonous than one thinks.

Grethe no longer plays tennis, she is now working at the Mühlberg, in a day nursery. Hertha is in Berlin at the Auguste-Viktoria House, a very exclusive affair that normally only accepts ladies of the aristocracy; but then one *is* aristocratic, at least almost.

Lotti is in the Harz Mountains, at a finishing school. The dear child is taking a domestic-economy course there.

> One, two, three,
> Dicke-docke-dee!
> Dicke-docke play the fife,
> The miller's lost his pretty wife,
> Searched the land for her in vain,
> I fear she'll ne'er come back again . . .

For the benefit of the neglected children, Grethe sings the songs she has learned from her mother and recites the sayings she has learned from Lene the maid: Peee, says the ol' owl . . . and the seventeen names of the Brettvogel family, she rattles those off just as fast as Lene can.

The day-nursery children, all sickly-looking and wan, cling to her apron, and one of them calls her "Mama."

They are pitiful children, with their cropped round heads, scabby and scrofulous. And that's why they must be nice and quiet after lunch and have a nap, though they aren't the least bit tired. A nap strengthens the nerves. And the little brain has time to digest all the benefits the children are receiving here, all the loving, healing care. Each child has a folding cot decorated with a deer or a mushroom. The blanket carries the same device as the cot: deer, mushroom, rabbit; to each his own. Grethe goes from one to the other, smoothing the blankets. Nap time: the little chicks must stop their chattering, they must lie quite still and not move. Here and there she pushes a cot to left or right so that the sun can shine on it with its strong, healing light. And here and there she lays a hand on a child's head, which gives the child a good feeling.

They must lie quite still, the little lambkins, and not move, otherwise it'll all be wasted, all the benefits they are receiving.

"If you don't stop talking this minute I'll close your mouth with sticky tape!"

Oh dear me no, Grethe doesn't beat about the bush! From spinking comes spunking . . . Those who don't behave are scolded, and some sticking plaster actually appears, together with a large pair of scissors.

Now at last they are quiet, and Grethe has a moment's peace and can join Thea, who is already making coffee, "nigger sweat." What fun it is to chat with Thea, she is always so understanding! She has already set out the two cups she brought along from home, and there is also a piece of sugar for each.

No, Thea is always understanding. August Menz being such a wonderful dancer, she has to hear that over and over again, a tango that nobody else could dance, and his *not* kissing her! Although he would have had every right to do so. She hears about that too.

Paints & Enamels, Wholesale.

The fact that Karl Kempowski isn't all that impressive is discussed, the human being is a sad machine, and that he has sloping shoulders? And such a broad accent? "Upon this baanch of wood let us repose . . ." How can anyone stand that? "The lake is roaring, seeking out its victim"?

And the way he kept on looking across at that actress at Silbi's wedding, instead of devoting himself to *her*. A bit wide of the mark, that boy (Grethe touches her cheek where she thinks she can still feel the wet spot from Graal), although—Rostock, that marvelous house, and: currant jelly with breakfast in bed?

Thea has an ear for everything, and understands everything, the two have sought and found each other: Thete and Grethe. In the morning they hug and kiss and in the evening they hate to part! (Actually from quite a modest background, but nice, so very nice.)

. . .

"Don't forget to bring home the soup!" says Father de Bonsac—the soup left over from feeding the children at the nursery. He reminds her every morning. It is a thin soup, a few carrots floating in it and a few dry shreds of meat.

"Don't forget, child!"

Even if one doesn't always finish it oneself, at least the fat can be skimmed off and the solids strained out and what's left taken to Mrs. Brettvogel, who has trouble satisfying her brood. (Four sons are at the front.) Or the soup can be poured onto that precious compost heap, for which one has recently scrounged some leather scraps, which are first pulverized.

He presses two jam pails into her hands, just to be sure.

"Don't forget to bring home the soup! D'you hear? Hm?"

One day Grethe leaves the empty pails behind on the streetcar; she runs after it like mad, with beating pulse. At each stop she almost catches up with it, and at the terminus she finally succeeds. And all because she is afraid of the dressing-down she could expect from her father: "My dear child, those lovely pails!" No, she mustn't risk that.

Another day she is lucky, a column of soldiers happens to be marching along the street, and the soldiers toss little bags of ship's biscuits to the passers-by: emergency rations, and she manages to grab one of the bags. She immediately eats up half the contents, and the other half is made into bread soup by her mother and Lisbeth and Lene, who also all taste the ship's biscuits.

"Why, that's wonderful!" says Father de Bonsac, although the soup has turned out a little thin from all the tasting. "Marvelous!" That's something to remember in peacetime, too, bread soup from ship's biscuits. Why not? Why hasn't anyone ever thought of it? And add a little fried bacon and onions and egg? Why shouldn't one have that in peacetime?

The caraway seed, though, will be left out, it gets between the teeth, it's enough to drive one crazy.

. . .

Grethe must bring home the soup and hand over fifty marks of her meager salary. "For board and lodging." Her father puts the money by without telling her, he'll give it all back to her again one day. With interest and compound interest.

"But Willi," says Hans, "a young girl like that surely ought to have a bit of ready cash . . ."

Ready cash? What kind of an expression is that? The only person capable of saying such a thing is someone who spends all his time in the café and takes a taxi to get to the office.

Ready cash or no ready cash—one is not going to accept reproaches from one's brother, it being absolutely none of his business. He'd do better to keep his mouth shut and look after his English wife, who used to be so nice and has recently taken to making such brazen remarks, always driveling about Belgium, about hands being hacked off and eyes being gouged out, and who fastens her blouse with safety pins. Who is being *tolerated* in Germany, although brave German soldiers at the front are sacrificing themselves to Albion's perfidy.

No, one doesn't wish to hear any reproaches from one's brother, nor later, possibly from one's own daughter. One certainly doesn't want to be accused someday of not having brought up one's children properly. Like in Hebbel's *Maria Magdalena*, the story of the little piece of sugar? No. He's not going to let that happen.

On Sundays Thea and Grethe go to church, where young Pastor Eisenberg has replaced Pastor Kregel, by now so very frail. Pastor Eisenberg preaches such "rousing" sermons, they call themselves the "Eisenberg people," and they revere him, although he is not exactly handsome, with his flat feet and big fish eyes. A Sunday without Pastor Eisenberg is no Sunday, on that they are agreed. The way he stands up there in the pulpit, a lonely apostle, and his sermons—so stirring and radical!

No, one must go to church, even if only for his sake, in order not to disappoint him. And they are not the only ones who think like that, people come from far away. Often they even sit on the steps of the chancel, it is so full, listening to him describe the struggle of the brave men in the West and in the East, and also regaling them with a vision of the Savior as a luminous figure hovering over the German trenches and protecting sons and fathers in this just cause.

Unfortunately this is always followed by reading out the names of the fallen, and it is a little embarrassing that this has to be done since one had just been saying that the Savior protects the soldiers. So one does it almost reluctantly and a bit helplessly. And one tries to lessen the impact by extended prayers, on each occasion, for *one* of those faithful men who is still alive and in the midst of the fray. The soldier is mentioned by name, and one can imagine how he is fortified when the wave of prayers engulfs him out there in the trenches.

Richard de Bonsac is one of the first to be so engulfed, in "the East," where he happens to be at this moment, plucking a chicken, a requisitioned chicken, and wearing slippers with his breeches.

Thea and Grethe sing in the choir, every Thursday,

Blessed are they that mourn . . .

and one day in St. Michael's Church too, for the benefit of the wounded, with their plaster-encased limbs sticking up in the air or a single eye staring out of a bandaged head: Who are these young ladies singing for us here, they must be upper-class ladies, mustn't they? Better-class, that is. That little blonde one with her hair parted in the middle? The one who opens her mouth so wide? D'you suppose she's had "one inside her"? Hm? Hardly, eh? Those young fellows singing there, they could certainly be used at the front . . .

Blessed are they that mourn—
That *mourn* . . .

Grethe sees the men on the stretchers and in wheelchairs, the men with their splinted limbs, and she can't go on singing, she feels choked up, and she has to hold onto herself not to burst into tears. Why is everything like this, she thinks, why must people be like this? Killing each other off? All those soldiers out there?

And she thinks of all those other men in field gray, and of a certain

XYZ in particular, with his handsome angular face and boyish laugh, she thinks especially of him.

. . . for they shall be comforted . . .

is now being sung, a few voices hold the note, others rise above it, and bows are drawn across bass fiddles, and suddenly she feels an almost uncontrollable sob rising in her throat, so that she has to slip to one side: No, she can't sing that now, and then come those oboes and now even the trumpets.

She is amazed that, under the impact of these sounds, the people don't all immediately rise to their feet and take each other by the hand and say: Yes indeed, we realize now, we'll stop it, all that bloodshed, we'll go to meet each other and say: Enough! It amazes her greatly.

When Grethe comes home she can see through the glass panel in the front door whether there is a letter on the hall table.

"Kindest regards, August." Or "Kind regards, Karl."

If there is no letter she takes her time, first greeting the dog who all this time has been jumping up at her, and she looks in the mirror, looks into it for quite a while, astounded by her own beauty.

But when there *is* a letter on the hall table, propped up between clothes brush and glove like a Christmas gift—particularly if the handwriting is vertical and not that rather feeble sloping one that might even be said to show weak character, it's hard to say, and which anyway is almost impossible to decipher—she pulls off her hat with all the hatpins, and Axel Pfeffer can whimper around her as much as he likes. While she runs up to her room she takes off her coat and throws it down onto the stairs.

"Do come in here, child!"

The coat can be hung up later, and the meal can wait. The main thing is that no one will come now to disturb her. "Yes, yes! I'll be there in a minute!" she calls—actually the best place to go would be the privy, *there* she could be sure of not being disturbed—and the envelope is ripped open with a hairpin, or rather it is not ripped open right away, it is first examined front and back and sniffed and pressed to her bosom, while she looks out of the window, beyond all the houses with all those people living in them.

The letters with the vertical handwriting contain photos, August Menz wearing a leather cap in his Albatross plane, his left hand raised, "All right, fellows, let's go!" In a moment the thing will start to move and fly toward the West, toward the gathering clouds.

That evening the neighbor is surprised to hear such beautiful piano playing suddenly coming from the de Bonsac house. "A-brim with Happiness," over and over again and with a very special emphasis. This happens once a week, that wonderful playing next door. And the neighbor decides that he must get his French horn out again.

33 A Comrade

My name is Neumann, and I knew Mr. Karl-Georg Kempowski in World War I.

More than sixty years have passed since I left Rendsburg to join the 210th Regiment—a regiment with a "high house number," as one used to say then, not *quite* out of the top drawer—as a volunteer with a thudding heart and fancy notions. One wanted to save the Fatherland, but ah me, those illusions soon went up in smoke.

After being unloaded we marched in pouring rain, still weighed down with packages from home, on a terrible road to Werckem, a small Flemish town. There we spent one night lying in straw on the floor of a pretty badly damaged house, dog-tired but still full of enthusiasm.

During the next few days we waited for our regiment that was up in the front line, and we waited in lively anticipation since it was going to be our home, as we knew, our crowd with whom we would be stuck for better or worse.

Three or four days later the time had come. Tired and dirty, the troops dragged themselves back from the front, all old people; we could hear them coughing before we even saw them, that's what I remember. I say "old people" for almost all of them had beards. But when they had shaved they had smooth, young faces, and before long they had also recovered from their exertions.

Among these "old men" I just mentioned was Karl Kempowski, an old man of seventeen. Those authorities should have been ashamed! At seventeen one is still a child. He came from Rostock, his father was a shipowner or broker or some such thing, "better class" anyway, you could tell that from his parcels. (Once he received a whole package of turkey drumsticks.)

He was a volunteer too, like me, not one of those conscripts who really had no liking for their job and some of whom were not even fit to be soldiers. Men with little aches and pains for whom the whole thing was too much of an effort, who groaned and complained and had their minds on home, on wife and child. (Today one can understand that.)

I quickly became friends with Kempowski, if only because the majority of the regiment came from the former province of Posen, and those people really seemed very strange to us. They were almost all Catholics, they'd cross themselves and recite the rosary when the going got tough. They smoked strong cigarettes and would rather have done without sausage and bread than their beloved *papyrossas*. We new fellows were immediately besieged for cigarettes, for cigarettes those men would drop everything. I gave away all my tobacco but got no thanks in return, on the contrary I was robbed blind. I had joined the company with a complete brand-new uniform, and within a short time all I had left was dirty old ragged duds and bashed-up rusty bits of equipment.

The same thing happened, of course, to the other newcomers. We were robbed by the "Polish sons from the Farthest East," as we called them, but among themselves they were as thick as thieves.

It is hardly likely that any of the members of the regiment at that time are still alive today; they were either killed in the war or have died of old age.

On Kreuz-Strasse in Hanover I once got to know a barber by the name of Scheibe who had served with the 6th Company. But that's more than forty-five years ago, and I'm sure Mr. Scheibe is no longer in the land of the living since he was quite a bit older than I.

I well remember one of the volunteers, a Wilhelm Kaiser, a middle-aged Alsatian, he was almost toothless and looked like an old woman. When we were tired and fed up, he managed to cheer us up by suddenly shouting: "War is a glorious thing!" At roll call he always had to call out his name as "Kaiser, Wilhelm!" which never failed to provoke roars of laughter.

I also remember dear old Kuplinsky very well, I had a real affection for him. It was he who called out to me during a hand-grenade battle: "All for de Fadderland, comrade, all for de great Fadderland!" He was already an old man and I'm sure he's no longer alive, even if he came through the war—or the wars, perhaps one should say.

I'd also like to mention our topkick, Sergeant Zarbock. He was a good soul who proved to be a real father to the younger soldiers especially. He always wore a long sword, and when he arrived in the morning a murmur would go through the ranks: "The cavalry's coming!" Carrying the sword was one of his whims, but no one minded for he was a good superior and a good human being.

Life in the trenches was pretty miserable. There weren't many who received as good parcels as Karl Kempowski, who whenever the mail was distributed was surrounded by so-called friends who would polish his boots for a cigarette butt. I can still see him pulling a whole side of bacon out of a carton. It really embarrassed him. The others might receive a bit of lard or woolen earmuffs knitted by devoted ladies—I had three of them—but certainly no sides of bacon.

I wasn't lucky enough to be blessed with wealthy parents, I'd get a parcel at most once a month, and then only a few cookies or those earmuffs, for my people in Rendsburg had barely enough to keep body and soul together.

We couldn't buy anything in the canteen either, since our pay amounted to all of fifty-three pfennigs a day! And you were really supposed to send some of that home to your family. Now and again, of course, there would be booty money, always a welcome extra allowance. This was paid when war matériel fell into German hands. The higher ranks used to get quite a bit of money then, we ordinary soldiers received proportionately less, but still it was always very nice.

Once we captured a heavy English machine gun, I was supposed to take it back to staff headquarters that night with another buddy. We had hardly started back when the barrage began, and my buddy took off. I fell with that heavy thing headfirst into a shell hole, into barbed wire, I was bleeding all over, and my uniform was torn. Finally, under constant fire on both sides, I crawled into a totally demolished forest, known as the "Polygon Forest," there was nothing left but tree stumps, I was at the end of my tether. And I said to myself: "I can't carry this thing any farther, I'm going to put it down right here!"

I leaned it against a tree and crawled to the rear, looking for some kind of protection or shelter. Next morning I went forward again with a buddy during a break in the firing, between four and five, and I actually found it! I made my way toward it by pure instinct, and there it was. I would never have believed I would ever find it again.

That's a job I'll never forget, as long as I live.

Toward the end of the war our pay was increased to one mark. A truly princely wage. But otherwise, of course, we lived for free, at the expense of the state. The state even provided a free funeral, always supposing some fragments were still available and hadn't been torn to shreds by heavy grenades or mines. In 1918, at Château-Thierry on the Marne, seventy kilometers from Paris, I happened to see a group of senior officers standing at a road intersection when they were suddenly hit by a heavy grenade and torn into a thousand pieces. In that instance the state saved on funeral expenses, for nothing of them was ever found.

Because of the shortage of wood, when there were heavy losses, the dead were simply wrapped in their tarps and buried in shallow graves. It was all the same to the dead. When there was more time, we dug up our hastily buried comrades and carried them back to the rear and buried them there with full honors. This always upset us very much. Corpses lying between the trenches in no-man's-land that couldn't be removed because of the virtual certainty of getting killed didn't prevent us from polishing off all the dried vegetables in our mess tins while in their immediate vicinity. One merely turned to one side to avoid some of the stench.

Often when we were digging trenches we came upon dead soldiers who had long lain covered by the mud and had served to feed the rats.

Almost every fallen Frenchman wore an amulet around his neck, with *"la vierge immaculée"* inscribed on it. We also found photographs, letters, and notebooks containing rhyming couplets. In the early days we would read the letters. I can remember one, a letter from a young wife: *"Petit-petit est toujours bien sage,"* it said at the end. She told her husband that she was sending him two pounds of chocolate and some gloves that wouldn't absorb the fog so much. We found the chocolate in his pocket, and we ate it up. We did indeed.

All through the war one felt under a heavy pressure that didn't go away until the war was over and one no longer had to listen to the incessant roar of the guns.

34

Karl's first weeks at the front pass quietly. They lie facing each other, "armed to the teeth," and do each other no harm; they lie in wait, merely trying to discover whether the other side is planning an attack. To the rear are the cannons, silent. Here and there a shot is fired that raises the alarm in some rear base or other. Then it is quiet again.

At night they dig trenches or do sentry duty. The sentry stands slightly raised in a niche against which he can lean and survey the approaches. Over his head is a metal sheet to protect him from aerial darts, and in front of him is a wall of sandbags: he has a blanket around his shoulders, his rifle beside him, and hand grenades at the ready.

To make it possible to observe the enemy, a steel plate with a narrow slit in it has been let into the sandbags. If the trenchscope is not used, the sentry looks through this slit to see whether anything is moving on the outer side. There are some Frenchmen who are such good shots that their bullets go right through the slit. There are also some who put their red *képi* on a stick and wiggle it about. The stupid Germans are supposed to think there's someone walking there.

When Karl is posted as sentry for the first time, he can hardly believe that he alone has been entrusted with the entire responsibility, and he stares across, straining his ears for the slightest sound. He's heard that there have been times when they have crept up, those *poilus,* and suddenly appeared right in front of the trench! What a ghastly thought!

It would be even more embarrassing if one were to sound the alarm by mistake. If one were to hit the metal sheet, bong-bong!, by mistake, and everyone came running up, fastening their helmets as they crawled out of the dugout, and asked: "What's up, for Christ's sake? Have you seen a ghost?" And the captain shouts: "What colossal idiot raised the alarm?"

No, better to keep a sharp lookout for anything that moves.

Empty cans have been hung in the barbed wire that clatter when anyone tampers with the wire. Moreover, one has binoculars with which to search every little mount, every crack. And sometimes one actually does see something; the fellow over there who is looking across to see if anything is moving on this side. One could "pick him off," but: shoot him down like on the practice range? Karl isn't keen to do that either, he feels inhibited. "A man who has never offended public morals lying in wait to murder someone?" he writes to Erich Woltersen in Rostock. That can't be what this war is about. If they were to charge shouting "Hurrah!" it would be a different story.

Erich Woltersen carries this letter around with him when he goes for a walk with his girl on the Unterwall—imagine having to storm up this slope while being shot at from above!—and also when he sits in his room sorting his stamps—Germania head overprinted "Belgien 3 Centimes," and when he stands outside the door to the study where his father is preparing for the next semester.

As he stands outside his father's door, he is actually holding the letter in his hand: mightn't he be allowed to volunteer after all, what does his father think . . .

"No, not until you've finished high school."

On this point the professor is adamant.

One day Erex rides his bicycle to the Warnow meadows. There is the willow tree where he lay so often with Karl. He would like

to do it again, but it seems rather absurd. Besides, how is he supposed to get across the river?

An old man cutting dandelions for his rabbits looks up at him:
"Well, young man?"

At night, too, Karl has to sit in the "blind" and wait. The whole
sky flickers and flares unceasingly. One can hear the Frenchies' field
kitchen driving up close to the front lines. Flares are sent up, green
or yellow, one can see right across the whole valley. (Back there
is a road with tall poplars, all bending to one side. It belongs to
"them.") No, there'll be no shooting, for over here on this side they
are also waiting for the field kitchen, and then those over there
won't be shooting either.

What will it be like when the Negroes come?

"Alarm!"

At first one will be able to hold them off with machine guns and
hand grenades—if one has any left by then! They have to climb
over the barbed wire, that'll slow them down.

But maybe there has been an artillery attack first? A concentrated
barrage? And the barbed wire has been ripped? Maybe the whole
trench will have been mashed and pounded by the artillery, and one
will be lying half buried under the mud and only at the last moment
will one stagger to one's feet, when the barrage subsides and the
Blacks come storming up: maybe one's even lost one's rifle or it
won't function and the fellows step coolly over the barbed wire
and stick their bayonets into one's belly? Coolly and expertly? A
Zouave maybe, or a Senegalese?

Would one try to speak to him? At such a moment? They say
the Senegalese even carry knives in their mouths when they attack.
They are given liquor to make them do it—attack. They had come
in great waves, according to the soldiers in the dugout, and our men
caught them with machine guns, swiveling the guns back and forth
twice, aiming slightly higher, just a few degrees higher, and wave
after wave collapsed.

"Ah yes, the Negroes. Clumsy clodhopping brutes . . ."

.   .   .

They also tell about their own attacks, back in 1914, and why everything was suddenly halted. Things were going so well. And there are rumors that there was something fishy going on in the high command. And all those sacrifices for nothing?

No, there's no more attacking now, just waiting; Heaven only knows what for. Time passes with sentry duty or playing cards, with reading or sleeping. Now and again shells land. When they are big ones, the candle in the dugout goes out.

"Trump! In a minute we'll be apple sauce!" the front-line soldiers say casually, and shuffle the cards again.

The whining tells them whether they will hit close or land farther away, the "comfort parcels" from the other side, greetings from Buxen & Full Limited.

When the *German* minethrowers fire a salvo, Karl looks through the trenchscope into the wrecked communication trench of the French. He can clearly see the frightened men over there bolting toward the rear. But there must be someone standing there with a pistol, for one after another they re-emerge.

Strange, one can't take one's eye from the glass, and one laughs at those Frenchmen, holding onto their *képis* and scurrying back and forth.

Russes en retraite—Qu'est-ce que vous faites?

is written on a large board and held up for the Frenchmen to read. The following day comes the reply:

Why did you
declare war on us?

Many soon get fed up with army life. Attack and fight—that they'd willingly do, but not this sitting around! And the moronic talk of one's comrades and those filthy obscenities.

One day they are asked whether anyone will volunteer for a patrol, one more man is needed, "playing Red Indians," the old-timers call it. Karl calls out: "Here!" and scarcely an hour later finds himself with ten men in a roadside ditch, inching his way along on his stomach.

The ditch is about five hundred yards long and some fifteen inches deep. The men have to press themselves into the ground if they don't want to betray their presence.

Frenchie hasn't noticed anything yet or he would undoubtedly have started up his "coffee grinders" as some wits call the machine gun out here. "Stutterteddy," "lawnmower," or "crap cannon" are other word-inventions. No, Frenchie isn't "raking": the group slides forward in jerks. Yard after yard. With both hands Karl pushes his rolled-up greatcoat ahead, then draws up his knees, and hitches himself forward. He moves along like a caterpillar.

After thirty yards his greatcoat bundle splashes into wetness. From here on the ditch is flooded, not deeply, but deep enough. Dragonflies hover in front of his nose . . . The water has a poisonous green color. That green: is it a fungus? A sort of duck-weed? (He has to laugh at his ignorance: so that's all that's left of his biology lessons, that he doesn't even know the name of the stuff he's lying in.)

They come so close to the enemy positions that they can hear the *poilus* talking. A group of six or eight Frenchmen appear very nonchalant. They walk through the barbed-wire entanglement and leave a sentry behind at the opening, probably so they can find their way back again. They busy themselves on this side and then disappear the way they came.

The soldiers are finding it too wet in the ditch, they become careless and raise their behinds. This draws fire. Three machine guns send them a hail of bullets. Shrapnels burst in the sky and scatter their pellets: they rattle into the trees. One man is hit in the back, "bites the dust," as they say. And when at last he is dead and the group is allowed to creep back, Karl sees that the man's side has been torn open: human flesh is bulging out of the field-gray tunic, and it looks exactly like the meat they feed the bears at the zoo.

. . .

Karl would like to know whether the reconnaissance party has been useful and whether they'll soon be starting on their victorious attacks. He would also like to tell all his comrades about the thrilling patrol, how he inched his way along the wet ditch on his stomach. But the others just say: "Shut up!" And so he *writes* home about "raking" and about "inching along." "You should have seen my uniform . . . !" and that he's "heart and soul" a soldier, he writes that too.

"I leaped into my field-gray tunic as if into a refreshing bath!" he writes. "To share in the greatest struggle of all time—that makes me proud and happy." And "We live in an age of greatness, perhaps the greatest Germany has ever seen. Our sons and grandsons will envy us!"

Anna reads this letter about the greatest struggle of all time, written on poor-quality gray paper that has made the ink run: among the other letters with their pretty stamps from Berlin and Bad Oeynhausen it strikes a solemn note. The clock under the glass dome tinkles, the grandfather clock across the room starts to whir, and now its bom-bom joins the dinging and chiming of the other clocks: five o'clock, in a minute Mrs. von Wondring will be arriving and one will have to offer her a cup of real coffee in the new vine-leaf cups. What a good thing Robert has managed to get some coffee again, he has really been fortunate with his two ships. They are continually carrying ore from Sweden, day after day.

Mrs. von Wondring's visit is enjoyable and not unimportant, for Mrs. von Wondring has a cousin in Berlin, a general or something in the Ministry of War. Tomorrow Mrs. von Wondring will have to sit down and write a letter to this cousin, or the day after, or next week, regarding "a son of my best friend . . ."

And Anna will sit down at her desk, dip her pen in the Meissen porcelain inkwell, and write to her son that he mustn't be surprised if something happens, if he is recalled from his position for some more important assignment. And she will have some parcels packed up for him in the kitchen.

A great deal will have to be written in the next little while. The parcels are packed by Giesing, who puts in whatever she can find: bacon, marinated goose drumsticks, smoked eel, tobacco, and some Swiss chocolate.

On one occasion Karl receives twenty mouth organs, and the result is a terrible cacophony. The company commander finally puts his foot down: "What next?" Only Corporal Schultze—Schultze with "tz"—is allowed to play, for not only can he hammer beautiful signet rings, stamped with an Iron Cross, from copper shells, but he is also a master of the mouth organ: with full chords and tremolo he plays Handel's

See, the conquering hero comes!

and everyone enjoys that. Even the *poilus* on the other side listen and clap and shout: "Bravo!"

A parcel of cigars and fruit drops arouses benevolence among the higher-ups, and Karl reaps the benefit: he is posted to the rear just when the order arrives to straighten out the position.

And Karl is counting loaves of bread in Werckem when his comrades climb out of the trenches and storm the enemy, and he weeps when he hears about this and sees the wounded and is told who was killed and how.

35

Margarethe de Bonsac sits in her white, sunny room looking through the window into the formal garden that is buried in snow, as if into an enchanted world.

Down below, the neighbor walks through his garden with his bare chest uplifted to the winter sun. Sun! Light! Strength! That's roughly what he is thinking, and between upliftings he checks on whether there is anything he can start doing in his garden, but it's still too early in the year.

Much bread is growing in the winter night . . . It is sleeping under the white blanket, waiting to thrust itself up toward the mild sun.

Outside Grethe's window hangs a bird-feeding ring, now and then a bird alights on it and clings upside down with its claws, pecking at whatever it can get.

How strange that these little birds don't feed *continuously*, Grethe thinks; sometimes they do and sometimes they don't. Instead of feeding continuously as long as the supply lasts! How can they know whether there'll be anything for them tomorrow?

A mystery. Remember to look up Brehm's *Lives of the Animals* tomorrow, why this is so and why sometimes they don't show up at all.

Great tits and blue tits come to Grethe's window, and chaffinches too, of course, those dear little creatures who, strangely enough, peck at each other no matter how cute they look!

"Stop that!" says Grethe, rapping the window, with the result that *all* the birds flit away, the pecking and the pecked, and don't show up again for a long time, and that the neighbor down below turns his head to look up and see which window that tapping came from and whether it was meant for him. And he is glad he did not relieve himself just at that moment, on the compost heap, which was what he had actually had in mind.

Grethe's room is cozy and snug: to the left of the window stands a glass cabinet inherited from her grandmother, containing rows of cups, big ones and little ones, with or without inscriptions, and also the doll Mary, with whom she cannot bear to part.

"What a lovely room you have here, child!"

And to the right of the window stands a graceful escritoire of cherry wood with many little drawers, its upper section supported by ivory columns.

Photos stand on either side on this desk, in order of size and importance: dear Uncle Hans is there, what a lot of trouble he has with his English wife, who only recently proclaimed yet again that the German soldiers are all criminals, and Uncle Bertram with dear, beetle-browed Aunt Minna, both of whom haven't been to the house for such a long time, they must have taken something amiss, oh dear, so touchy. There is also a photo of her brother Richard, head erect in his stiff collar, how brave he looks! One may be proud of him, and indeed one is. How comical he was as a child when he ran around the table on all fours like a dog. And kept raising one leg. Oh, how funny that was! And always galloping along the garden paths on his hobbyhorse . . .

Grandfather with his patriarch's beard has been dead for four years now. "My little gal," he used to say, and he was always so sad on Wednesdays that his grandchildren wouldn't learn the catechism.

Await, my soul,
Await the Lord!

Those lovely Wednesdays . . . Now everything is so different, no sense of unity, so cold and impersonal.

. . .

The photos on the desk, lightened by the snow outside, are under thick beveled panes of glass, fastened at the back with elaborately twisted brass wire. Grethe slides her grandfather's picture out of its stand and puts it in the top left drawer.

Enlargements up to life size.
Made to last indefinitely.

Grethe takes another photo and slips it between glass and stand, the one of August Menz: "All right, fellows, let's go!" It was taken at the Somme, just where the danger is greatest, where they shoot from below with machine guns at the intrepid riders of the clouds, which is somehow unfair, Grethe feels. Down below, yes, they bang away with their big shells, obviously, war is war, whee, what a racket that must make! But up there, in God's free air . . . No, if *she* had to shoot at those intrepid men she would aim right past them: just to show.

She looks at the picture and thinks she can smell that sharp, masculine aroma she was aware of in Rostock when they danced the tango, the one with sixteen different steps that no one else could do yet. And she takes a magnifying glass to see whether she can make out the little scar on the angular forehead.

"Do you know that I am now allowed to kiss you?" That's what he said because she was standing under the mistletoe, and she said: "Oh, please don't . . ."

Instead of saying: "Oh yes! Do. Please do!"

No, she can't make out the little scar, so instead she looks her fill at the gleaming teeth.

She also looks her fill at herself, for her mirror image suddenly appears on the glass covering the photo. And now the setting winter sun strikes the beveled edge and reflects the colors of the spectrum on the wall: It seems like a miracle, and she stares at it until it gradually fades away.

In the top right-hand drawer there is a soft dust cloth with which Grethe polishes the glass until it shines. "August Menz" is written on the back of the picture. "For Grethe de Bonsac." And only then does she set it down, placing it at precisely the right spot.

· · ·

Now Grethe draws the muslin curtains, for it is almost dusk. She draws the muslin curtains and the heavy drapes with their little woolen pom-poms and turns on the light that falls on the round table and on the sweet little sofa with the color print of the Savior above it. She nips off a few leaves from the potted palm standing beside it and walks up and down for a few minutes: her lovely room, *her* world: the table with the sofa, the glass cabinet, and the escritoire.

Beside the door hang the Suhr drawings of the French using St. Peter's Church in Hamburg as a stable, really quite shocking.

To the right of the door stands a bookcase—*The Sweet Girl* by Zobeltitz—most of the books bound in red with gilt embossed lettering.

One book among them is actually inscribed—"Tears"!—written in the poet's hand. *The Daily Round and Sunshine* is the title, and she still remembers the poetry reading in Graal where someone kept calling out "More carbide!" because the lamps were dimming.

Mr. von Büschel is also thought of, *briefly* thought of, how he sat on the sand wall playing with pebbles: "Upon this baanch of wood let us repose . . ." The rowboat *Irene*, and the kiss that landed in the wrong place.

And then the other one blots it out, that man whose strong shoulders she could feel under his jacket.

"Do you know that I am now allowed to kiss you?" . . . Instead of saying: "Oh, yes! Do! Please do!" she thinks, and she throws herself into the corner of the sofa: please do! And again her thoughts keep rolling around in her head like billiard balls, and she can actually feel him lifting her up and carrying her from one room into the other, all the guests have gone and only a few lights are burning. And he carries her out of the house and sets her down in his car and roars off, far away . . .

Grethe gets up. Go downstairs and play the piano? No, one will only be given some chore to do: somebody will ask one please to tidy the pile of gardening magazines. Or lend Father a hand by holding the planks that he is just about to glue together. Tongue and groove neatly chiseled.

"Grethe, can you spare a moment?"

No, better not go downstairs, one will only be spoken to and questioned, one will have to read the latest letters from Hertha or Lotti, how hard they are working, and then one's thoughts come to a dead stop, and it is hard to get them going again.

She wouldn't mind having a little piano up here, she thinks, a square grand piano like the one her grandmother used to have, yes, then she would be able to play "A-brim with Happiness" for hours on end.

Grethe straightens the dried flowers in their vase, sits down at her desk, and first writes a postcard to Karl Kempowski, a card with a view of the Bismarck monument. That seems appropriate to the struggle of the times. She draws an arrow and writes underneath: "Behind Bismarck is the day nursery." That's where she is working now. Montessori, Kerschensteiner, and Berthold Otto, she's read them all, and how to occupy children, she knows that now. Paper-folding and raffia work: one need only encourage the children and the rest will follow, and one mustn't force anything on them. She is fully aware of all this, and she has also discovered that it works.

Grethe de Bonsac first does her duty and writes to Karl Kempowski, that she is well and she hopes he is well too, and did he receive the cake she baked for him?

When that is out of the way she writes to August Menz, and she writes a *letter*, a longish one on a sheet of letter paper that she has been keeping among her nightgowns next to the soap: pale blue, fine laid. The letter has to be drafted first, drafted several times, torn up, redrafted: how far one *may* go and how far one *wants* to go, that is the crucial question.

She is writing to August Menz, who at this very moment may be soaring above the clouds in a wire and canvas contraption, wind goggles over his face. Looking down to see if he can help somewhere with his machine gun. Maybe he can throw a hand grenade overboard, onto that railway station down there? Won't that make the little ants scatter!?

Yes, it is true, Grethe trembles for him: all that flying, it *can't* be safe, something is *bound* to happen, it's just a matter of time!

And something actually does happen: as August Menz is returning to his air base, his engine starts coughing and he has to land on a field. During this emergency landing the bouncing plane tips over, the wooden propeller shatters, and August Menz fractures two ribs.

36 The Friend

In the summer of 1915 Grethe and I attended the Fröbel Institute where we took our kindergarten teachers' training. I really had nothing particular in mind, but Grethe was doing it, and so far we had done everything together—"Grethe and Thete"—so what could be more natural than to apply for this training? Paper-folding, knitting, gluing, that's what we learned there: in other words, how to keep children occupied. The Montessori system with its lovely educational toys was all the rage at the time, and the idea that one should not behave in an authoritarian manner toward the child but be indulgent, patient, and helpful. We learned about "child-oriented education," and handicrafts were also all the rage. We had Plasticine, building blocks, and silhouette paper: once Grethe cut out a Cinderella freehand, I can still see it lying in front of me. Without drawing the outline first!

Of course we also had scientific courses, we took Psychology, Social Science, Pedagogy, and Health, all that kind of thing. We read Pestalozzi, Rousseau, Kerschensteiner, and, of course, *The Century of the Child* by Ellen Key.

After a year and a half we had finished our training and were then posted to a nursery school down by the harbor: a terrible district! Only the poorest of the poor lived there, dirty, bedraggled, and louse-ridden.

I can still remember some of the children, Willi Heinbockel for instance, he was an awful little creature, he had a head like a fish, running to a point on top, and fish eyes, just like a carp. He was always soiling himself, it really was disgusting! His mother worked in a fish-packing plant, and when she brought her boy to school we could smell her a mile off. In her hair, her clothes—she had fish scales everywhere. Sometimes she brought us fresh kippers wrapped in disgusting newspaper. They turned my stomach, but my father was in ecstasy when I took those kippers home, and he couldn't understand why I wouldn't eat any.

There were some frightful cases. We had one child whose mother was seriously ill with V.D., it had never had a hot meal. It was a wonder the child was still alive. It couldn't even walk properly yet.

Most of the mothers worked in munitions factories and couldn't deliver their children to us, so we had to pick them up. I never told my parents: living conditions you wouldn't believe! There was one lane, for example, in the so-called *Gängeviertel*, that warren of sordid back alleys—I never went there without having my heart in my mouth. One courtyard after another, and the courtyards surrounded by houses with washing hanging out of the windows and noise and stench. One had to climb narrow chicken ladders to get to the upper floors. Sometimes there was just a string hanging down instead of a handrail: there's nothing like it today. An appalling district. Some of those alleys were so narrow that a single person could barely squeeze through. If one had come face to face with some ruffian there—after all, we were still young. I just wonder . . .

One of the women, I can still remember her, was always sick; first you went into the kitchen, then came a kind of wooden partition with just a bed in it. And in this bed, wrapped in rags and newspaper, the child would be lying, and I had to dress it. God, how repulsive that was. And the state of the kitchen! The comb really did lie next to the butter.

There were body lice, too, of course. Lieschen Pump had some. The doctor came once a week, and the children had to undress and be examined. We were there to supervise the children, and that's where I heard Lieschen Pump talking to another child about fleas.

"My fleas never jump, they're here inside my vest, crawling around, and it tickles and itches."

I made her show me the "fleas," and lo and behold, they were lice. The child was taken home and not allowed to come back for so-and-so-many days. The mother kicked up a terrible row, she was a regular virago, the child had got the lice from *us*, she screamed.

I sometimes caught five or six fleas on myself when I came home in the evening.

Once a week the dirtiest children were given a bath. There were some we put in the tub *first* and took out *last*, they needed to "soak." We knew what we were up against. There was no other way of getting them clean. Oh my God!

Mrs. Holle, she's another one I remember. She had three illegitimate children, one more pitiful than the next. Finally she found a man who wanted to look after her, a sailor, and he was killed right away.

Once Grethe put those three children in a baby carriage and took them to the doctor, they had a rash. The doctor asked: "What does the father do?" "I don't know." "What? You don't know what your husband does?"

Our nursery school was at the Mühlberg, right by the Elbe where the Bismarck monument stands. Behind Bismarck was where we worked. Our salary was one hundred and twenty-five marks a month, social workers really were terribly underpaid. Once a week one of the committee ladies would visit the school: Did we have any problems? Countess Berghausen, Mrs. Lassmeier, Mrs. Uppschleiger, wife of the privy counselor, and then another one, a particularly obnoxious one, she gave herself such airs, she simply ignored us as we worked around the place in our blue smocks. One day she turns up in her carriage, the coachman wearing a skunk collar and cap. I open the door to her and offer my hand, whereupon she gives me a withering look and sails past me. I should have waited, you see, for her to offer her hand. What a snob! Right in the middle of the war, too! Incidentally, she looked a bit like the Empress, and her husband had a center part running from his forehead right down to the back of his neck.

Countess Berghausen was nicer, you could see what a difference established wealth made. She was our favorite among all the committee ladies.

"Which of you has the afternoon off?" she always asked. Then one had to change in a hurry and was allowed to drive with her as far as the main station. Actually this didn't suit us at all, for it took longer than if we had taken the interurban. She meant it as a gracious gesture.

Once she arrived when the children were about to have their nap. They were making a terrific racket as they took off their wooden shoes. One boy really stood out; he was pestering the others, which, of course, redoubled the racket. She grabbed hold of the boy and raised her umbrella to strike him, but he was faster than she was, he ran round and round the table with her after him in her hat and billowing cape! It was like a whirlwind, I could have laughed myself sick.

In 1943 she was killed in an air raid. A charming woman, quite delightful, so full of understanding for us and our work. After all, our job was not an easy one.

On one occasion we were invited to her house. Gertrud Bäumer gave a talk, and there were more than fifty ladies there to listen to her. The driveway had been carpeted, and a dignified old manservant took our wraps.

After the talk—I forget what it was about—we were actually asked to stay for dinner. The meal was served in a small dining room, paneled from floor to ceiling, with built-in cupboards in the paneling where the silver dining service was kept. We ate off this silver service (potato soup, by the way!), and the old manservant handed round the dishes. Grethe and I felt rather out of place, we were glad when we could leave.

Such wealth, such solid wealth, is a thing of the past these days, just like that poverty: there were families where the mother boiled potato peelings for dinner!

I wonder what's happened to all those children! They came to us from the most squalid parts of town. Yet I was happier working there than at the upper-class kindergarten on Ritter-Strasse. The poor children were grateful for everything, they were pleased by the smallest thing. The upper-class children, on the other hand, were demanding and arrogant and treated us like servants.

37

In February 1916 Karl-Georg Kempowski reaches the "highest degree of the lowest": he has been made a private first class. A few days after his promotion he leads his unit into a ruined farm lying about thirty yards ahead of their own lines. It would be a good idea, Captain Brüsehaber had said, to occupy the *ferme*, as they are called here, before the others got the idea.

Karl Kempowski was actually supposed to be counting loaves of bread again in Werckem, but it hadn't worked out. "Why always me!" he had said: damn it all.

There are five men in Karl's unit, a butcher and two Polish workers, a high-school student, and a farmer from Teterow. They look at him, wondering whether he'll be able to swing it. At seventeen? The farmer is forty-two.

They start out that evening. Stealthily, like Red Indians, they move along beside a hedge, weighed down with hand grenades in bags and spades and gas masks, rifles slung around their necks and packs on their backs. The last few yards they have to crawl.

The *ferme* consists of three buildings. The farmhouse is a pile of rubble, as is the big barn. Only the stable is still standing. Several holes have been shot through the walls, but the roof is in good condition. In one corner there is even some straw. The men scrape it together, then lie down side by side, making Karl think of the Warnow meadows, with Erex in the willow tree. Or in the cabin of the *Gaudeamus*. The cavernous twilit cabin where the bright sunlight outside had been reflected in bright rings on the mahogany lockers.

. . .

One of them stands guard, the others lie side by side, whispering. Karl looks at his watch every five minutes. Should he tell the sentry that he is soon going to be relieved? He can't settle down: he has all the responsibility here . . .

He gets up, goes over to a corner, and sits down. From his breadbag he takes out the Globus edition of *Faust*—not much bigger than a matchbox—and a clipping from the *Rostocker Anzeiger* that had been sent to him from home, listing who has died and who has been killed, and "I gave gold for iron," a gold watch chain can be donated in exchange for an iron one.

He is surprised that the others haven't brought along any books in their baggage. Those two Poles there. Whispering together, incessantly. What have they got to whisper about? Their Polish homeland? Where the wind whistles over the bare fields?

The butcher, in his calm and steady way, does not whisper, nor does the farmer. The farmer with his leathery face.

Karl can't settle down to read. He takes writing paper from his breadbag, field inkwell and pen. In the corner is a wooden case he uses for a table, putting a candle in an empty bottle on it. And against the candle he props a picture postcard of Hamburg showing the Bismarck monument and an arrow: "This is where I work!" Maybe something will occur to him now, a poem or a profound thought, to this Mr. von Büschel, something truly magnificent, now that he is so completely on his own in this great hour: a poem, like the one long ago in Graal? About the "brazen tongue" of the artillery, perhaps, or one's longing for home?

Where is home, anyway? In which direction? Over there?

The wind blows through the hole in the wall and swells the tarpaulin he has hooked up to keep the light from showing outside. Here he sits, Karl-Georg Kempowski, son of the shipowner Robert William Kempowski: sitting at a wooden case, and over there lie "his" men, side by side, sleeping, just as soldiers slept in 1870 or in 1813.

Frederick the Great, sitting outside the mill and drawing in the sand with his stick, comes to his mind. Or the Thirty Years' War? Harlequin-like men with stolen chickens? They toss the chickens to their buddies, a pot is hung over the fire, and soon the jolly feast begins.

Ala mi presente al vostra signori . . .

Soldiers—in every age and every land. Jolly and sinister at the same time.

> A bullet came a-winging:
> Aimed at me or aimed at thee? . . .

Next morning, when they have finished washing under the pump— the handle squeaks infernally—Karl stripped to the waist and spluttering, the others taking a mouthful of water and spitting it into their hands, when they are just peeling a few half-rotten apples found lying in a corner, a shell suddenly explodes twenty yards from the stable. Shit and spit! Out of a clear sky! (It's aimed at *them!*) Immediately after, a second shell explodes close to the stable, the splinters rattle against the wall, and then a third one right inside. The roof collapses, and three fingers are torn off the farmer from Teterow.

The men lie behind the shattered walls. They look at Karl, who looks at them: Which way? What do we do? Holy Mother of God! *Pica krew pioron!*

More shells come flying, crashing and bursting: What's going on? If only it would stop soon . . .

But it doesn't stop. It has only just begun. Even though there are pauses from time to time, pauses in which the fellows over there are presumably bringing up more ammunition and adjusting the sight: Fine thing if we couldn't manage to smoke out the Boches! One shell after another comes whining through the air. Not exactly in rapid succession, but steadily: one to the left, one to the right, and then again into the middle.

. . .

The soldiers have pressed themselves against the wall and keep their heads down, the two workers from Posen, the butcher, the farmer with his bloody hand, the schoolboy, and Karl. For the nth time they tell themselves: the shell that hits us we don't hear. If it whistles, it's *harmless*. Death comes *soundlessly*. But still they are afraid. "Dear God," maybe they are thinking, "dear God, help me just this once, you needn't ever help me again."

Cautiously Karl slides down into a nearby shell hole. It would have to be a miracle for a shell to hit the same place twice, and just as the others have also slid down into shell holes, into separate shell holes, the wall they have been lying behind collapses.

The shells crash tirelessly into the farm. Here, that corner's still standing, we'll have to put another one in there. Each shell can mean the end, Karl knows this now, and he wonders whether he had imagined the end to be like this. He had pictured it as a victorious attack, receiving the deadly bullet as he advanced, and falling to breathe his last on the blood-soaked earth.

> Lifts up his hand to reach me
> While I my rifle load . . .

That's how he had imagined it, but not this! (Perhaps it would have been a better idea if he had gone to Werckem to count loaves of bread?)

It's close to noon, Karl sees by his watch, his gold pocket watch. He winds the heavy chain around his finger: if he gets out of this alive he'll exchange it for an iron one, he vows to himself. "I gave gold for iron," as the citizens did in the Napoleonic Wars.

The firing continues until almost five o'clock. When the last shell lands, the men know: that was the last. Altogether they were favored with one hundred and fourteen rounds. Apart from the farmer, no one was hurt, not the two Poles, who kept on crossing themselves, not the butcher, not Karl, nor the schoolboy either. The farmer doesn't say a word, he looks at his bandage as it turns red and redder.

That evening the company commander himself arrives and is glad to see they are still alive, he hadn't expected that.

"And you're all right, Kempowski?"

Certainly that bit of a racket, he hadn't minded it at all. But the bottle of red wine, and the bread and sausage, he'd be happy to accept that now.

Yes, he's all right, so are the others, who all stand around the company commander. Except for the farmer, of course, who holds up his bloody bandage like an admission ticket.

Would Karl mind hanging on for one more night? he is asked. Since he knows the ropes now?

No, of course not, be glad to, and his men also say: "Yessir!" because that's how things are done in the army, because one just says "Yessir!" Only the farmer doesn't, he goes back. He is sent to the field hospital and from there to Teterow, to his home, to his wife and child.

That night Karl Kempowski has a deep hole dug under the barn and roofed with beams, boards, straw, and earth.

> Holy Night, Oh wilt thou pour
> Heavenly peace into this heart!

Into that hole they crawl, a Hindenburg light smolders, and they cock their ears, listening for any sound outside, footsteps perhaps, and hurried, gasping breath: whispered orders.

"Quiet, everybody!"

Karl leaves his *Faust* in his pack, also the *Rostocker Anzeiger* with all the announcements on the back: who's got engaged and who's got killed. Nor does he think of the Warnow meadows or of the yacht *Gaudeamus* in which the sun painted golden rings. He wishes he had a pistol, it's easier to handle than a rifle. Remember to ask Dad whether he can get him one of those. An iron watch chain and a pistol, surely it's possible to get hold of those?

. . .

The men lie side by side and look at each other. The two workers from Posen on the left, the butcher and the schoolboy on the right. They discuss whether the Frenchies will try to seize the farm or whether it wouldn't cost them too many lives.

Seizing the farm would be pretty stupid, for then the next day the Germans in turn would obviously fire one hundred and fourteen whizz-bangs into the farm, or maybe even one hundred and fifty.

"What good would that do them? No good at all!"

Come to think of it, it doesn't do the German High Command any good either, they think, letting themselves be mashed up here, but who knows what's behind it all. Perhaps they'll be told one day: "If you hadn't occupied the farm just then, the whole affair might have gone down the drain . . ." This somehow very important affair of which at present they know nothing whatever and of which one has no idea whether it will ever materialize.

So: keep one's ears open and listen for hurried, gasping breath. Even though it's unlikely they'll do it. Attack here.

Or will they?

Next morning they crawl out of the straw, stiff and still weary, this being the second night they have slept ready for an alert, which means with all their equipment buckled on. They don't wash, they don't handle the handle, nor do they spit in their palms. They look across to Frenchie and eat their army bread. A pot of coffee right now wouldn't come at all amiss.

Not likely they'll fire again today, most unlikely, for that would mean they had doubts about their own action, it would mean they thought yesterday's firing of one hundred and fourteen rounds had been pointless.

The schoolboy, a pale, skinny youth, is about to say that, strangely enough, he feels no fear at all and that he is glad to be lying here in the mud for Germany and so on and so forth, when the firing actually starts up again, at eleven sharp, hard to believe, as punctual as the Prussians. And the Prussians count the impacts: twenty-eight, twenty-nine, thirty . . . If it's going to be one hundred and fourteen rounds again, they have already survived one quarter (*si* takes the indicative: "if, in case").

The hole proves to be safe, they lie pressed close together, ears cocked.

At five o'clock it is all over again, they dig themselves out and look at each other. Strange still to be alive (although with powdered hair). And that lark up there? As if making fun of the somewhat battered warriors down below, who are now stretching and pissing wherever they happen to stand.

Karl picks up the detonator of a shell, it is still warm. It is a nice smooth one, the numbers clearly legible. He'll take that home to Rostock when he goes on leave. And when they ask him: "Well, how was it?" he'll place this dramatic object on the table, place it there *without a word*.

What will Schenk say to that? There couldn't have been anything like that down there among the Blacks.

Then they are replaced.

First of all Karl and his men get a hot meal. Others try to line up with them to get something hot too, but they are chased away. Now it's the turn of these brave men: "Or they won't be able to shit tomorrow!"

Karl reports back to the captain, and the captain is glad he's all right and promises him the next promotion. Moreover, he proposes to nominate him for the Iron Cross, an agreeable prospect that pleases Karl no end: second class or right away first class? He wonders about that, but he'll find out soon enough. Better not to set your heart on anything, then you won't be disappointed.

Perhaps Karl's men will also be pleased at his prospects of being decorated. The workers from Posen have brought back apples from the farm, and the schoolboy goes from one to the other saying he is glad to be out here at the front.

But the one who is most pleased is the farmer from Teterow, who is already on his way home, he is pleased about his lost fingers. For the rest of his life he now has a story to tell, while playing cards at the tavern in the evening: "When I was in the trenches near Ypres . . ." (And perhaps someone will come by with pad and pencil and write it all down.) Thank God he has kept his thumb. Without a thumb a fellow's really stumped. Without a thumb he can't do a thing.

38

In March 1916, on March 12, at two in the afternoon, a large open Opel drives up to Number 7a Bären-Strasse in Wandsbek. In it sits August Menz, his arm resting casually on the door, with his two cracked ribs, wearing a leather jacket with its collar turned up, and a woolen scarf.

He wipes his elegant boots on the doormat, which is fastened to a chain, and listens for any movement in the house.

He rings the bell; first the dog barks, then—what luck!—a maid actually comes to the door, wearing a white apron, a *young* maid, not at all bad-looking, who is embarrassed as she lets in this elegant gentleman who seems to be a real live airman, for heaven's sake!

"Axel! Down!"

From the back, another maid approaches, shorter, with a humpback, who also becomes embarrassed and calls out: "Axel, *kusch!*" because the dog is carrying on so crazily, running from one to the other and into the kitchen and back again: Have you ever seen anything like it?

That the word *kusch* comes from *se coucher* is something these simple girls don't know, but Lieutenant Menz knows it, and it flashes through his mind. Ever since he has been in France, French words constantly flash through his mind: *Je me promène* = I me go walking, for example, or *Je ne me promène pas* = I not me go walking.

He takes off his gloves, and at last Martha de Bonsac, the countrified-looking mother, emerges, not in the least embarrassed, pinning up

her hair, for she had lain down for a nap, it's just after lunch, isn't it?
Actually not the proper time to pay a call, she thinks.
"Bong!" goes the grandfather clock.

Bonum bono

is inscribed on the pendulum: "Bom!" And the family coat of arms
is carved on the case: goblet and grapes.
"Axel, *kusch!*"

What a surprise, calling at *this* hour!
Yes, the Lieutenant happens to be in Hamburg to pick up two
monkeys, just imagine, two monkeys! Hagenbeck has donated them
to the squadron, and he wouldn't like to pass up the opportunity
. . . He really would like to pay his respects, and . . . He would
never forgive himself if he failed to pay his respects since he happens
to be in Hamburg anyway.
And he looks for a place to put down his gloves and wonders
when he is going to be asked to take off his coat.

He has brought along a sliver from the shattered propeller, from his
own aeroplane in which he almost met his death, as a souvenir,
carved into an ashtray—instead of flowers, if that's all right?
"Oh, how very nice!" says Martha de Bonsac, but Grethe isn't
here, she's sorry, what a pity! The two maids are sorry too, listening
open-mouthed but now being sent back into the kitchen. Grethe is
at the day nursery, looking after the children of working mothers.
Would the Lieutenant care to come in for a glass of sherry? she asks
him, and a slice of bread with ersatz butter, she is sorry she has
nothing else? Or would the Lieutenant prefer to drive straight to the
Mühlberg?
Yes, he would, if she wouldn't mind, and he says it straight out
and pulls on his gloves again and roars off in his car, and when he
arrives at the Mühlberg the children call out: "Look! The soldier's
come for his girl!" and Grethe blushes deeply.

They then sit in Winterhude eating wartime cake. How nice it is of
him to have come, and: "Really because of two monkeys?"

. . .

Outside the River Alster is frozen over and covered with snow; the
weeping willows reach down with their frost-covered branches onto
the snowy surface and draw fine, delicate circles in it. "Filigree,"
Grethe thinks, yes, the word is appropriate. "Like an enchanted
world."

Yes, he has come because of two monkeys, and as long as he lives
he will remember that he came because of two fully grown monkeys
and that he has no idea how he is supposed to get these animals
safely to France.

Half the empty terrace outside has been cleared of snow—the broom
is still lying there. They stir their coffee and fall silent.

The silence is broken with: Ah yes, the great struggle of the nations,
how powerless one is, but one will do one's duty no matter where
one is placed. It is Menz who says that. And: God created war and
God loves the stronger warrior. He has never yet been on the side
of the weaker battalions. Isn't all Nature a hymn to victory?

Grethe can't think at all. She looks out onto the gray-white Alster,
and it seems to her like a fairy tale, all she can think is: Like a fairy
tale! Winter outside, and here inside an angular airman. And how
amazed the children must have been at the shiny automobile and her
driving away in it.

Grethe can't say anything at all, somehow she is on a higher plane.
"He has really come," she says to herself at last, over and over
again, and she can ask for nothing more.

Meanwhile August Menz provides the conversation, he tells her
about flying: "When you pull, the crate goes up!" And to climb
above the other, that's all there is to it.

In winter one looks down on a whole labyrinth of trails, he tells
her, also on snow-covered earthworks: like veins under the skin. In
spring, the sun turns the deathly pallor of the ground brown—and
in summer all the fields, wide and narrow, turn yellow and green and
lie spread out like carpets, one this way, one that. Hill and dale,

with the pale ribbons of roads, with rivers and villages, with barracks, with vehicle parks, tents, occupied trenches, and hovering
bursts of shrapnel: one great tapestry on God's loom . . .

That's how August Menz talks, accompanying his description with
frequent gestures, and managing to make the eyes in his angular face
look quite dreamy without losing any of their determination. (He
has a large Adam's apple.) And then he says that he was lucky as
Hell to have time to land his two ribs here . . . Supposing the
machine had caught fire? Click-click-click the gasoline dripped, and
him hanging in the straps? And the gasoline dripping click-click-
click right onto him? A single spark would have been enough. But
he won't talk about that now . . .

Grethe feels so small, so insignificant.

Peee, says the ol' owl . . .

All she could tell him about would be Willi Heinbockel, who has a
face like a cod and is so filthy that it is easy to be repelled by him,
which indeed she was at first That she found him absolutely disgusting, but that she suddenly saw him in a different light, in his
trusting helplessness, and that the other day he painted a truly delightful picture for her, which one would never have expected from
a child like that. Coming from such a background!

Or about Pastor Eisenberg, and what an extraordinarily good
man he is. To be able to preach an entire sermon with his eyes
closed, on the struggle of the times, about the just cause we are
defending, and about the Savior Who is sitting beside our men in
the trenches, the men with their—what do you call those things?—
gun machines.

She feels small and insignificant, but then again exhilarated: to
be sitting here, in Winterhude, with a real live airman. And at the
door a magnificent automobile. Green with red upholstery. And she
looks to see whether the old waiter back there, the one with the big
moustache, isn't looking at it too. Is he aware that that shabby leather
jacket hanging over there is worn by a highly important person?

How fortunate that she happened to be wearing her beryl today of

all days! The green stone surrounded by sapphires given her by
Aunt Luise of Doberan.

August Menz pays for the ersatz coffee and the wartime cake,
" 'garçon,' " he thinks, "in France I would have said 'garçon' . . ."
He takes down his jacket, which is hanging beside her coat, and
allows her to help him into it, oh, thank you! And now do up the
buttons in front. Wonderful. Then comes a walk around the Alster,
he on the left, his collar turned up, and she on the right. All those
lovely, elegant villas, and the gardens buried in snow.

As has been said, he is wearing a somewhat shabby airman's jacket,
and Grethe is wearing a long coat lined with finely striped yellow-
and-black silk. She has tied her hat under her chin with a scarf.

August Menz, broad-shouldered and virile, looks right and left,
wondering what people are saying about him as he strolls along the
Alster in Hamburg with such a pretty, patrician girl. And he also
looks down, onto the path, to make sure there isn't a slide made by
street urchins on which Miss de Bonsac might slip, or to see whether
there are any stones or something Miss de Bonsac might trip over.
And if there are any, he footballs them to one side.

Does she know that joke? "Lift your footsie, tootsie," is what you
say when you're in love, and: "Lift your paw, Ma," once you're
married.

Does she get the joke?

Of course she does, she wasn't born yesterday, was Miss de
Bonsac. For instance, the spires of the city over there beyond the
Lombards' Bridge outlined between the huge iron candelabras, she
knows them all: over there St. Michael's, good old St. Michael's.
Wasn't it funny, that night Uncle Hans brought them the molten
glass from St. Michael's after the fire—"Oh, it's still warm!"—
Uncle Hans who's rather stuck now with his English wife.

Lieutenant Menz lights one of his curiously long cigarettes. First he
inspects it to see whether it is properly packed, at either end, then

he puts it between his wonderful teeth, lights it, and puffs the smoke into the air.

The average type of German airman has undergone a considerable change since 1914, he says, although actually he has been talking a little too much about flying, as he admits to himself, but he can't think of anything better, and he has no choice because Grethe has already gone back to Willi Heinbockel with his pointed head, saying that even this child can be led to better things and that a very great deal of patience is required for that.

Or Lieschen Pump, that diminutive little person? And coming from such a background!

No, Menz has to go on talking about flying, no matter what, otherwise he might have to listen to still more stories about Lieschen Pump, and somehow that's more than he can stand.

In the early days, he says therefore, they had been tremendous fellows, when the flying corps was still a small, untried unit, real daredevils they had been, reckless men! He can still remember the race he arranged with his friend Ferdinand von Maltzahn. His friend in a car on the highway, and he in an aeroplane thirty feet above him! There was nothing like that today, today only boring types got to the front, hard-working, undemanding fellows: the élite quality had gone out the window.

He shapes a snowball and throws it at the streetlamp, hitting it fair and square! But—oh!—he grabs his chest, the ribs, the pain! He hadn't thought of that . . . and Grethe de Bonsac clasps his elbow: Is the pain going away? she asks with a woebegone look on her face, or would he care to lean on her?

No, thanks. No, it's all right. It's already gone.

And when it has really gone he tells her, in his unquenchable way, all about LVG's, Aviatiks, AEG's, Albatrosses, Fokkers, and about "spotting," and how it's done: a pretty responsible thing, for, with 42-centimeter mortars, every round costs a small fortune, doesn't it? And it's quite a ticklish thing, too, for the enemy "grid tails" can see what you're doing, of course, and hasten to spoil your game.

He grinds out his cigarette with his heel.

Does she understand all that? he asks her. "Forty-two-centimeter shells? Those are things as long as from here—to here. And that thick, Miss de Bonsac, *that* thick!!" Does she understand all that?

Of course she does, for, to repeat, she wasn't born yesterday.

Will the ice carry them?

They climb down the embankment, he in front, and he holds out his hand to her, careful, careful . . . and with her right hand she holds onto the branches of the weeping willow, causing little strips of frost to fall off.

Her heel catches in the hem of her coat and tears it, but it doesn't matter, no, no, it doesn't matter at all. (Her hand lies in his perhaps a shade longer than necessary.)

The ice holds, it cracks but it holds. If it were peacetime now, the ice would be crowded with skaters, swooping around, alone or in pairs, one would be eating toffee apples at steaming stalls, and there would be music to waltz to. But actually it is good to be alone like this, the broad white expanse, and over there the first street-lamps being lighted . . .

"Like an enchanted world," Grethe thinks, "fairylike," and she turns around to look for a tree with white branches, so that the word "filigree" can come once more into her mind.

Lieutenant Menz has stopped thinking about flying. *"Nous nous promenons,"* he thinks, "we us go walking." Quite funny, really.

After August Menz has left, they both think of that short walk across the ice: he in his wire contraption on the Somme, she in her white room. How stupid to have taken a short cut, they both think: they should have taken the longer route, there would have been plenty of time.

And then she does it, she writes him a long letter. Telling him that she loves him terribly, she writes on the sky-blue, fine-laid paper, which smells of soap, that she cannot live without him, and that she would like so much, oh so very much, to be his dear wife.

Then the sky-blue letter is placed in a dark-blue-lined envelope— but just unfold it once more and read it over again, one last time, and one last, last time, and all the desk drawers, big and little, are pulled open, what is she looking for?—(what will he think when he gets the letter?)—what is she looking for in all those drawers? A stamp? No, that's not required for an army post letter. Nor is it the plaster bee, the one from Rostock; she's looking for some little object, nothing special, and she finds a glossy picture, from childhood days, still lying there, a Sistine angel, she puts that in the letter and laughs as she does so: What will he think, what will he say? And she closes the drawer, then licks the envelope, and presses it flat. There.

The dog Axel Pfeffer, who happens to come into her room (as the house policeman, this is his duty), is lifted up and swung around, despite his struggles and howls. Grethe runs out onto the street, without coat or hat, Axel Pfeffer leaps up at her and runs along beside her, and there it is, the Imperial mailbox she always used to bump her head against as a child.

As she is about to slip it in, she hesitates: Should she? Shouldn't she? Next collection 6:30 P.M. . . . Shouldn't she rather wait for him to do it?

No one, no one to discuss it with, and the letter plops into the mailbox.

39 The Comrade

So then with Karl Kempowski I shared pretty well all the joys and sufferings of the front-line soldier. We carried out our duties as ordered and were filthy and lousy and no different from all the others.

This changed for him when he was made a corporal and eventually vice-sergeant-major and thus a platoon leader. Then he wore a silver sword-knot and a silver cockade on his cap and had a dugout to himself with a batman who cleaned his boots and kept his uniform in order.

Some time before I was wounded, I shared a dugout with him near the Kemmelberg in Flanders. As a telephonist it was my job to repair telephone cables when they were severed by artillery fire. (That sounds easy enough, but just try leaving a bomb-proof dugout and laying yourself open to those whining shells!)

This meant, of course, that he was now in a position of authority and had to give orders. But this didn't go to his head. The shouting and bellowing one so often hears from superiors wasn't his style. He asserted himself in a quiet, more gentlemanly way. Incidentally, in those days every soldier was so deeply imbued with militarism that insubordination virtually never occurred.

1916: that was the time of the so-called matériel battles. It will remain forever in my memory: the whole horizon dipped in red and everything under a pall of smoke.

We were often bombarded, even by naval guns, shells of 30 to 38 centimeters caliber. You never heard the discharge, only suddenly a soft whoosh in the air swelling to a thunderous roar. The shells would then land in the trench or behind the line and gouge out enormous shell holes.

In addition to this shelling, heavy mines also fell on our position. These mines are thin-walled but loaded with a very powerful explosive charge. The detonation of such a mine produces a fantastic racket, they rip open even bigger holes than the heavy naval shells. You hear a light discharge in the enemy trench, and you know: Here comes a mine. Everyone looks up and tries to spot the twisting mine in the air before it falls. Then you dash along the trench to seek shelter behind a traverse. Sometimes you succeed, sometimes you don't, and if someone's already standing there, you're out of luck!

Not every mine or shell hit the trench, quite a few dropped behind or in front. But when it made a direct hit a number of men were wiped out.

It was ghastly. Soon there were no positions left at all. Sleep was virtually impossible, at most you might nod off briefly from sheer exhaustion.

Hour after hour of incessant barrage, that was bad, I can tell you. We, young though we were, had a feeling we would never get out alive. That appalling noise and the flashes of the impacts and all that. How are you going to survive that? you thought. Whether you'll ever get out of this, there's absolutely no telling.

Running away was out of the question. Somehow you had a feeling: You mustn't do that, you can't do that. The thought may have occurred but it was brushed aside, for one simply mustn't: Running away and being caught: that was the equivalent of death.

The various units were always relieved after a few days, otherwise it would have been unbearable. On top of everything else there were the hunger and the vermin!

When I felt something crawling for the first time—I had just arrived at the front—the old soldiers said: "Don't you ever wash yourself, you filthy pig? You've got lice!" They all had them, of course, it was just their rough and ready way of pulling the leg of an upper-class recruit. The straw or wood shavings in the dugouts were never changed or renewed. Hardly had one arrived at the position than one was already full of lice. The cleaner the underwear, the more one was tormented by these creatures. And the more one scratched and scraped, the worse the crawling sensation became. It often happened that the company leader and the newest recruit would be sitting peacefully together in the dugout picking lice off each other, and as a result of cracking the dear little creatures we had permanently red fingernails.

The louse is actually a good-natured animal with a certain relaxed way of life. Quite different from the flea, which is more passionate, more impetuous and impudent. Individually a louse isn't that much of a torment, with touching innocence it allows itself to be caught quite easily. But when it has multiplied, and that happens very quickly, it becomes a real terror. The old mother-lice have dark, heavy bodies. To burst them between the nails is a joy for every soldier.

At the appearance of a flea, the louse retreats. These pests can't exist side by side. A flea is if anything more unpleasant in its effect. Its bite can rouse a grown man from the deepest sleep.

> The father picks lice,
> The child picks lice,
> The mother picks lice,
> It's not very nice.
> I sit here as guest
> Among the whole crew,
> At first I look on,
> And then I pick too.

That was one of those jingles that were in everybody's mouth at the time. Another one I remember goes:

> When silence settles in the night,
> You chase your lice by candlelight.

Rats were something else again that gave us a lot of trouble. In the dugouts we used to hang our bread on strings from the roof. The water rats would run over our stomachs, jump up to the ceiling, and pull down the bread. They gorged themselves on half-buried corpses that hadn't yet been recovered. The battle against these revolting beasts was one of our daily tasks. Rats are extremely dangerous and can pass on all kinds of diseases, they can cause plagues. For that reason we were constantly being inoculated against every imaginable disease. I can't tell you the number of times I've been inoculated in my life. Perhaps that's one reason I have never suffered from any major disease.

Seen from today, it's hard to imagine those daily ordeals. Lice, rats, barrages—that was only part of it. Front-line soldiers are also working soldiers who, apart from the constant threat of death, have to do shovel fatigue. "Shovel fatigue" is the front-line expression for hard work. For three days in a row we would be in the very front line, then for about six days behind the front in reserve, and every night we had to do shovel fatigue.

Shovel fatigue meant really hard work. From the sapper vehicle park in Werckem, where the materials were stored, we drove coils of wire, logs, bags of cement—under constant artillery and infantry fire—in trucks across open terrain up to the front-line position, where the stuff was used to build bunkers or repair destroyed sections of the trenches and dugouts.

At night, flares rose almost incessantly into the sky. The German flares dropped quite quickly, whereas the English and French ones were usually equipped with parachutes that stayed up in the air for incredibly long periods. The men working above the shelter had to stand stockstill or fling themselves to the ground so as not to be recognized by the enemy and shot at immediately.

Shovel fatigue lasted for eight hours without a break, and during that whole time one was constantly exposed to enemy fire. Every night there were a number of dead and wounded. Up front in the trenches a man often felt safer than when digging at the rear.

Toward morning, when we marched into our rest area, frozen through and totally exhausted, as often as not we would be greeted by the regimental band. Then the tired limbs revived, and the ensuing parade past the regimental commander, Lieutenant-Colonel Kümmel, known as "Dauntless," went off without a hitch. Dauntless was of the opinion that a parade of exhausted troops returning from battle and filth was the only kind worth having.

The "Helena March" was our regimental march. Even today, if I happen to hear it, my muscles respond, and all the old images rise up, you see yourself standing there in the trench in wind and weather, surrounded by your comrades, all sharing in the agony.

It was deeply moving to hear the band play a full tattoo. That wonderful music, crowned by the theme of love, with the thunder of the artillery in the background, the flashes of the guns, the incessantly rising flares . . . I'll remember that as long as I live.

For a while the Bavarian infantry was posted in our neighboring sector. We also frequently met the Bavarians in the rest areas of Menin, Comines, Werwik, and other places. Since Adolf Hitler also served in these units, it's not impossible for us to have glimpsed our future Führer around there.

Let me bring this sad chapter to an end. It was a time of greatness, and I thank God that on the whole I came through those trials and tribulations more or less in one piece and in good health.

Two million soldiers gave their lives on the German side in the First World War. But we managed to survive. Thank God!

40

In April 1916 Karl Kempowski is transferred to the rear, to Bruges, with instructions to report to local headquarters. His Excellency General von Benseler wishes to speak to him. Something to do with Rostock.

Bruges is a queer city. Its many churches and convents and the white bonnets worn by the women of Bruges give the impression that the whole city is inhabited by nuns.

The melancholy streets, the Gothic buildings with their tall stepped gables and steep roofs beside the canals where white swans stand in the murky water: again and again Karl walks through the streets, and he cannot imagine why he never looked at his own home town properly, for there were gabled buildings and old convents there too . . . Next time he goes on leave, he decides, he'll poke his nose into every nook and cranny: who knows, maybe he'll make some great discoveries?

Headquarters is bustling, what a vast apparatus of offices, of personnel! Whole armies of clerks populate the enormous building, platoons of orderlies with briefcases under their arms weave their way about, swarms of officers and officials enter and leave the offices.

Karl feels a bit out of place as he wanders along the corridors.

"His Excellency General von Benseler?" Over there, two floors up, you'll find the receptionist up there. "What would you be wanting with our General?"

Yes, what does Karl-Georg Kempowski, recruit, born 1898, want with his General? Or rather: what does the General want with him?

(Hints in the last letter from Rostock, Mrs. von Wondring, one
of his mother's cronies, whose cousin at the Ministry of War in
Berlin . . .)

Karl does not get to see the General, he is told to come back tomorrow. And the following day: "Come back tomorrow." And that
becomes his daily pilgrimage, and he walks through the town and
looks at everything, the churches and the courtyards; he watches the
swans, and the mongrels peeing at every corner. "Come back tomorrow!" And the longer he waits the more agreeable this life appears to him.

He enjoys sitting in a restaurant where violinists fiddle away at
"The Watch on the Rhine," it didn't take them long to learn that,
and little boys go from table to table selling hazelnuts. Officers sit
here with their surrogate-wives.
    Or he goes to one of those marvelous pastry shops where they
have little rice cakes with hot milk, and that is a delicacy.

Karl buys a lace handkerchief in a small shop, his comrades have
advised him to be sure and do so. Such lace handkerchiefs simply
don't exist in Germany, they're just wonderful. The young salesgirl
helps him choose.
    "She has coquettish hands," thinks Karl, and notices that they
are none too clean.

Sometimes there is an open-air concert. "Boys" in blue or green
stroll up and down with their Belgian girls to the strains of the
military band.
    After every piece the bandmaster looks around to see whether
he is being properly appreciated. He has chosen the pieces for their
sentiment, "The Thieving Magpie" and "Mignon." That's what the
spa orchestra in Bad Oeynhausen used to play too. Today would
be just the day to make peace, Karl feels. Then the band strikes up
"We Must Be Victorious!" and he remembers: Oh of course, that's
right, the war still has to be won.

. . .

One of the largest hotels has been turned into an army recreation center. Here they are performing Theodor Körner's *German Loyalty*. Highly appropriate for these times, in Karl's opinion. They are bound to go straight to the heart, those powerful words: "No one is too good to die for the freedom and honor of his country, but many are not good enough!"

Then when all the soldiers join in singing the old German song: "To thee my Fatherland I yield . . . ," Karl's chest feels ready to burst. Yes indeed, the Fatherland, he has yielded to it heart and soul, and if he isn't summoned to the General soon he'll report for duty at the front again. The dugout with the Hindenburg lamp on the rough table . . . that's what is calling him, that's where he belongs. But: Can he risk doing that? Wouldn't his mother be offended? And: Who knows what General Benseler really has in mind for him? Perhaps he is needed for a difficult secret mission that has to be accomplished with intelligence and skill?

Time enough to report back. One must not put a spoke in the wheel of Destiny.

After a week he is told he needn't come back. They'll call him when the General is ready.

Karl thereupon takes up his quarters in a small village. Here attempts have been made to introduce German spirit and German style. The houses have been painted a pale yellow, the windows picked out in brown, with green shutters. The houses are further adorned with folksy sayings. They are to be seen everywhere.

> While water's to the donkey dear,
> We men rely on wine and beer!
> So let us therefore raise our glass,
> For no one wants to be an ass!

The object is to display German words to native eyes, and to impress German ways and German humor upon the local populace. This village has felt the breath of the German spirit! it seems to

Karl. And: The age-old German delight in the hop and the vine, how irrepressible it is!

The streets have also been given names. Carved wooden signs are hung at the street corners. In the "airmen's quarter" they read: Immelmann-Strasse, Boelcke-Weg, and Zeppelin-Platz.

> Flight Lieutenant Immelmann
> Twists his way the heavens to scan,
> While bold Lieutenant Boelcke too
> Disports himself in yonder blue.

The main street has, of course, been named Kaiser-Wilhelm-Strasse, even though it is unpaved.

Now the villagers at least know what street they were born on!

Karl lives at the corner of Hindenburg- and Ludendorff-Strasse. His room is the "holy of holies" of a young schoolteacher's wife that has never been used. A black-and-white cat stands in the doorway when he looks at the room for the first time. Overstuffed furniture with antimacassars, a piano, tinted plaster statuettes.

On the table lies the latest issue of *L'Illustration*, with a drawing on its cover of a kneeling German soldier who has thrown down his sword and raises his hands in supplication: *"Pardon—Camarade,"* the caption reads.

Karl immediately tosses the magazine into the waste-paper basket. He picks it out again, shakes his head, and throws it away for good. He wonders whether he shouldn't go to the kitchen and confront the schoolteacher's wife. Did she put the paper there as a provocation, or what did she have in mind?

If she weren't so pretty, that's what he would do, no question.

Unfortunately the piano is out of tune. The strings jangle and tinkle. "Rustle of Spring" can't be played on it, neither can Schumann's "Soaring." Karl unscrews the front panel and tries to tune the instrument with pliers: he manages to get the middle octave more or less right, but then it becomes too difficult. Strange, in a way, and he's trying so hard.

. . .

The bed is wonderful, a thick down quilt and a huge pillow into which Karl sinks his head. From here he can look at the picture of "The Guardian Angel" in peace and for as long as he likes as it hangs there on the mauve wallpaper; from here he can also listen to the mice scrabbling, though it's impossible to tell exactly *where* they are actually gnawing.

His watch lies on the bed table beside the glass of water for his dry throat: this is the life! If his throat gets dry in the night, he'll have a sip of water, and if he wakens he need only pick up his watch to see what time it is.

"I gave gold for iron": it was possible to arrange for the exchange of his gold watch chain; he wears an iron one now.

The schoolteacher's wife can't understand what Karl is getting at. *"Pardon—Camarade"*? What does he mean? She can't understand. On the other hand she cures a sty in his eye. She smells of garlic, pleasantly.

The schoolroom in which her husband had taught the village children is desperately poor. Battered desks, a peeling blackboard, a closet full of dog-eared books, a rusty fish tank, and a cane, splintered at one end.

Did this man keep bees too? Karl wonders. Windmills, water mills, powder mills, and treadmills. And the boy way back there, he must be dreaming . . .

The husband is a soldier. God knows where he is now.

Running around in the muddy schoolyard are three chickens, each tied by one leg with a string to prevent it from being stolen.

"A disgrace," Karl thinks, "really a disgrace that German soldiers should give rise to such suspicions."

With God for Kaiser and Reich!

Surely German soldiers should be an example of integrity and decency. And he looks out the window to make sure the chickens are still there. He could almost wish that a Schippanowski—meaning one of the supply-corps soldiers from that area—would try to snatch one. Wouldn't he make it hot for him! He would have him court-martialed.

"Just a moment!" he would say. "Aren't you ashamed of yourself?" And he pulls up his chair to the window the better to look out.

After doing that for long enough he goes out into the kitchen. His sty is gone, true, and there is no sign of one in the other eye. But he might need some water for shaving. Or for the fish tank. Couldn't the fish tank be fixed up again? Surely that shouldn't be too difficult?

Yes, she says, by all means try, and Karl obtains some putty and seals the fish tank, puts in some gravel and water, and in Bruges buys a goldfish that actually swims around in it—mouth open, mouth shut—to and fro with undulating fins.

So that job's done. Time to look out the window again to make sure the chickens are still there. Looking by turns out the window and into the fish tank to make sure the fish is still alive. And then Karl goes into the kitchen and asks whether he may sit down for a minute.

Wait, first cover the fish tank with a sheet of glass because of the cat.

May he sit down for a bit? Yes, says the schoolteacher's wife in her own language, wiping the stool with a cloth, of course, and: Why not? And then she goes out into the yard, where the chickens are fluttering about, and brings in some firewood. Of course he may sit down, she says, and not the least reason for her saying so is that he has brought along half a loaf of bread as his price of admission.

Now he tells her about the goldfish, that it seems to be perfectly happy in its surroundings, and he enjoys sitting in her kitchen and does so very often. And each time he tells her about Graal, about the fisherman who threw the little plaice back overboard because they are too young to die.

He tells the cat sitting beside him that at home he has a "bow-wow" called Stribold, he's very nice too.

He watches the woman as she busies herself at the stove, below the pots and pans hanging on the wall according to size, the way she pushes the iron rings to one side, her face lit up by the leaping flames, and sets the big pot on the fire for the chunk of meat he has also brought her. For normally in this house they have only a thin gruel and at best a small piece of cheese.

Her movements seem unfamiliar yet familiar. Everything done deftly and smoothly, and now and again she scratches herself. Karl wonders why it seems familiar, the sight of a young woman busy like that at the stove, and he believes he has preserved an atavistic image deep inside himself: it must have been like that then, and it has always been like that.

As she busies herself, she lets him know that she once went to Lyons, she really did, and that she even has a cousin in Brussels.

"Cousine" is not the word she uses, but *"nicht,"* that's what they call it here, and Karl understands that too, although *Nichte* in German means something quite different, for her speech sounds almost like Mecklenburg Low German. *Almost.* Slightly more absurd, to tell the truth, than Mecklenburg dialect:

> *Klabastert upp de Biesters,*
> *noch net—aber nu!*

Often downright ridiculous, isn't it? That's supposed to be a military command! He demonstrates to her how absurd Flemish sounds to his ears and in comparison how easy and agreeable the German language sounds:

> *Füllest wieder Busch und Tal . . .*

To speak only Low German, and nothing else, is almost like walking bent over all the time, in his opinion, and he persists in demonstrating to her how he thinks Flemish is pronounced until he finally realizes that this isn't getting him anywhere. That if anything it is making her gruff and obstinate.

So instead he takes the "Markopano" from his pocket and looks at the meat he has brought her, a really good piece, isn't it? He says that and gives her some of the marzipan.

He has been to Lyons too, he says, passed through there one night, and: Hamburg, he intends to have a close look at it next chance he gets, he says that too. Does she know where it is? On the Elbe? Vistula, Oder, Elbe, Weser, and Rhine, those are the quintessential German rivers that make a man's heart swell. And the Danube, flowing straight across down there.

"Isar, Lech, Iller, Inn . . ." This flashes through Karl's mind, and he says that too.

Where is the German's Fatherland . . . ?

This also flashes through his mind, but he doesn't say it.

And Rostock? Does she know where that is? Far away, on the Baltic, that's where it is, where the forest with its storm-tossed pine trees comes right down to the dunes, where one can find amber that can be polished into necklaces.

There are wrecks there, washed by the waves . . .

Rostock, that's his native town.

He looks at her feet, she is barefoot, her strong, none too clean feet on the worn tiles: the hem of her skirt is slightly frayed.

Her two daughters, aged five and seven, who in the beginning always ran away when he entered the kitchen, then started looking around the corner, then became interested in the goldfish, are now sitting on his lap and covering him with so many kisses that his glasses mist over. He lets them listen to his watch and paints flowers on their new wooden clogs, daisies and forget-me-nots. He even allows them to spoon out the "sugar fish" from his coffee cup and tells them his father always let him do that too: unfortunately he doesn't have a picture of his father with him, or he would have shown it to them. "Always frank and honest . . . ," really rather an unusual man.

. . .

"Hest du ok eene Fru?" the children ask him (or that's what it sounds like); they want to know whether he has a wife, and the young schoolteacher's wife listens intently for the answer.

A wife, no, a girl friend though, yes, says Karl, or rather, actually no girl friend either. No girl friend. No. Footloose and fancy-free.

The water hisses on the stove, the meal is ready, the kitchen table is cleared and wiped with a cloth that is also used to swat flies on the windowpane and that has also once been thrown at a mouse which the cat allowed to pass unmolested. The children bring over the bowls used here, kneel on the stools, and look at the chunk of meat that their mother is cutting up. They get their wrists slapped when they try to snatch bits of meat, and Karl sits at the end of the table humming with contentment, the stove back there with the pots and pans above it, arranged according to size, the worn red-and-white tiles, and the rough wooden door to the yard, its cracks stuffed with straw: yes, he likes all that. This is a lot better than fighting. And: this is how he wants it to be one day, in peacetime, when he has a wife and child of his own—it has to come sometime, there's a lid for every pot. And vice versa.

Sitting at the end of the table, that's how he sees himself, and his wife will have to carve the meat.

He gets up once more, brings in the fish tank with the goldfish and places it on the kitchen table. He wants the goldfish also to see how cozy it is in here, poor creature, always alone. Perhaps they should give him a little wife. Or, if he is a little female, a little husband.

Yes, this is how he wants it to be one day, this is how Karl imagines it, so simple and so uncomplicated. Armchair and sofa, buffet and rug? They're not really necessary. A simple, rough-hewn table, a stove, tiles, and a big bed.

In Bruges Karl buys himself some wooden clogs. He puts them on and walks out into the muddy yard past the fluttering chickens and also carries in some firewood, although there is really plenty of wood stacked up beside the stove; he even picks some flowers, and tomorrow he'll get hold of some more wood and split it with his very own hands. But as for painting his clogs, as he had intended, he won't do that. He can't very well have flowers sprouting on them, can he? Or an Iron Cross?

At night, when the young wife is asleep and the two little girls are also asleep in their room upstairs and have stopped coming down and saying: *"Wij kunnen niet slapen . . .,"* as regularly happens when he has been sitting for a little while longer with their mother, Karl walks up and down in his room. The ceiling is low, if he stretches a bit he can touch it with his fingertips. A pity he threw away the magazine: *"Pardon—Camarade."* He wonders what other thumping great lies it contained. About German nurses, probably, who attack wounded enemies with knives.

Absurd.

Karl stands at the door and listens. He has only to open it and walk across the corridor and in through the other door. And he would if she gave him a sign, any sign.

Perhaps the young schoolteacher's wife is also standing behind her door, and perhaps she, too, is thinking: "He must give me some sort of sign . . ." But then there's her husband, huddled in a trench somewhere in the West, his rifle between the sandbags . . .

What German nurse would ever do such a thing as gouge out the eyes of wounded men, Karl thinks. And why should she?

A pity the piano is out of order, otherwise he would now play "Rustle of Spring" or, even better, "Dreaming," that most German of all piano pieces.

Then that sturdy young woman across the corridor, with her healthy teeth, would listen and be full of admiration and no longer think of German nurses doing God knows what, or of German soldiers spearing Belgian infants on their bayonets.

Karl sits down in the armchair and stares in front of him. Every so often his gaze falls on the mirror over the washstand and he sees himself sitting there, his head resting in his hand, the Iron Cross on his chest and the Golden Mecklenburg Cross of Merit underneath it, the one that is awarded automatically. It looks exactly like the Iron Cross, just that it is "golden," and it looks very decorative.

Karl gets up, smooths down his tunic, and turns this way and that in front of the mirror as if at the tailor's. "I'm really not bad-looking," he thinks. Although only five foot seven. But still, five foot seven.

He won't cross the corridor, he knows that now, with or without a sign, even if she should want him to. He will prove to her that German men are not like that, not as immoral and dirty-minded as people here imagine.

Would August Menz already have the Iron Cross? He'd like to know that, but he doesn't ask in his letters. His letters are limited to: "How's everything?" Whatever else may have happened.

What he would really like to know is whether his parents are terribly proud of their son. They are not exactly terribly proud, they are more surprised. Vice-sergeant-major? Iron Cross? And: he's still alive?

No, he won't go across to the young woman, if only because of her husband, who is also doing his duty, after all. Whom one may even have met, without knowing it? Perhaps he was the one on the other side whom, *although* he had seen him, he did not "pick off," as they say in the trenches.

He won't go across, instead he'll go into the kitchen and get himself a pitcher of cold water.

He picks up the pitcher, and there is a light in the kitchen, the young woman is sitting there wearing her necklace and looks at him. And Karl has a hard time setting the pitcher down onto the tiles without breaking it, the blood is throbbing in his throat and head, and he doesn't know how to reach her. He suddenly feels quite ill from the blood throbbing in his head and his stomach and all over. The black-and-white cat jumps aside. And many skirts envelop him, all of a sudden, and bare limbs inside the skirts cling tightly to him: that it could be like *this*, he hadn't thought, so flaming and elemental. So utterly without any thought?

He lies with her for a long time on the worn white-and-red tiles, *"Pardon—Camarade . . . ,"* and the cat comes closer and looks at them. Karl has never experienced anything like it. And he never will again.

41

August Menz is living with his air force comrades in an abandoned château. The rooms are sumptuously furnished, the invasion having fortunately bypassed the estate with almost no trace. The oaken closets and tables with their twisted columns stand there as of old, "awe-inspiring" as August Menz writes to his parents; and in the mahogany and walnut beds sleep airmen of whom some, appropriately enough, are of noble descent.

During his leisure hours August Menz wanders from room to room. In the music room he admires the black grand piano, the one his blood brother Ferdinand von Maltzahn always plays so beautifully.

He also admires the rooms of the chatelaine, the glass cabinets with their inlaid borders, and the dressing table with its many little drawers and pigeonholes, a masterpiece of artistic detail. He sits down at this dressing table and looks at himself in the triple mirror, first from one side, then from the other, he leans closer and flattens his unruly hair with two fingers. His moustache, what's happening to his moustache? Is that a gray hair?

It is not surprising that August Menz should find a gray hair in his moustache, it's all been a bit much, the experiences he has gone through. With a pair of nail scissors he snips it off: August Menz from Rostock, six enemy planes shot down. Maybe, if he's lucky, it will soon be seven or eight, and then ten won't be far off. Ten kills, that sounds much better. "I've ten kills to my credit . . ." Or, better still: "That's Lieutenant Menz. Lieutenant Menz has ten kills, but he doesn't want it talked about."

August Menz puts away his nail scissors and gets up. He smooths down his tunic. Six foot one, he's all of that, there's no denying.

The park is an invitation to a stroll: ivy-clad trees and stalactite grottoes artificially constructed from cement. The French gardener, who has stayed behind to watch over his master's property, raises his hat. Yes, true, the paths need raking again, the Lieutenant is quite right.

It's all right, don't worry, the Lieutenant hadn't meant it like that. He starts talking about new rose varieties: the Lyons rose, that's a really beautiful one. The *Juliette* and the *Soleil d'or*, and all the rest of them.

August Menz intends to acquire such roses after the war, when maybe he will be the owner of an estate like his uncle's. Why shouldn't he buy himself an estate? What's the objection to that?

The gardener is still annoyed at someone having chopped down those fine mirabelle plum trees. Whatever will the Count say when he returns one day? Chopping down all the trees, why would any-one do such a thing?

He thinks it was the Prussians, and August Menz thinks it was the English, that mob. The English, who systematically destroyed many of the homes of their allies. A strange thing: and in the air they are such fair opponents.

"*Gott strafe England*": this saying does have its justification, he finds.

He reassures the gardener, he mustn't be afraid of what the Count will say when he returns. The Count won't be back for a long time. For the sake of this château, August Menz hopes that a German master will soon move in here once and for all, someone who will repair all the damage, who will also do away with all the surround-ing mud hovels and replace them with trim cottages, and who, for all he knows, will also plant new mirabelle trees. Then this château, this jewel of a vanished civilization—so he writes home—will be set in a golden ring of German diligence, German order, and German civic pride. For it must surely be beyond doubt that the coming peace will bestow upon the Fatherland a Greater Germany, greater than anyone could have dreamed at the beginning of the war.

Kurland, for instance, can't possibly be left to the Russians, they would obliterate all trace of German culture there, root and branch.

And Belgium, this "pistol aimed at England's heart," Belgium can only belong to the German Reich, that much is sure. One owes this to the Flemings, this vital, energetic, and highly individual race of people. "Flanders," that's what this province should then be called. And one owes it to oneself, too, to Greater Germany's own prestige.

Inexplicable that Scheidemann should want to renounce all this, even war reparations! That unpatriotic fellow need hardly wonder that his Socialist party remains beyond discussion among people who understand something about politics and have a sense of history.

When the war is over, it will be as well to keep a watchful eye on him and his ilk.

For himself, at any rate, August Menz wishes, someday, somehow, to own a similar property—more modest, of course, simpler, more "bourgeois," if you like. A small estate in Mecklenburg (Paints & Enamels, Wholesale!), a white house behind a linden tree. A property something like Glüsenberg, his uncle's estate. The only daughter, Anna-Mathilda, quite a girl, come to think of it, the way she galloped across the meadows. On his next leave he will have to see to things there, no doubt about it: have a pavilion built, with a copper roof and a cupola on top, and sit and read and watch the swans on the lake to be created there.

And from far away the sound of scythes being sharpened.

"Cela suffit!" he would think, then, so he imagines. Or: *"Je suis d'accord,"* that would probably be appropriate, too.

August Menz looks down from the stone bridge into the moat containing a little murky water. He sees the stone bridge in the water, and he sees himself looking down, and he can't resist the temptation, he has to spit down and watch the circles set in motion by his spit.

. . .

The possibilities of walking in the park are limited. One can walk along the paths this way around or that way around. In front one has the advantage of the fine view of the façade of the château, at the back there is a dilapidated chapel, a family vault that lets the fancy wander.

In a deserted corner stands a conservatory with green cast-iron decorations, a greenhouse in which the air is damp and smells of exotic plants. In this greenhouse the two monkeys presented by Hagenbeck to the squadron disport themselves. Sometimes they chase each other with shrill screams, but sometimes they are quite sedate and pick minute scales out of each other's fur.

However, a giant eagle with clipped wings that has also been placed in here, a gift of the Grand Duke of Baden, has already given up. It no longer comes down from its perch, even when offered the finest meat.

Lieutenant Menz looks up at the eagle: such a giant creature and so melancholy? Couldn't it at least stretch with some semblance of majesty? Surely some vestige of strength must still be alive.

The eagle turns its head to the right and blinks its white eyelids just once. Otherwise it gives no sign, although it can very well see that someone is standing below. Instead, the monkeys come romping up, Heini and Rieke, and look at the airman who brought them in a jolting box from Hamburg to here. He has his hand in his pocket, is he going to take out something? An apple perhaps? Or a few hazelnuts?

August Menz doesn't stay for long with these odd humanoid caricatures, just long enough to take a cigarette from his case. The two monkeys stare at him fixedly as he looks up at the eagle and taps his cigarette. How strange, the fellow is leaving again. Hasn't he only just arrived?

"Lieutenant Menz has ten kills, but he doesn't want it talked about. Ten kills means ten human beings who gave their lives, you realize." Who gave their lives for their country. Even if it is a foreign country.

. . .

After August Menz has walked along the paths this way around and that way around, he goes up the steps to the château again—a piano is being played indoors—step by step, with a little bounce on each step as he goes up, and pulls off his gloves.

In the library Ferdinand von Maltzahn is playing Chopin, up, down, on the melodious grand piano. This is something one may someday hear again somewhere, and one will remember how pleasant it really was. This polonaise. Or this nocturne.

Close the door softly so he won't break off.

Menz goes into the room with a fireplace where the batman has just started a crackling fire. Ah, that feels good. He rubs his hands. Ah, that feels good.

On the mantelpiece lies the mail, sorted according to size. Well! A letter from Margarethe de Bonsac from Hamburg, isn't that nice, and his mother has also written, as he can see. Very nice.

The *Rostocker Anzeiger* has become thinner again—"Strikes in Russia!"—soon there'll be nothing left to read in it.

He puts down the paper, also his mother's letter (". . . and so we think of you every day and pray God that everything will turn out for the best . . ."), and sniffs at the little sky-blue letter from Wandsbek. He sits down and stretches his feet toward the pleasantly warm flames. The feet in their ultra-soft boots, bought in Brussels, just before everything was confiscated there.

First light up one of those extra-long cigarettes that he obtains from God knows where, then a liqueur from the cut-glass decanter, and then, with slim letter-opener, slit open the sky-blue letter, which once again probably contains some delightful bits of nonsense.

To his annoyance, something immediately falls out of this letter and he has to stoop down, bumping into the little table with the liqueur decanter as he bends, and dropping the ash from his cigarette. A childish glossy picture, as far as he can see, one of the kind with which his two sisters so often used to plague him.

August reads Grethe de Bonsac's letter—strains of Chopin still coming from the other room—and he reads it a second time and a third time, he straightens up and he *gets* up and he walks to the wide window: Chopin, up and down, and the park, so green, so vast: my God! She wants to *marry* him? So this child has developed a crush on him? Misunderstood the pure friendship in which he had enveloped her?

No! *C'est impossible, absolument!*

Swiftly and purposefully he sits down at the desk, dips the pen in the cut-glass inkwell and, in his angular handwriting, writes a brief letter. "No," he writes, no, he can't do that, he mustn't do that, marry in these uncertain times, the war, how long may it still last, this cruel struggle of the nations? He may be killed! Has she never thought of that? Has she forgotten that it must pain him to receive such a letter in the face of death? And to have to refuse?

Any day, any hour, it can overtake him, and she would then be alone!

No, he cannot take that responsibility. Every day Fate can overtake him, as he has said, any day, any hour. And if it does not, which would really be a miracle, he must still somehow build up an existence for himself, after the war. Or does she expect him to join his father's firm? Paints & Enamels, Wholesale? Never! She must understand that. A quiet estate in Mecklenburg, like Glüsenberg, that's what he wants, but first he must have it.

He looks at the portrait of the French lord of the manor hanging over the fireplace, and the batman brings in the silver candelabra with the five burning candles, and he folds the letter and licks the envelope and seals it: A.M. Then he throws the childish picture that has slipped out of Grethe's letter, the little Sistine angel, into the fire and goes across to Ferdinand, his blood brother, who immediately stops playing, who senses something of the burden of the decision that August Menz has quite obviously just shouldered. And they drive out to the airfield and get into their machines and climb up into the cold blue air and almost forget that there is an earth and that there is so much grief and misery on this earth.

Two weeks later this letter stands propped up on the hall table in Wandsbek, and the dog barks, and Grethe can see the letter from outside through the glass panel and breathlessly unlocks the door. She runs upstairs holding the letter, wildly pursued by Axel Pfeffer —"Do come and have your dinner first, child!"—and as she removes her hatpins she reads the letter, and that day she doesn't come down for dinner. She hurries off to her friend Thea, who immediately knows that something terrible has happened.

Another two weeks later Karl is sitting in the schoolteacher's wife's "holy of holies," drinking a glass of near-beer and holding a pale-blue letter that smells of soap and is different from what he usually gets from Hamburg. Not: "How's everything?" No, this letter is serious. Short and serious. That she is standing at the edge of an abyss, Grethe writes, and that she needs someone who will jump into this abyss with her.

> What, oh what, can be the meaning?
> Can there, can there be, better times coming?

Karl doesn't understand this letter, and he turns it over to see if there is anything else on the back. Somehow the tone is different from before, not unfavorable, it seems to him. Somehow not unfavorable, he finds.

The next day Karl has his photograph taken, he has grown more virile, a little more angular, and the picture is sent to Wandsbek, a machine gun in the background, painted on a backdrop, and a bridge of papier-mâché. And in Wandsbek it is placed in the frame that used to contain a different photo.

42 The Friend

I was in on it all! What a disappointment! I felt so sorry for my poor Grethe, oh what a tragedy that was. And she was so in love with him . . .

Our circle was having its weekly get-together, and Grethe turned up a little late, which surprised us, she was always so punctual. There were five of us, and Grethe rings the doorbell, I open up and look at her and say: "Grethe, whatever's the matter?" She looked completely changed, all the life gone out of her, drained, and she had always been such a radiant creature.

She wasn't crying, but she was rigid, and somehow inwardly dead.

"What is it, Grethe?"

"He's written," she said: "Out of a mistaken concern for me, he says he can't marry me . . ."

So he had backed down, and Grethe was left high and dry. Oh what a tragedy! All through the war they had corresponded, letter after letter, back and forth. He had also once been in Wandsbek, had called on her, an airman, with decorations, very dashing. And now this rejection. Why? Perhaps he felt pressured and that's why he said "No," short and sweet.

Probably he would have preferred to ask the question himself, whether she wanted to become his wife, some men are funny that way.

In any event, there was Grethe, letter in hand, completely devastated.

"What on earth is the matter?" I asked her.

Out of a "mistaken concern" for her he couldn't marry her. (Don't really know what that meant.) I suppose he had no career yet and probably wanted to remain free for the time being.

I don't think Grethe ever got over it. The "blond scalawag," as Mrs. de Bonsac used to call him. And Grethe was so in love with him!

43

In the trenches the mood has changed greatly. Of the solicitude for the soldiers so frequently mentioned in the newspapers, precious little is to be observed out there. "Never again will I thoughtlessly shout Hurrah in a café when a victory is announced . . . ," thus the soldiers write home.

He reigns, her reins, it rains . . . The trenches and dugouts are filled with mud and water. Water from below and rain from above. Day and night earth must be shoveled and water pumped out, but the water remains, and rain falls incessantly in sheets, making underwear stick to thighs. In addition, the depressing darkness at night: the least light would give away their position. A nocturnal darkness illumined only by flashes of the shells—painful for the eyes. And ears buzz from the mines.

Resentment grows against this life in mud and filth and against the incessant wet, cold, futile labor. These are hardships that no one would tolerate in peacetime for a civilian cause.

Every morning, when all is quiet, Dauntless goes through the trenches with his retinue. Extra gratings are laid down. The sentries, who have to keep their eyes constantly on the French lines while they are speaking, are questioned about the positions and about the names of their superior officers. He asks a newly arrived Mecklenburger: "What is the name of your regimental commander?" And the fellow says: "The name of my regimental commander is Lieutenant-Colonel Dauntless!"

Three days' solitary confinement (to be served after the war).

. . .

One of the young volunteers raises his head above the parapet as he reports. Ping! Shot through the head: dead.

Every two weeks they are relieved. They march back to the rest area, heavy and soggy with mud and, incredible though it sounds, the last hundred yards have to be covered in goose-step. It is a strange sight, Dauntless on his horse and the filthy, exhausted fellows in their flapping greatcoats.

As soon as they have had enough sleep they emerge from the barracks, blinking into the sunlight, their faces covered with dust and dirt. They wash and sit on the grass, stripped to the waist, and search for lice. The captain goes around and talks to them, and the barber gets busy.

But to sit back and relax is out of the question, the thick layer of mud has to be scraped off their clothing with a knife. Furthermore, every spare minute is taken up with drill or inspections.

While they are sweeping the road, the divisional general arrives; he senses their feelings and calls out to them: "It can't be helped, boys, someone's got to do it!" and nods to them and looks kindly enough through his spectacles. He's a reasonable old gent.

Road-sweeping and road-building, they'll put up with that. But when an order comes at night to move up to the front on "shovel fatigue," the soldiers get angry. They have to march for three hours, without weapons, lugging coils of wire, wooden posts, and tools, and it's so dark that they're constantly afraid of losing contact.

Sometimes the platoon leader loses his direction, and then, cursing and swearing, they have to climb over barbed wire, through muddy holes, across steep slopes and water trenches in impenetrable darkness.

"Close ranks!" comes the order, but many soldiers play deaf, slip off into the darkness, and lie down in some shell hole or other. They don't appear again until the following morning. And many of them not even then. They hole up for days in abandoned huts or wander from one group to another, asking: "Where is the two hundred tenth Regiment?" Whole hordes of stragglers are wandering around in the rear, laggards and shirkers of all kinds.

In March 1917 Karl was made an ensign. He has a dugout to himself and a batman to look after him. When another batch of new men arrives, Karl can't believe his eyes: Why, it's Erex Woltersen! . . . They fall into each other's arms: What's Rostock doing, good old Rostock, and: "Now nothing can go wrong anymore . . ."

They talk about Valentine Becker, how terribly pretty she really was, and about the Warnow meadows, how they used to spy on lovers, and the hollow in the old willow tree. So nice and warm and snug . . .

The two men exchange books, the Globus *Faust* and the little Reclam paperbacks, and when they have finished reading them all they spend their time studying the Reclam catalogue. They go through the authors one by one and are thrilled with the knowledge picked up in this way.

They are agreed that the German soul is that part of the German heritage that endows it with its greatness. What they are fighting for is German culture (over there are the Zouaves), German poetry, art, and philosophy: for Goethe.

> River and brook are freed from ice
> By the lovely enlivening glance of spring . . .

and for Strasbourg Cathedral (though with only one spire, but that one so unmistakably German!). Or for the St. Matthew Passion: "Cru-ci-fy Him!" The way the whole orchestra throbs and swells and the chorus sings: "Cru-ci-fy Him!" Forgotten for a hundred years and then suddenly performed again: the St. Matthew Passion. (And by a young Jew at that.) Bach, that fifth Evangelist, whose compositions are the basis for all Western music of the last two hundred years!

What may still lie hidden in the womb of the German spirit, waiting to be discovered? . . .

How they will enjoy everything once they are back home again!

. . .

Erex has a gift for drawing in pen and ink, on good days he portrays the rats scuttling across the footplanks, the soldiers picking lice, and Karl sitting on the latrine. *"De profundis,"* Karl writes under that and sends the drawing home, and it still exists, there is a coffee stain on it, and *"De profundis"* is still written under it. (It is a moot question whether Anna Kempowski has shown it to her cronies. She certainly never had it framed.)

One day a sapper passes by with six prisoners. That's drawn too. The sapper with his fixed bayonet and the prisoners frantically saluting, apparently afraid they are about to be killed off: they walk so fast that the sapper has a hard time keeping up with them, and they brandish their *képis* with shouts of *"La guerre est finie. Patrie allemande!"*

On clear days Karl and Erex watch air battles: deftly the opponents circle each other, and one can hear the tak-tak of the machine guns. And then suddenly one of the planes starts spiraling toward the ground, faster and ever faster. Or suddenly one of them flares up: it has been set aflame! A plume of smoke in its wake, it spins to earth. That is a sight that never fails to fascinate. If only one knew whether it was friend or foe.

Erich, who has a good memory and a nice talent for reciting, sometimes declaims ballads in the men's dugouts when the exhausted soldiers huddle against the walls, unshaven, their fatigue caps pushed back. Or he reads Homer aloud, and the fellows listen:

> And vividly pictured for him the horrors that people
> Suffer when enemies take their town, reminding
> Him of the men all slaughtered, of the city reduced
> To ashes, of children and fair-belted women dragged off
> By the foe.

Unfortunately there are always those types who belch loudly during the most beautiful poetry or even release black-bread farts of the very worst kind, and as loud as possible.

. . .

In March 1917 a bad thing happens: "Who'll volunteer for Finland?" and of course they all step forward. They would all like to go to Finland, but the destination isn't Finland, a so-called "ridge" is to be recaptured. The 210's are picked to do this, and they are put on a train.

That afternoon they arrive in "S," as it is known in the code language of the war bulletins. As soon as they are on the road they encounter one automobile after another, crammed with groaning wounded, others drive back empty. These alternate with lightly wounded men hobbling along and men with stretchers.

Now they can see the "ridge" lying in the distance, it is number 63, and on the ridge all hell has broken loose.

This is no longer a matter of single detonations, it is an incessant blood-curdling thunder. The impacts can no longer be distinguished, the scene resembles a fire-spouting volcano.

And this is what they have to go into! Quickly they swallow a few mouthfuls of food, and quickly they scribble a few last words for the field post (from many probably the very last), then comes the order: "Fall in! Forward march!"

The officers hurry back and forth, a certain tension has gripped all of them, there is cursing and swearing, everyone is on edge. In such a situation Karl always displays an unnatural calm. He doesn't suffer from the "jimjams," as the soldiers call the anxiety-state of frightened men.

They march slowly up the steep slope in bottomless mud toward the firing. Here, as in a forest of felled trees, lie the dead—mostly German soldiers. And each one lies differently: with outspread arms, a hand firmly gripping the rifle. Officers, their swords thrust forward, face down; others kneeling, their heads buried in the soil: with their pale limbs they look like figures in a wax museum.

A soldier's life, hurrah!
How merry we will be!

One man is lying on his back in a wheel rut, his right hand grasping his rifle, in his death throes his left hand has ripped open tunic and shirt: the bloody death-wound lies exposed. An officer lies surrounded by fifteen motionless figures, all face down, on the other side they all lie in firing line, shoulder to shoulder. One of them was just about to shoot, his finger is on the trigger, his left eye screwed shut. Even in death he stares at the enemy, after the bullet has struck him.

Appalling, the horrible stench of corpses!

Suddenly the barrage subsides, a miracle! The firing dies down, the dust settles, sparrows can be heard quarreling.

Advancing through a communication trench, the 210's reach the forward trench on the slope of the north face of the wooded hill.

One after another they force their way through the trench, where corpses block their passage forcing them to clamber over them and thus come into contact with the cold hands and faces and the still bleeding wounds. Mud and blood mingle on their boots.

Thirty yards away are the French trenches: as soon as a helmet shows above the parapet, bullets whistle over their heads.

The trench is a chaos of earth, rocks, logs, and corpses, and the farther they advance toward the left wing the more ghastly it becomes. The corpses lie closer and closer together inside and outside the trench. On the left wing the trench looks more like a shallow trough—so badly has it been shot up—a kind of improvised barrier has been erected, the other end of the trench being in French hands: their flanking trench is clearly visible.

In the trench, which is choked with all kinds of equipment, one sits and stands on the dead as if they were rocks or chunks of wood. Brains, limbs, blood everywhere. Whether one man has had his head pierced or torn off, whether another has a gaping chest, or a third shows bloody bones sticking out of his tunic—no one cares: out there in a shell hole sits a young Frenchman, his rifle under his arm, his head slightly bowed, holding up his hands as if to shield his chest, which gapes from a deep bayonet thrust.

·   ·   ·

A pile of five corpses lies in front of the barrier, one has constantly to step on them and squelch them down into the mud.

Suddenly Karl notices that one of the corpses, lying under three others, is starting to move, a bearded, sturdy Frenchman who opens his eyes and moans horribly. He is pulled out, given something to drink, and lapses into unconsciousness.

The 210's settle in as best they can, digging little hollows for themselves as shelter in case the artillery should start up again. Once Karl raises himself incautiously on his knees to get a better look across: instantly it rattles, whistles, and buzzes around him! Dirt sprays into his eyes. Over there are machine guns, and the French shoot with their pipes in their mouths.

The following morning there is another whopping bombardment, and toward nine o'clock the fire is lifted, and from the French on the other side come shouts of *"Allez, allez en avant!"* From behind shrubs, trees, and hillocks they come darting out in a crouch, and the Mecklenburgers sit there as if on a rifle range. Whenever a Frenchman tries to leap from one cover to the next he is stopped by a bullet. Karl fires with a French rifle until the barrel is red hot; water runs down his body, and his glasses are smeared with sweat and earth. From beside him comes a low cry: "They've got me!" Schultze with *tz*.

> See, the conquering hero comes! . . .

His right arm hangs down limply, badly torn. He crawls back, and as Karl looks over his shoulder at him something buzzes past his left ear.

The French advance to within ten yards, then they retreat. That is the moment for the counterthrust, to scramble up out of the trench: "Hurrah!" and into the enemy trench.

> The assault is the peak of springtime
> in a man's life . . .

These are the images that Karl will never forget, leaping down into the shell holes, young fellows raising their arms, others running away: so this is what assault means, he thinks over and over again.

Enthusiasm is not the right word to use here. During an assault each man wishes he were a thousand miles away, and a nice little wound to send him home is the unspoken ardent wish of each man. But if next day they had been ordered to advance again, they would have climbed out of the trenches again, from a sense of duty or from habit: the order comes and is simply obeyed.

Some are also motivated by fear of ridicule from the others if they stay behind. For even though a soldier will normally boast that he has managed to duck his duties, after such a day each man is sternly judged and thoroughly quizzed as to whether he was there, or whether he stayed behind, and how he behaved.

In the evening, quiet descends, not a Frenchman to be seen, and the 210's can catch their breath. They search through the packs of the fallen French and find rusks, chocolate, sardines, and bread. That lovely white French bread. One man shows up with a whole loaf one end of which is covered with blood. After brief hesitation the blood is cut off, the bread is divided and eaten up.

Cigarettes, too, are found, strong cigarettes, soothing to those shivering, jangling nerves.

Karl holds a pistol in his hand, he has taken it from a dead French officer. It is a German pistol that the Frenchman must have pried loose from the rigid grip of a German officer.

It feels good in his hand, Karl finds. More practical than a rifle. More pleasing, somehow, than his heavy service pistol.

Karl huddles against the trench wall and stares in front of him, the pistol in his hand. One of the men passing by nudges him, thinking he is dead.

44

In Rostock it is raining. People have become gaunt, they look haggard and hollow-cheeked. Bread rations have been reduced, and the winter allotment of potatoes is a hundredweight less. Although the stores still display huge cheeses in their windows, these are all dummies.

Pompeius et erat.

The newspaper says: "That's the very thing that is good about the war-time diet: the incidence of gout, obesity, liver disease, and diabetes has been reduced, indeed in some cases they have entirely disappeared. War has taught people simplicity and thrift. It has virtually done away with all big and little abuses of the body—coffee, tea, tobacco, and alcohol."

For the women, life is hard: hour after hour they have to stand in line for a bit of fruit or fresh meat, always worrying that something more essential might be available on the next street. Or that they'll be told "Sorry, that's it!" just when it's their turn. It's exhausting, standing in line or roaming the countryside to beg or to collect wood on Rostock Heath, or berries and mushrooms, always in fear of the forest warden, who demands to see a "permit," a "berry-picking permit" with an official stamp on it, which, of course, can't be produced.

Mushrooms are much prized, meadow mushrooms, boletus, and chanterelles, not that there is any nourishment in them but their meatlike flavor takes the mind off hunger. Too bad that people know nothing about the many other kinds of edible fungi, such as the masked tricholoma or the shaggy mane or the honey agaric. It's really up to the schoolteachers to spread the word.

They hang up posters pointing out how stupid people are: mountain-ash—that is, rowan berries—they're free for the taking! Are *they* to be left to the birds?!

And couch grass? The white roots of couch grass? Full of albumen! They have to be chopped up and scalded in boiling water, it's a real treat. How far removed one is from natural life. Too far.

The children go to school in patched pants and wooden clogs, they eat turnip slices instead of bread. They sit eighty to a classroom or even ninety, because the young teachers are all at the front and the old ones have to take over their work.

Heads up: le roi!

The wrinkled old teachers also bring turnip slices instead of bread and also wear patched pants. And when they cane the children, because they don't know what else to do, they think of all kinds of things, but not of the children.

In the pseudo-Gothic post office pitiful figures stand about on the cast-iron rosettes from which warm air rises. Warmth! They are discharged soldiers, with one leg or "shell-shocked," the fellows who tremble all over because they have been buried under the earth. They are waiting for someone to throw away a cigarette butt, one of those dashing lieutenants, or fat Sodemann, who happens to be collecting the mail: the mail with the heart-warming news that further sizable ore contracts have been concluded. Good ore from hard-working Sweden for the hard-working German armament factories in Silesia.

At the Hop Market, shabby old men stand around reading the newspaper in the display box: 183 kilometers of front line taken back? Planned retreat? What's the meaning of all that? . . . The casualty lists in the *Rostocker Anzeiger* get longer and longer, and saluting the wounded has become less common. If one were to salute all the wounded, people say, one would soon be doing nothing but raising one's hat. Salute every single wounded soldier? A well-meaning person suggests some kind of salute-badge to be stuck in one's cap.

On the market square a soup kitchen has been set up, brought there for the poor; each one gets a mug of thin soup against a voucher, it tastes of kerosene.

One day even a horse-drawn cart arrives loaded with army bread. That leads to a free-for-all, and the soldiers trying to distribute the bread say: "What the hell, let's forget about it!" and trot off again.

In City Hall a mockup of a naval mine is displayed into which, for a donation, nails can be hammered on an outline of the German war ensign.

> To thee we'll ever faithful be
> Where'er we may be led;
> To thee we dedicate our lives,
> O flag black-white-and-red!

This large wooden replica bears the outline not only of the German war ensign but also of a design consisting of one laurel and one oak branch, also for nailing. In order to achieve a pleasing effect it has been mounted on other, smaller, naval mines, also of wood.

The nailing was started in 1915, Mondays and Wednesdays from eleven to twelve. A maiden stood beside it and handed you the hammer, and it's still incomplete, there being no more nails, neither "golden" ones at ten marks nor "silver" at five, that's why.

The ducal chamber at City Hall, which is normally only opened up on special occasions, is now the home of the Patriotic Clothing Salvage Society. Under the gilt-framed portraits of long-deceased mayors, wearing fur collars and velvet caps, there are now piles of ladies' evening shoes, white, pink, sky-blue, silver, and gold. Tail coats are there too, with dangling swallowtails. Volunteer members of the Patriotic Auxiliary Service are busy turning old into new. A newspaper photographer arrives and photographs the activities, and the picture appears in the *Rostocker Anzeiger*. The tail coats are to be seen, and the evening shoes—no ski sweaters or furs: since 1914 no patriotically minded citizen has donated any of these.

Church bells are rung less often now for victories. During the first year of the war it had been very difficult to agree: Lodz? The capture of Lodz? Is that a victory or not? The pastor of St. Nicholas's said yes, that was a victory, and had the bells rung so that the dogs ran barking through the streets; the pastor of St. Peter's said no, that wasn't a victory, and didn't have them rung.

So of course the authorities had to intervene: Yes, the word was from then on, this one today is a victory, bells are to be rung and flags hung out. A policeman makes the rounds of the churches on his bicycle, and the schools too. And in the schools the bells are given three long rings, which means: Victory! And now the church bells begin to peal too, which means: Schools closed!

But, as has been said, the pealing of the bells is heard less often because of the absence of victories, and it has also become less loud because so many of the bells have had to be turned in.

Before they were thrown down onto the paving, garlanded as if for a wedding, there had been a great farewell peal from all the churches. People stood on the roofs to hear it; the old women were in tears.

Only the oldest bells were allowed to remain, those from medieval times that had been sounded when the great fire broke out in 1677, on the fourth of August, when seven hundred were reduced to ashes.

The turning in of the bells also means the end of the art of bell ringing: Who can remember how it goes—the gentle introductory peal of the first bell, the precise chiming in of the second and third bells, the swelling and dying away? Who is there to remember the plaintive sound of the Poor Sinners' bell when yet another sinner was led to the gallows, the dark swell of the deep-throated Feast

Day bell, the silence of the bells during Lent in the days when people still longed for Easter: "Brothers, it's over!"

The great metal pipes of the organ in St. Mary's, the ones from the front, have also been removed, melted down, and replaced by cardboard dummies. Pastor Schaap delivers himself of some inspiring words for this action: how wonderful for the great organ to be participating in the struggle of the nations! He also delivers himself of some inspiring words for those fighting and dying at the front: "We love united, we hate united, and we all have but one foe: England!"

He has lost two sons, he doesn't mention this but it is known, and when the great clock in the transept chimes and the apostles make their round, as of old, every stroke seems to be the death knell for a soldier.

In the house on Stephan-Strasse the tail coat has not yet been donated, nor have the evening shoes. Although Silbi has knitted a few earmuffs for the men out there, one can't go on doing that forever. Now she is crocheting lace for a bedspread: it is to have long fringes hanging down on all sides. Let's hope Arthur is going to be home for his weekend at least, he's always having to sit around in Schwerin in the war enlistment office, they hardly see each other at all. He has to sit around in Schwerin, with all those ladies working there, like a cock of the roost. Where is it all going to end?

There are no children yet. For the time being, no children, first wait and see, that's their motto.

On Stephan-Strasse there is no such thing as thin soup. The master of the house sees to that. Sometimes the maids have to spend all night in the kitchen putting up preserves. Twenty-five pounds of butter arrive one day, or rather: one night. At the rear, at the servants' entrance, there is a knock on the door.

"What do you think, shall we take it?"

This butter has to be melted down to prevent it turning rancid, at night, and they sing while it's being done and no one blabs, for everyone gets a share.

> The gypsy's life is a merry one,
> Faria, faria, far!
> Roaming freely under the sun,
> Faria, faria, far!

When too many geese are delivered, they are pickled. Candied drumsticks—there's nothing like it! That's something to be eaten one day in peacetime, too. Tomorrow the "opera crowd" will be here again, and they'll be served this, and old Ahlers will come with his measured tread and Mrs. von Wondring, who has a cousin at the Ministry of War, and Gahlenbeck, who can't serve at the front on account of his kidneys.

Sometimes there are twenty people around the table in the evening, the longer the war lasts the more there are, two maids have to serve. Stribold the dog gets a piece of the good liver sausage.

After the meal Bobrowski, the wheelchair attendant, stands behind Robert's chair and makes comments on the guests. He also talks about the war of '70/71, how his comrade did in that Frenchman in the trench: "I never did that!" he still says.

The joke about '80/81 is repeated and "This time I'll pay like this!" Then Professor Volkmann recites the best lines from his third volume of war poems: "Beside the Kemmel, and the clock struck three . . .," and at nine o'clock Robert has himself carried upstairs with all his magazines, and perhaps those who come to wake him the next morning will still be holding a glass of champagne. They will stand by his bed and shout "Prosit!" and "You only live once!" for they have been celebrating all night.

"Year after year a dove descends from Heaven!" sings Müller the tenor in some of the quieter hours, and he sings it more softly than usual, and Anna is sad because he wants to move to Berlin. She can't imagine how she will carry on without him, and she considers moving with him to Berlin, leaving everything behind. After all, she's not that old, is she?

But desert Robert? With his rubbery legs? Who'll be there to clean him up? And now with his hemorrhoids bleeding too.

And she thinks back to her wild days when her carelessness caught up with her suddenly, and it was her husband who had to pay the price . . .

45 The Housekeeper

All through the war we went on living as if nothing had happened. From Sweden the old gent received tobacco and real coffee, which he exchanged for whatever he needed.

"Boiled or whipped?" he'd ask whenever lemon dessert was served. Whipped lemon dessert is made with egg whites, of course, and plenty of them, and Robert much preferred that to the potato-flour mush. You simply can't imagine how well we lived, even in the worst times. When the head clerk celebrated his twenty-fifth year with the company, that was in 1916, we had roast venison and a Pückler ice-cream bombe. Once a week a farmer called Witt came in from the country, after dark, and brought everything one could possibly wish for: fresh vegetables, eggs, sausage.

Employers are always employers, of course. But the staff downstairs in the basement kitchen got the same to eat as their masters upstairs.

I have very happy memories of that time.

Everyone's Fate is decided at birth, my mother always used to say, and I suppose this was fate too, in a way: in 1917 a young man was taken on by the Kempowskis, he had been wounded, his name was Heinz Grewe, a fine figure of a man but at that time a bit run down from all he had gone through. His job was to look after the garden and if anything needed repairing. We immediately took him down into the kitchen, put a pot on the fire, and tried to fatten him up a bit, we all stood around him

And later on I married him, I did. And trouble enough it brought me, too, all the time we were engaged, for our plans to get married had to be kept secret, because of the mistress, she mustn't find out. I would've been kicked out immediately, and Heinz too, and then what would we have done?

"Listen to me now," she said once. "Don't you go and get married, just stay right here with us." For decency's sake a furnished room was rented for Heinz on Lloyd-Strasse. A man couldn't possibly be allowed to live in, with all those girls around, that wouldn't have been proper . . . But that was no problem for us two, we saw each other all day long so there was always some opportunity. At night, of course, it was not so easy. We could only do it outdoors—be together, I mean.

In summer we went for lots of walks, in the Warnow meadows or in Barnstorf, and in winter we bought tickets for the cinema, Asta Nielsen was a star in those days, and we would go dancing at the "Schuster." There was a piano there, and a violinist. Once we even went to Lütten Klein, walking all the way, in the snow! In Lütten Klein we danced to the phonograph, in a tavern.

When I got home from my afternoon off, a bit puffed and rumpled, the mistress usually opened the door to me: "Come in here for a moment, will you?" and, just as I was, I had to go into the living room and talk over the whole week with her. Once her hair was all mussed up, her singer friend must have just left. And once when I go in she's sitting there with him on the sofa fumbling with his fly. That was 1917, and the master and mistress were always at each other's throats. She had her singer friend, and he had Miss Linz.

Once the old gent got so mad at his wife that he wanted to kick her out. So she says to me, "If I went to Berlin, would you come with me?"

I think, "Nothing'll come of that," and say, "Yes, I'd come with you."

And then when I go upstairs to take the old gentleman his cocoa, he says, "Gertrud Elisabeth Hedwig, if my wife does go to Berlin, will you stay with me?" I say, "Of course I will."

I reassured them all.

.   .   .

Heinz was in charge of the gardens, front and back. Not that there was much to do, the gardens weren't that big. But he managed to keep busy.

He also kept the stoves going. Once it apparently wasn't warm enough for the mistress: "It's so cold here! Are you letting the fire go out completely?" she asked.

So he dumped the coal scuttle in front of her and said: "If it isn't warm enough for you, you can look after the fire yourself."

He had been through a lot at the front, he simply didn't care. On the balconies, all around the house, there were geraniums or petunias or whatever they're called, very pretty. But to get to them he had to go through the rooms, and through *hers* of course, too. To avoid that, he had put up a ladder from the garden, because when she lay there in bed she always gave him the eye.

"Like hell I will," he said, go through her room. "Like hell I will!"

Each of us had a certain bell signal. Housemaid was twice, I was four times, Heinz was five times. Once it rang five times, and Heinz went upstairs: "No!" she said. "Why don't you pay more attention? I rang only four times! I want Miss Obermeyer to button up my petticoat . . ."

So Heinz said: "If that's all it is . . ."

We got married right after the war; the old man was generous as always: the wedding had to be at his house, of course. An altar was set up in the alcove, and three musicians played, it was just lovely. He was generous, he really was. Quite the opposite from her: not a single bedsheet did she pass on to me. All I had was two sheets, and she had whole closets full of them.

46

In the spring of 1918 Karl is made a lieutenant, and on March 2 there is a gas alert. From the English trenches rise white clouds. Gas masks are put on, the men wait to see what happens. The stuff lies densely massed on the forefield, the barbed wire is scarcely visible, and there is no sound, just the occasional click or rattle. Like monsters, the soldiers look at each other with their huge glass eyes.

Five times an unbroken curtain of gas clouds is blown toward the German positions: the soldiers wait, rifles at the ready. But on the other side, not a soul is in sight. Finally the men shout across to the English that they should hurry up and come; they brandish their bayonets and hand grenades. In response further gas clouds appear, and then some thirty Englishmen jump out of their trench. But they advance only a few steps, crouching low, before running into fire, and they hastily turn back.

By eleven the wind has driven away the gas, and after hours spent under their masks the air now seems particularly aromatic to the men.

The last vestiges of gas are driven out of the dugouts. Blankets are flapped, and wood is lighted.

However, the hope that the dugouts have been thoroughly disinfected turns out to be illusory. The rats and mice are very much alive, and the "Reich bugs" quickly recover. Only the rabbits have copped it, all thirty-five of them are dead.

During the night Karl notices that something is wrong, his skin is itching and burning. He reports to the field dispensary: "Off to the hospital!" he is told. Low-level gas poisoning is diagnosed.

. . .

After a week in the field hospital, where they smear his skin with all manner of ointments and lotions, he is allowed to move into private quarters, his hands bandaged and a turban on his head, a cause for much merriment among some: "Sultan" they call him.

Karl is glad to be allowed to leave the field hospital. Coarse types had said that his beard was sprouting as sparsely as poor people's grain. They had also loosened the supporting plank of his bed, and when it collapsed they lit into him for making such a racket: "What the hell d'you think you're doing?"

Karl moves into a dugout that he shares with other lightly wounded officers. It is furnished almost luxuriously. Comfortable beds with spring mattresses, soft feather pillows, and even down quilts from the nearby château. A folding table occupies the middle of the room, surrounded by armchairs upholstered in red plush. All very comfortable. There is even a flowerpot stand, and a tall vase beside the door to hold walking sticks.

The evenings are particularly cozy. A lighted kerosene lamp stands on the table, and the officers read—"*Lecture pour tous*"—write letters, or play chess. Over in a corner one of them is making coffee, and another is drying his socks. Outside somebody is playing the mouth organ, and without meaning to one hums the tune, and without warning one's eyes fill with tears.

"This is how somebody should paint us!"

No, nobody paints them, but they are photographed. Karl is photographed too, and one of these photos has survived: a young lieutenant with a bandaged head. In Rostock his mother sends the photo to the newspaper *Mecklenburg's Sons in the War* and has it published in the column "Our Heroes."

Karl also receives a copy of this paper, he sees his picture in it and quickly puts the paper away. "Our Heroes"—he hopes to God none of his comrades gets to see it!

It is always a special event when the field post arrives: greetings from home! The mail is sorted on big tables, the sacks quickly get thinner and the piles grow bigger. Then names are called out, and the men sit in silent groups, or off by themselves, and all the grumbling about the field post is forgotten. (A letter takes two weeks, that's not too bad.) Karl still receives regular packages of cigars and "Markopano," it almost embarrasses him.

From Wandsbek come homemade cookies and sky-blue letters smelling of good soap. Isn't he coming on leave soon? And he must be sure to travel via Hamburg! A photo is enclosed in one of those letters, Grethe in the midst of her children: the boys with close-cropped heads, the girls with braids. She writes that she loves what she's doing, really loves it, looking after the children, and that the children give her so much pleasure.

The field-hospital library consists of English and French books: it is the former château library. The first book Karl reads is a German grammar in French, intended for the use of French soldiers when they have conquered Germany.

> "Hir istt mainn kouartirtzêtl."
> "Habeunn zi kainn bett?"
> "Brinnkn zi vassr ounnd saifé."
> "Habeunn zi guéheurtt?"
> "Chlisseunn zi di thur."
> "Kainné luknn, ich habé dess recht, zi erschissn tsou
> lassen, venn zi luknn."

Next he reads the *Contes drôlatiques* (a dog-eared copy): first laboriously spelling out the words, then more fluently, and finally quite speedily: What an amazing collection of filth . . .

On Sundays brief lectures are given at the casino, on the theory of heredity, for example, or "What Is Courage?" There is also a talk on the dispute of the monists with the Christian doctrine and on the pronunciation of the Latin *c*, as in "Kikero and Kaesar ate kippers," which, however, is of no great interest to Karl. He pronounces the *c* like *ts*, and that's all there is to it.

A garden has been laid out around the dugouts. Broken treetops have been dragged over from a nearby pine forest and planted; for a few weeks they stay green. The stream that runs through the area has been cleared of all debris, little dams have been built and water

mills constructed to act as clocks, which, as they turn, count out in
minutes how long the war is going to last.

Each dugout bears a name, carved on a wooden board, appropriate to the mood: "Villa Forest Glade," say, or "Heart on the
Rhine," "Eagle's Eyrie," and suchlike. And outside the dugouts are
little tin figures that turn in the wind: a German endlessly knocking
down a Frenchman.

"Pardon—Camarade."

Karl likes sitting out of doors, the warm spring sun does him good.
He removes his bandages and exposes the affected areas to the
warmth: very odd, these scabs. They weep and itch. Itching is
supposed to be a sign of health, but this itching certainly isn't. He
longs to scratch at it with a knife.

Sometimes he goes for long walks. At "Dri Grachten" he is fasci-
nated by the flooded areas. ("Dri Grachten," the very name is so
interesting.) Broad expanses of reeds, interspersed with muddy
ponds full of waterfowl and marsh animals. Narrow canals bordered
with poplars.

He is struck by the clouds, the clouds are so beautiful. He finds
himself a boat and rows into the rustling reeds, and there he lies
down in the bottom of the boat and looks up into the sky bristling
with towering clouds: How odd, to be lying here in a boat, in
Flanders, Mr. von Büschel is thinking, and between him and the
deep water, where the fishes rest among the waterweeds, only the
flimsy boards.

> Sing me a little song, O mandolin mine!
> But not of today!
> Sing me a song of times that are gay . . .

Should he pop over to Bruges? he thinks. Sit in the kitchen and
watch the young schoolteacher's wife switching the iron rings back
and forth on the stove?

What is the goldfish doing? he wonders.

Better not go to Bruges. Best to let that kind of thing rest. One
might even be confronted by a fellow in suspenders and slippers

who demands to know one's business there. One should have done things differently, right at the start, he thinks. And what's more, he knows how.

A few times he goes horseback riding. The horse is called "Fessel." In the dusk a captain drilling his battalion mistakes him for a high-ranking officer (as he comes trotting up).

"Attention! Regimental adjutant from the right!"

For God's sake! A quick salute and hurry past.

The horseback riding comes to an end when someone places a small piece of wood under his saddle.

On one occasion the Crown Prince is driven through the place, he has a gray automobile and a special horn. He salutes. And on another the Grand Duke arrives on a visit to his Mecklenburgers, but his interest is slight, he hardly gets out of the car.

The "enthusiasm" of his Mecklenburgers likewise holds itself within bounds:

> And there we saw him, one fine day,
> Our Grand Duke riding on his way,
> Riding on a grenadier,
> Legs dangling o'er the cooking gear . . .

They sing that in the background, and the Grand Duke smiles faintly and drives on, his shiny spiked helmet under its field cover.

Actually he had intended to have the holders of the Mecklenburg Cross of Merit presented to him, but he now decides to let that go. (Karl had already pushed his way toward the front and made his eyes light up.)

The best part is still, yes that's true, sitting in the dugout in the evening, felt slippers on one's feet, a long pipe, and one's comrades sitting there too, also with pipes—there's such a comfortable hum, and one wishes it could be like that always.

47

After his convalescence Karl is given a short home leave.

He goes by train, a brand-new lieutenant. The journey takes thirty-six hours. The female train staff irritates him, everything run by a pack of women. There are stationmistresses, conductresses, and stokeresses, and they all try to flirt.

"Rostock! Rostock! Everybody out!"

There's Platform 3, the station clock points to four, and Plückhahn the porter, tottering with age, lifts his hand to his red cap.

In the house on Stephan-Strasse they sit around the coffee table. The son, the mother, and a Mr. Hasselbringk.

Old Ahlers is there too, with his impressive leonine head, but he doesn't sit at the table, he sits by the stove.

Anna is wearing the high-necked black dress that suits her so well, and she scrutinizes her slim, serious son, by now so masculine, and she does so in the pensive way that she so rarely displays, and at the same time she touches a certain spot in her abdomen where today she is again conscious of a slight pressure.

That skin trouble of her son's, is it going to stay that way?

Mr. Hasselbringk comes from Berlin, he has brought a letter of introduction from Müller the tenor ("Be sure and go there, the Kempowskis keep a good table"). A wonderful person, an ornithologist; looks like a bird himself, like an owl. He has acquired a stork for the Rostock Museum, a stork with a Negro's arrow stuck through its neck.

He was introduced by Müller, who left Rostock quite a while ago.

(The little Linz woman hasn't been to the house for a long time either, *although* she is still in Rostock.)

Good Swedish coffee is served and Madeira cake, the kind whose crumbs so easily go down the wrong way. And the "incident" on Stampfmüller-Strasse is discussed, where women and youngsters stormed a bakery and stole the bread. Even the window was smashed, they say, and the bread thrown to the rabble that had collected outside!

The police had been powerless.

Mr. Hasselbringk fails to understand: powerless? What do you mean? Rabble? There's only one thing to do: clobber them—clobber them ruthlessly!

Karl, who is pensively scratching his hands, is asked whether he doesn't agree that they should be clobbered—ruthlessly?

But Karl has no opinion in this case, he is remembering that occasion, long ago, at the tennis court, the mob in violent mood marching past shouting "Hunger!" or rather, not shouting, and how good bread can smell, he is remembering that too, in Werckem, a whole wall of bread. How good bread can smell, he thinks, and he remembers how he used to pick up some of the larger crumbs as they fell. And how he had made sure that some did fall.

Mr. Hasselbringk has had many experiences, in Africa, no doubt about that. When the bull elephant charged him, for instance, that must have been quite something. And how well he tells it!

"Dangerouth that wath, very dangerouth," says Mr. Hasselbringk, who has a slight impediment. Indeed, Mr. Hasselbringk knows what it means to be mortally afraid. And while he talks about it he takes his watch from his pocket to look at the time.

"Exthtremely dangerouth . . ."

Before old Ahlers, who has been sitting over there by the stove and clearing his throat for some time, can get a word in to tell them that in Rio he also saw a lot of rabble but that somehow it was different there, that the people had danced and sung and hadn't looked so grim and bitter—before he can regale them with that, Karl is asked to tell them about the tanks careening about over there on the Western front, as one has read in the *Rostocker Anzeiger.* "Tanks": they give it the English pronunciation.

What? Never seen any?

No "male" ones and no "female"? So he has never known what it's like to have a thing like that roaring down upon you?

Oh well, never mind. And isn't it wonderful, really, that the business with America has come to a head, open hostility is always better than hidden, isn't it? And: one more or less doesn't make any difference, many enemies, much honor.

Our men will teach those young fellows from the Wild West a lesson. That's his opinion, anyway, says Mr. Hasselbringk, and old Ahlers never does find an opening for his rabble in Rio.

They are joined by Silbi, smiling and trim. No, she has no children yet, but she has grown plumper, which suits her. She pulls out a bag of bright-green fondant candies from her pocket and shakes them into a little cut-glass dish. Only then, after she has thrown away the bag, does she fling her arms around her brother's neck, a little too ecstatically, they were never that close, and kiss him: Oh, how pale he looks, and his head all shaved!

Whatever's the matter with his skin? It's all scabby and cracked! Is he doing something about it? He can't possibly run around like that, can he! That's what she asks him as she holds him and hugs him to the rhythm of her speech.

Does he still remember the Hairy Man? Does he? Gilly-gilly piccalilli? In the picture book? Who puts the naughty children in his sack? And does he still remember the fire in the lumberyard outside St. Peter's Gate? All those bells ringing, and the shouting and running?

"Long, long ago." And now she's already been married four years —and he'll do her the favor, won't he, of having a look at the new house Papa has bought her? The villa, hm? won't he? And she is positively shaking him, as if she had to wake him up, and she still has her arms around him.

No, Arthur's not at the front, he's in Schwerin, that's what's so dreadful, every day he groans about the work he has to do there, he'd much rather be at the front . . .

He comes home only every second weekend. Awful, when you think you're only just married. Isn't it? And hardly get to see each other? And his parents down there in German Southwest Africa? You wonder how they are, interned all this time . . .

Hm? He'll have a look at the house, won't he, her dear brother, and he'll be very, very nice to Arthur, won't he?

She still has her arms around her brother, who hardly knows what to do with his hands and has let them fall several times to indicate that enough is enough, but she holds onto him, unyielding.

When at last she lets go, her new blouse, which she has embroidered herself with leaves and tendrils, catches on his decorations, and Mr. Hasselbringk wonders whether that isn't downright "thymbolic."

Good coffee in the Meissen vine-leaf cups, and the good old silver spoons from dear Grandma in the Home of the Holy Spirit who has been dead these three years now, the old silver spoons worn thin from constant use.

The clocks tinkle, and the parakeet up there on the curtain rod is pulling out all the pins again. At a clap of the hands, the bird flies once around the coffee table and alights on Karl's shoulder and nibbles his earlobe, he is gentle and warm and smells a little of dust.

The lovely Meissen vine-leaf china. And the lovely tablecloth.

Don't soil the tablecloth, for heaven's sake! On this tablecloth all those many actors and singers have immortalized themselves, and the signatures have been embroidered over. Here's "Müller" and "Volkmann," thick and heavy. Mr. Volkmann no longer appears in this circle because he is working on his great war book that will put everything published to date in the shade, according to rumors. But perhaps the reason Professor Volkmann no longer comes is a different one, that business with Silbi years ago, which no one is sure about, something in the garden. Had he clasped her bosom?

. . .

Now Mr. Hasselbringk will be allowed to immortalize himself on the cloth, that is, if he behaves himself, he is told. Eagerly he licks the gold pencil hanging from his gold watch chain, and eagerly he gets up steam for the flourishes that customarily precede his signature.

Old Ahlers, sitting back there by the stove and gently stinking away, does not appear on the cloth. But then, he has been to South America, and he wonders whether it really is such a good thing for the Americans to have entered the war. Maybe, maybe not. That's something "about which" he doesn't feel qualified to give an opinion "about," he thinks.

Karl isn't on the cloth either, of course not, he's not a guest, although he feels like one here. Karl is still one of the family, after all. If he shouldn't return one day, presumably they'll put a photo of him on the grand piano and fresh flowers daily.

But—what can happen to him now? After all this time out there! And not a single scratch! says Mr. Hasselbringk. The very idea!

Pipsi, the parakeet on Karl's shoulder, coos and ruffles his feathers, and Stribold the dog jumps on his lap, in spite of the medicinal smell on his hands, and Karl fondles him.

"Is the poor old doggie sick then?" he asks, and Stribold wags his tail as if to say "Yes." How we all laughed when he stepped in the butter . . .

Tonight Karl will be playing on that grand piano, playing for a long time when he is all alone, he is looking forward to that. And there, that picture of Rostock in a thunderstorm, he's never looked at it properly before, in the middle St. Mary's Church harshly illumined, flanked by the other churches. And in front the churned-up harbor, dotted with boats and steamers—how is it possible that he has never really looked at this picture before? One day, when his parents have died (he decides at this moment), he will appropriate it. Remarkable, that technique. The colors all mixed up like that, yet everything perfectly distinct!

. . .

Now Giesing comes in bringing some more cake. She used to help him put away his "Anchor" building blocks, and look at his stamps through the magnifying glass: Karl isn't sure whether he should get up and say "Good afternoon!" . . . but then there's the parakeet on his shoulder and Stribold on his lap, so he can't, Stribold the mongrel who probably won't last much longer.

> Korli with the big red nose
> Which from too much brandy glows!

Giesing's face has become firmer, and there are lines around her mouth. Her brother has been killed at the front—but that isn't what gave her those lines.

Karl shoos the animals away, gets up, and goes from one clock to the others as they tick away on the chests of drawers. Little gilt ones with shepherdesses under a glass dome, their arms tenderly draped around the clock face, or youths playing the flute, entire scenes complete with flower baskets, fences, and dead trees all in gilt bronze and all under glass.

Yes, they are on time, he establishes, all the clocks are on time. And those people over there in the alcove look like silhouettes against the window: his mother with her piled-up hair and the gesticulating Hasselbringk, the coffeepot and the potted palm.

Karl walks through the dining room, past the long, extended table where he used to swap stamps with Erex—if the serration isn't perfect, it does make a difference.

And he walks onto the veranda, where there is a draft.

> Gilly-gilly
> Piccalilli
> Boo!

He is reminded of the paper cutouts, the villages with chickens, cows, and pigs, and that they had been set alight one winter and that it had looked amazingly lifelike.

Karl goes out into the hall with the pale birchwood furniture he has never sat on, and with great deliberation puts on his coat.

On the round birchwood table stands a silver bowl filled with calling cards. Geraldine Meyer-Ney and Joseph P. Böcklin are among the visible names. Some cards have a corner turned down, on others is written: p.f. or p.c.: *pour féliciter*, that means, or *pour condoler*—*"pour condoler"* because of the dead grandmother.

> For me the sun is risen,
> And golden shine his rays,
> I know a heart for which I pray . . .

is being sung in the basement kitchen. And Karl considers for a moment whether he should go downstairs. (Had he done so, he would have come upon Giesing standing by the coal cellar.)

And the watercolors, the little Rostock watercolors, his sister probably won't have her eye on those either, he thinks as he goes out onto the street.

"Ohmygoodnessme!" shrieks the parrot from across the street as he steps out of the house. He is determined not to look that way, Mrs. Jesse will be sitting over there by the window wanting to greet him and tell him how big and tall he has grown and that she almost didn't recognize him. In the old days she used to scold him when his ball fell into her garden, and then she would pick up the ball and take it into her house.

> Abo, Beebo, Ceedy-Reedy, Dead-as-Doornails . . .

And next morning one had to go and ask for it back and apologize, and that's why Karl won't look across now.

"Ohmygoodnessme!"

He walks along Stephan-Strasse, under the leafless linden trees, wearing his spiked helmet, without its field cover, and his sword quite properly at his side, sharpened and never yet used. One has to be careful it doesn't get between one's legs.

He looks at the villas, the comfortable ones and the pompous ones, that of Consul Viehbrock and that of Judge Warkentin with the laughing and weeping masks in the gable.

> Tradesmen Use Rear Entrance!

Menz has had a grotto built of clinkers among the rhododendrons. Move on quickly, before someone comes running out of the house to tell him how August is doing, that strange fellow one will have nothing more to do with. Interfered, that's what he did, intervened, and for no good reason.

Everything had been working out so well!

Wind sweeps through the street and bends the treetops this way and that. Risse the hairdresser is not sitting outside his door, it's too cold for him. He is looking over the curtain rail in his window as he hones his razors. The brass basin swings back and forth in the wind.

On the Reiferbahn they are still twisting ropes as of old. The men carry a bale of hemp tied to their stomachs and, walking backward, pluck out threads and twist the ropes, as they are expected to do.

The ropes are white when they are dipped in the tar barrels, and black when they come out.

Over there is Stone Gate.

A baro- and a thermo-
Journey to Palermo . . .

The streetcar tracks run straight toward the gate and through it. Stone Gate with the Lagebusch Tower where criminals used to be confined, in darkness, on rotting straw. Debtors were kept there too, people who couldn't pay, sometimes for years.

The city wall is overgrown with ivy, as is Stone Gate.

Karl walks along beside the Rose Garden as far as the high school. "You see? You see?" Go in and say hello to the teachers? No. They might ask about one's decorations (which actually one wouldn't mind at all), or say: "Yes, was there something?"

No, he'd rather just have a look in the basement to see whether the daughter of Lange the janitor is sitting on the counter—Karl counts on his fingers: she must be over sixteen now too. She used to have grubby feet in those days, and she was cheeky.

But no, better not go into the basement, she might wonder what was the matter with his skin, or on the Wall, with its three ramparts one higher than the next, although the sun is just beginning to come out a bit.

The paths on the Wall are slippery. He might soil his new half boots.

Karl walks through Schwaan Gate, and suddenly he catches sight over there . . . surely that's not Miss Seegen? Yes it is, and one can look her confidently in the face, she won't recognize one anyway for she never did in those days either.

"Korl, I can see you!"

"I can see you too!"

She has aged, with her tentative gait: Is it safe to put one's foot there? she seems to be thinking at every step. Will it hold . . . ? It must be a strange feeling to spend so many years teaching little boys to write:

> Up, down, up,
> A little dot on top!

Teaching them to count with eggs, and the story of the different types of mill: windmills, coffee mills, paper mills, and treadmills, and then those boys are suddenly dead? A single bullet in the head, and everything gone to pot!

Rostock is not as beautiful as Bruges, but nicer. The market square with City Hall, quite romantic really, and mentioned in every encyclopedia.

> Green herring and cod!

A subterranean passage is said to run under the paving, dug in the Middle Ages as an escape route. The little snake at the base of the third column from the left—no one knows what it's supposed to mean.

In olden days they used to sit in judgment under the arcades. The weirdest punishments: "pillory" and "stocks." How would they have stopped the blood in those days, chopping off a hand must have produced terrible bleeding?

Being hanged—Karl doesn't imagine that to be so hard to take. Or having one's head chopped off, he'd be able to stand that.

But the rack?

Or—or to have one's intestines cranked out of one's stomach, as he had seen on an altar painting in Bruges?

And anyway in the churches: each saint depicted with his instrument of torture, Saint Lawrence with his grill and Saint Peter with his upside-down cross.

He walks once around St. Mary's Church: "a pretty fine pile," he thinks. Unfortunately it is closed, someone happens to be practicing the organ: terraced dynamics, very loud and then suddenly very soft. Karl would play extremely softly, barely audibly, he knows that. As if from distant worlds.

The sundial over the entrance is something he's never noticed either. Is it showing the correct time? He pulls out his watch on its Hindenburg chain, and at that moment the sun disappears. It would!

Krüger's Delicatessen with the stuffed boar's head over the door: where there used to be pineapples and grapes, there are now turnips, and in ample quantity. On the Kistenmacher-Strasse side there is another entrance, the bell is rung there at night and people come with baskets, empty or full, or they leave with baskets, empty or full.

On the "promenade" there is no one to be seen, no saunterer in a brand-new boater and no row of girls, white and giggling. A few young louts stand around in doorways with young hussies, smoking cigarettes.

"Callow youths, that's what they are," Karl thinks. "They're callow youths." He'd push them off the sidewalk if they stood in his way. Too bad they don't.

No, he doesn't belong here anymore. Everything seems so shabby. In the old days, with Valentine Becker and Erex and all those corps students—when those fellows raised their caps, what a difference! "Let Obotritia be the banner!"

Where are they all now?

CLOSED
Have enlisted in the Army

This sign lies in the window of the military outfitters', and the epaulets are covered with brown paper to prevent them tarnishing.

Karl would have liked to look at some dress uniforms, what choices were being offered to a lieutenant, or to find out what provision there was for wearing decorations with mufti: surely there must be miniature replicas, discreet but clearly visible?

To his great satisfaction he has just been awarded the Hamburg Hanseatic Cross, Second Class, for his participation at Ridge S. The effect is highly decorative.

Old Rostock: he looks at the gables on the Wendländer Schild, they are still there, as of old, and next to it the house of the Jew Gimpel to whom he used to sell his father's empty wine bottles.

Two little boys come up to him and ask whether he has any French uniform buttons or a French *képi*? And Gimpel the Jew says: "Well, Lieutenant!" and tries to start a conversation. But Karl gives a curt salute and walks past him.

The Lieutenant knows everybody, doesn't he?

Karl walks along Grosse-Mönchen-Strasse where the booths always used to be at Whitsuntide, the roller coaster, and "Schichtl's Marionette Theater":

Manna! Manna! Good for de tummy!

The man at the "Test Your Strength" used to have two studs. The shorter one was put in the hole for the strongest customers, then they could hit it as hard as they liked. "Hit it! Hit it! Hit it!" They never managed to reach the top.

Plain gables, small courtyards, and shoulder-high walls. Outside the ground-floor windows, so-called spies, window mirrors through which one can observe the street, and *inside* the ground-floor windows cactus trays with little bridges and pagodas. Karl needn't worry about running into bankrupt old Gütschow, for on New Year's Eve Gütschow drowned in the Warnow, having fallen in, it is said, because he was so nearsighted. He was found under water caught on a post, his spectacles still on his nose.

Now a harbor train comes puffing by preceded by a bell-man, on foot, and the engine driver looks out the window to see that he doesn't run onto the bell-man's heels. Cling-bing! Cling-bing! that's how it goes, and Karl remembers: Yes, as a child he liked hearing that too. Even when he was a child it had always had a lovely sound. But: such a big engine and only a single freight car?

Being in business, he thinks, can't be that difficult. Like the fishermen in Graal: first the net is empty, then full. One sits at a desk, dictates letters, and telephones. Running a business, one should be able to manage that.

Karl walks through Monks' Gate, past the fountain, the bottom for dogs, the middle for horses, the top for birds, where his father sits at the window in his office looking out to see who happens to be passing by. He must always have a view.

Old Mr. Kempowski sees a young lieutenant walking by under the window, with a fur collar on his custom-tailored army greatcoat: why, that's his son! That's Korli! He taps against the window: Come in, come in! And when Karl enters, they embrace, the seated father and the stooping son—this is the first time they have ever embraced, they both become aware of it at the same instant—and the father has tears in his eyes: over there, at that empty desk, over there, that's right, his place is waiting for him, that's where Karl will sit, and why doesn't he sit down there now and tell him a thing or two!

(In the bottom right-hand drawer lies an envelope containing stamps that he has gone on collecting for him. Danmark, Norge, and Sverige, all those countries with which one is doing such good business these days.)

Karl sits down. The office needs to be done over, he thinks, the walls are positively grimy with smoke. And such a small room? Is it really so small?

His father sits in front of the Gothic safe, Robert William Kempowski from "Kayniksbarg," his fair hair streaked with white—at this very moment he has pulled out a large white handkerchief and is holding it up to his eyes. He has already bought three good-sized villas, one for Silbi, one for Karl, and one just in case. And the ships continue to ply back and forth between Sweden and Stettin, and down below, his arse, at the moment it's giving him no trouble, but he is in pain day and night, can scarcely sleep, Togal doesn't help anymore. If only he could sleep, have one good night's sleep. He has already read all of Fritz Reuter.

This is news to Karl. Never before has his father spoken of his pain. Sometimes clutching the arms of his chair and sometimes a sudden display of temper—but pain? This is the first Karl has heard of it.

Karl looks out of the window while his father talks about the new "favorite," meaning Mr. Hasselbringk. Over there lies Gehlsdorf with the white lunatic asylum behind the tall trees.

> Gehlsdorf opens wide its gate.
> Korli run, and don't be late! . . .

is how they used to tease each other as children.

> Gehlsdorf opens wide its gate,
> Erex run, and don't be late! . . .

had been the retort: simple but effective. Now it is a. hospital for soldiers who aren't quite right in the head. Shell-shocked.

His father is talking about the new "favorite," wondering whether he has been sitting around again with his wife today—always leaves when one arrives—and spouting about Africa, about elephant hunting and crap like that?

So this fine new desk will be his when the war is over, Karl thinks. On the right the "In" basket, on the left the "Out." The drawers are empty except for the bottom one on the right containing those stamps. Sverige with such unusual perforations. Funny, to go to all that trouble. And Norwegian stamps with a lot of little holes in them so they can't be stolen.

The empty desk, that's no problem. First empty, then full. There'll be plenty of work to do, and they're all looking forward to having him here, as his father has just been saying—Gladow the old book-keeper, and Sodemann the obese head clerk, and the other employees at their desks who are looking through the windows of the private office and aren't doing a stitch of work at the moment. As of late, there is even a female clerk who sits at a real typewriter that rings at the end of each line.

Robert William has now lighted a cigar, he continues to wave the burning match to and fro until it finally goes out. His son gets one too—"Never smoke cigarettes, d'you hear?"—beer is brought from Alphons Köpke, from "The Jolly Teapot," and schnapps is poured.

"First slosh the beer around in your mouth, otherwise it'll be too cold in your stomach."

And now how about telling him a thing or two, dammit all, young rascal, what things are like out there—"Up, down, schnapps!"—with those Frenchies? And has he ever seen any tanks?

"First slosh it around in your mouth," he keeps saying to his son sitting there with his decorations, "otherwise it'll be too cold in your stomach."

Those tanks are fantastic things, so they say, regular monsters. Funny we don't have any. "Are they asleep up there? And he pronounces it "tahnks," in the German way.

"Just take care you don't get killed!"

His son looks so scaly, he thinks, he'll have to have a word with Anna about that. He's got real cracks in his skin, and: Whatever's the matter with his ears? They seem to be weeping. Will it go away again? A person could think all kinds of things, seeing that.

And Karl wonders what sort of a flap that is in the floor, could it be a trap door? An entrance to the cellar?

Has he had a look at the house yet, on Schiller-Platz, he is now asked, third from the left, the house he has bought for him? He hasn't? Well, he's in for a surprise!

Yes, profits aren't bad at the moment. Business with Rawack & Grünfeld, the ore importers in Silesia, is humming along nicely, day after day. From that point of view one might almost hope that the war won't end too soon, if it weren't a sin to talk like that. And he taps the desk top from below: "Touch wood!" Ore for Stettin and coal for Sweden, a very sound business.

His father pulls his expanding purse from his pocket and takes out ten marks. Puffing out a cloud of smoke, he tosses the bill to his son. Here! That's for him! He can use it for a visit to the "Villa Mary," he knows the place, doesn't he? He must be at that age now . . . Or has he done enough screwing in Belgium?

"To be quite frank . . . ," the father says to his son, who is grown up now after all, and he leans forward so he can lower his voice, although no one can hear him here in the private office, and he removes his cigar from his mouth: to be quite honest and in absolute confidence, he—Robert William Kempowski (and this is news to Karl too)—sometimes goes to the "Villa Mary" himself. He does. He frankly admits it. He sometimes goes there himself, that's to say, he has himself *driven* there.

That night Karl lies awake for a long time, the rain splatters into the linden trees below his window.

DFUTSCHES REICH

How small the room is, he remembers it differently, and how quiet it is. Only the sound of the rain.

Miss Seegen with her Bible pictures: the children of Israel walking dryshod through the Red Sea. Will they make it? Will they all make it? On the ocean floor lie starfish and shells, and in the distance the pursuers are already being swallowed up by the waves. "I've been to Rome, and I've also been to Athens . . . !" Write a novel about the war? How can one write a novel about this war? So Karl thinks, and his head is filled with all manner of things that will stay with him for the rest of his life.

· · ·

At that moment a carriage rattles past outside, and now, yes, now at last he hears footsteps outside his door, bare feet, and the door opens: "Koarl?" comes a whisper. Yes, Karl has already lifted the quilt, and Giesing slips into the tent, cold as she is. She presses against him and lays her head on his shoulder.

Lower down, the feet are bare and, well: a bit sticky.

He has changed, she feels that, but she doesn't mind. She has changed, too. She just wants to snuggle up a bit. And he thinks: Is she disgusted by me? My skin? *He* would be disgusted, to be sure. And he has to think of Ludwex the Secondex and how he tended to avoid people. He can understand that.

On his way back to the front, Karl travels via Wandsbek. There are no upper-class young ladies on the platform now, distributing tea or cocoa, there is only the military guard who ask him gruffly for his leave-permit.

In the house on Bären-Strasse he drinks turnip coffee with Mrs. de Bonsac, at four in the afternoon, at the proper time. Axel Pfeffer the dog "sits," and looks at him attentively.

Has he heard anything about that blond scalawag, Karl is asked, about that—what was his name? Has he heard anything about him? Menz, of course, Menz. Extraordinary person . . .

Martha holds her coffee cup up to her imposing bosom. Actually quite nice, that Menz boy, and no doubt from a good family. But: drops in out of the blue and never shows up again? Right in the middle of one's afternoon nap? (He brought that ashtray over there on the Fanchon chest, carved out of a wooden propeller.) Never a word from him since. Extraordinary. Why did he come in the first place if he's never going to give another sign of life?

She sits on the curved sofa, and Karl sits in a curved armchair, and over there is the chest of drawers with the hollowed-out piece of propeller, and they both drink turnip coffee exactly as if it were real coffee, little finger crooked, and they do it in turns, first he, then she.

. . .

Then Martha puts down her cup on the curved table and calls through the open door, across the passage into the kitchen, where the door is also open: "Liesbeeth? Liesbeeth?" And from the kitchen comes a shout: "Ye-hes?"

"Oh Liesbeeth, please bring us a pear!"

"Ye-hes!"

"You'll have a pear, won't you, Mr. Kempowski?"

Yes, he would like a pear. That's good for his skin. After he has chatted a bit about his skin, telling her that he can thank the English gas for it, that it tends to weep and itch, and that he is curious as to whether he will be given a wound decoration for it—"Is it infectious?"—the conversation soon peters out, and Karl would really like to leave, "take his departure" as they say. If only he knew how to go about getting away. He wonders where Grethe is.

Lisbeth comes bringing the pear on a plate that is decorated with a pear (and below it the word: "Pear"). Lene, standing outside in the kitchen, humpbacked Lene, will be angry with her, for it was really her turn this time.

So the two of them sit there and talk about this and that and fall silent, and Axel Pfeffer sits there too, looking attentively from one to the other and twitching his nostrils.

Yes, as one was about to say . . . what was one about to say? Can he go and pick up Miss Grethe from the nursery school at the Mühlberg, that's what he meant to ask.

> No doubt you *can*,
> But whether you *may* is another matter.

Yes, he can, he must take a Number 14 streetcar.

"Oh, the soldier's come for his girl!" the children call out, they know all about that now, and Grethe blushes again. Actually she hasn't finished her day's work yet, but Thea will take care of that, she wasn't born yesterday. If Karl doesn't mind waiting a moment, she'll fix it up somehow.

.   .   .

The café in Winterhude is closed, and the paths around the Alster aren't in the least enchanted, they're just muddy. Moisture drips from every branch, and there is a cold wind blowing. Grethe pushes her bicycle. She is wearing her coat with the yellow-and-black lining, the hem showing the tear made by her right heel.

Did he ever get the cookies, the ones she baked herself? And had he liked them, she asks—the lace handkerchief he sent her from Bruges, yes, she got that. Like a filigree cobweb, that's what the hankie looks like, says Grethe, and then she's off on the subject of Willi Heinbockel, how he carved a dear little boat the other day—"I'll make you a boat"—and about Lieschen Pump, how she would love to take that little girl home with her if only she could, she's so sweet. "Such a sweet little thing!"

All the children are dears, each in his own way, even the naughty ones—that's how she talks, although she's been rattling on a bit too long about these children. One must see them "the way God wants them to be," that's all that's needed, then there'd be no problems, that's how she talks. To love a person means to see him "the way God wants him to be . . ."

She frequently buries her little nose in her handkerchief, and Karl pulls out his big white one and polishes his spectacles, which are misted over with fine raindrops, and to do this he has to stand still or his sword might get between his legs. He would like to tell her that this business with his skin isn't infectious, that it's already much better and will continue to get better—but she doesn't seem to be interested. Skin problems are familiar to her from her children, who are scabby and scaly too, it doesn't strike her as anything special.

They walk once around the Alster, the Atlantic Hotel and the Vierjahreszeiten Hotel, there's a difference, one must remember that, and over there are all the banks. The seventeen names of the Brettvogel family are reeled off, with special emphasis on the names of the seven sons who have fallen in the war, and Karl says: "To be more than one seems," that is *his* motto. He has no time for showoffs. At "Saint

Quen-ti-en," for instance, he had seen the "most incredible" show-offs, they run around there in droves. One of them, for instance, one of those fellows with a monocle—I ask you!

Does she remember Graal, he goes on—a white flag with a red eye means "yes"—and does she remember the wreck they always sat on, in Graal? And for him, being a Mecklenburger, it's not all that easy to pronounce the word "wreck," and for Grethe de Bonsac, being from Hamburg, it's not all that easy to understand it.

Oh yes, the wreck. Yes of course, the wreck.

Then he steps into some dog dirt, of which there are quantities lying about, and he has to scrape his sole sideways against the curbstone to get the stuff off again—his beautiful new half boots—and then they fall silent and finally not a single word is said, neither by Miss de Bonsac nor by Mr. von Büschel. Only the handkerchiefs are pulled out, alternately.

It grows darker and darker, and the streetlamps are lighted. And immediately beneath one of these just-lighted lamps Karl gives his Grethe a quite normal kiss, and that is their engagement.

In October 1918 Karl is certified fully recovered. A captain in the service corps, in charge of a field bakery, takes him along to the front in his smooth-running touring car. It is a breakneck journey, the car being driven by a volunteer recruit who in civilian life is a racing driver. When marching columns block the road, he sounds his horn furiously, and the captain shakes his fist and curses those unreliable customers from the East, those fellows marching to the front and infected with the weirdest notions. "World revolution"—he has only to hear the words. And: "Proletarians of the world, unite!"

The driver honks, and the captain fishes out his notepad, he's going to find out whether he can't have them disciplined. Deliberately taking their time to move aside . . .

A stale vapor hangs in the air, as if glue were being boiled: they are racing past the main cadaver-utilization depot of the army group. Here the fat of dead horses and cattle is being rendered into lubricating oil. The skeletons are ground to powder in a bone mill and added to hog feed. Nothing is allowed to go to waste.

In the trenches Karl is greeted morosely. This is not because they don't like him, no, their strength is at an end, that's why. In the morning they are given a turnip brew called coffee and some dry bread. At noon, sauerkraut or gruel. In the evening each man gets a spoonful of synthetic honey. Instead of tobacco they get dried beech leaves, and rationed at that! The eyes of many of them water from hunger.

It is a mystery to everyone what is happening to all the grain from Romania and the meat from Poland, it can't all disappear on the black market . . . If at least once a week they could have something decent to eat: meatballs, or even a piece of sausage.

The "fuel" situation looks bad, too: only some thin beer now and again. Wine is out of the question. Instead they are visited by a "sky pilot," an army chaplain wearing a strange hat, who gives them a talk on war loans. Wouldn't the soldiers like to subscribe to a war loan? Twenty marks would be quite a nice contribution, and once the war was won they would get back twice the amount.

Does he really believe that he can soften them up with such talk? This is his gospel: Germany, maligned and vilified Germany, has a mandate to teach reason and morality to the rest of the evil world. And in his sermon he says this more than once. He has a portable altar, an automobile that opens up at the back, called a "field chapel." After the service it is all closed up again and firmly secured and the clergyman gets in and drives off.

Forty-six replacement troops arrive from Graudenz. They are Poles, released prisoners of war from Russia. "How must laced boots be stowed in the pack?" they are asked by Dauntless in the wonted tradition. But the Poles don't understand him, inexplicably enough. What? What's that? They can't understand him at all.

"What do you do in civilian life?"

"I'm a butcher."

"Then now you can butcher some Frenchmen!" That's his brand of humor. And: "If each of you kills only eight Frenchmen, that will decide the war." That's what he has figured out: If every German soldier kills eight enemies, there will be no more enemies left.

"Don't put these new fellows together with ours," he tells Captain Brüsehaber, "they'll only contaminate our own men." They seem to be quite a bunch of bastards. They'll have to be put through the mill.

Shortly afterward, the 210's are moved to another sector. What a lousy sweat, having to pack up everything and who knows what you'll get in exchange? Here at least you knew what you had. Sullenly they march along. Shouts of "Fraud!" "Hit 'im!" "Empty stomachs!" come from the rear.

The officers hear them but say nothing, knowing the men would laugh in their faces.

To add to their miseries they lose their way: they toil up a slope and at the top are ordered: "Halt!" and "About-face march!" They are only one step away from open revolt. Slipping and sliding they arrive back on the road.

The new position is a paradise. They are wide-eyed with wonder: all the trenches—three systems, one behind the other, with supplies being brought up by field railway—all the trenches are reinforced with fagots and roofed over with logs. The floor of each trench has been improved with comfortable wooden grilles so boots don't get muddy, and there is a sign on a post: TO THE BARBER.

The very first day they are served a thick pea soup, it even has some bacon in it. A real miracle! Thick brownish-green pea soup with pieces of bacon as long as your finger! Those commissariat fellows seem to be very resourceful here, and one can only wonder at its being so different before.

.   .   .

They play blackjack, Polish bank, and three-card monte, quite openly, although it is forbidden, and they sing again, too, for the first time in a very long while.

They've really struck it lucky.

Karl has a nice dugout all to himself, with a table and an armchair knocked together out of birch branches. He places the books he has brought along from home on the narrow shelf beside the others that have been left behind. He dips into *The Daily Round and Sunshine* over and over again. "Who knows?" is written on the flyleaf in the poet's own hand; he is tempted to write: "*I* do" after it, for by this time he has learned a lot.

Karl and Erex see very little of each other now. Valentine Becker— oh yes, she was a pretty girl, we know that. And that business with the hollow in the old willow tree: Karl always wants to talk about the old willow tree. But Erex would rather know "what Silbi's doing." Has she written again, and might he have a look at the photo?

When Erex does come, he salutes Karl, then they both laugh: they agree it's funny, but if Erex were not to salute it would also be funny, somehow it wouldn't be right.

Erich asks whether Silbi's marriage to Schenk, to that "jack-anapes," is working out, and he asks Karl whether he can still remember how he let himself down in a basket all the way to her window—does he?

Karl says "Yes," he does remember, and he tells him about the Outer Alster and the pretty coat with the black-and-yellow lining that Grethe de Bonsac had worn. And that he is—"I think"—engaged. Yes. That he is engaged, he tells him that too, and as he is telling him he realizes that it is a wonderful thing.

The new position is a paradise.

Here friend and foe live peaceably side by side without losses and without damage: the men even visit each other in the evenings,

at twilight, and exchange tobacco for jam. The very first evening an
Englishman comes strolling over the parapet and says: "Is this the
enemy? I've lost my way . . ." He is a young fellow and quite
happy to be taken prisoner. He has brought along three jars of
orange marmalade.

The 210's would like to cultivate this good-neighborly relationship
—but Dauntless will have none of that! His orders are that any
sentry who doesn't shoot the instant an enemy appears is to be
court-martialed.

The next time the English turn up again with chocolate and white
bread at the edge of the trench, they are waved away: Get back—
quick! And a shot is fired into the air: bang! The following day
Dauntless even has the field artillery fire at the trenches on the
other side. They're enemies, aren't they?

When the Tommies have recovered from their initial surprise, they
hammer away at the German positions with the new American high-
explosive shells. Twenty, thirty shells explode simultaneously,
fountains of earth shoot up into the air! What a shame! All those
splendid logs and floor grilles are blown sky-high, even the sign TO
THE BARBER with the black pointing finger underneath. The field
railway that had always done such a good job bringing up the pea
soup lies twisted and crumpled. Twenty to thirty shells whine
simultaneously through the air, and the stench of powder makes eyes
water and noses run. Now the hand-grenade depot is blown up too,
with its sign saying HAND GRENADES, and the last of the sparrows,
which hadn't been doing badly around here either, leave the area
with indignant cries.

There are explosions right and left, and Karl has to keep on en-
couraging his men. He shouts into their ears that it'll soon be over
and that it's already getting less, haven't they noticed? And he
makes a point of not going into the dugout, where he would be safe,
but, like the others, burrows into the earth, clawing into it with both
hands, and waves of sand and stones cover him.

.   .   .

All of a sudden he is flung to one side by an appalling impact. Beside him he hears a brief gurgling, sees someone's legs twitch: a shell, three men hit, but Karl is unscathed.

"Immune," he thinks, this uncommon word comes to his mind. "Am I immune?"

The enemy's consumption of ammunition is enormous. Day after day now, the 210's are battered by hundreds of mines and thousands of shells. Their own worn-out field guns, which at first replied tentatively and sporadically, soon fall silent, and the soldiers burrow into the earth and listen, waiting for the end of the cataclysm.

Each night strenuous work has to be done to get the destroyed trench sections and dugouts more or less back in shape again. And then they are smashed up again anyway.

After one of these bombardments Karl is called away. With a gaping hole in his abdomen, Erex Woltersen lies against the trench wall, gasping for breath. Karl speaks to him: "Erex, can you hear me?"

"It's all no use," his friend says with a despairing gesture.

Karl cannot bear the sight; he moves on a few paces and looks across to the enemy. "Oh, my poor parents!" he hears Erich call, and: "Such a shame!"

When the stretcher-bearer wants to bandage him, he stops him and asks for a pain-killer, but this is not given him because of his intestinal injury. No one believes that he will reach "Point 80," the first-aid station, alive.

The last thing Karl hears him say is: "I can't see anymore . . ." When they lift him onto the stretcher, he is already dead.

Karl packs up his friend's things, with his scaly hands, putting the letters and drawings into a cloth bag; and when his batman comes in and asks if he can do anything to help, Karl turns on him: What does he think he's doing here, and: Get out, get out! Karl keeps one of the pencil drawings for himself, putting it in his wallet: a dugout with a Hindenburg lamp, bearded men around the table, like a Rembrandt drawing, at least so it looks to him.

The next day they can observe enemy infantrymen in the distance —they are Americans—walking quite casually across the open terrain into their positions. They encounter no artillery fire since the German guns lie crumpled in their emplacements.

Epilogue

Early November 1918, deputies from Berlin arrive at the front to try and reassure the troops. One of them, Friedrich Naumann, has a piping voice. What does he want? think the soldiers. Hand in pocket and cigarette in mouth, they listen to what he has to say. But the longer he speaks the more reasonable it sounds to them: the man is talking about an armistice, and that doesn't sound bad at all.

"We will be given very harsh conditions," he says, "but we'll have to swallow them."

So we're not going to keep half of Belgium, that pistol aimed at England? Don't we need Belgium, then? Don't we owe it to the Flemings, those vital, industrious, and independent people, to preserve them from irretrievable Frenchification?

"Flanders" was the name to be given to this Germanic province, hadn't that been said?

And weren't they to receive one square meter of soil for every dead German soldier, as had been figured out quite recently?

Instead, were they to give something *away*?

No, no question of keeping Belgium or Kurland. On the contrary, something *was* to be given away, although only border areas, presumably quite insignificant border areas.

One must be prepared for that.

On November 11, at twelve noon, Captain Brüsehaber says to his men in a loud voice: "It's all over, fellows!" On November 11, 1918, at twelve noon, or, more precisely, at eleven fifty-five. And to the machine-gunners, who have a hand on the trigger and a cartridge belt like a scarf around their necks, who are looking at him with no inkling of what that means, to those men he says: "Unload, at ease."

And, true enough, it is all over. A great sigh of relief goes through all the trenches, the men lean back and relax their muscles: "All over!" Really and truly all over. And then they fire into the air, on this side and on that. All remaining tracer bullets are used up, a spectacle without parallel.

The Germans are given two weeks to evacuate the occupied territory, otherwise military action will be resumed: those are the terms of the agreement.

"Can't be done," they say, but in the end it can.

The retreat is carried out in good order. A cold, strong penetrating wind is blowing and sprays needle-sharp, icy rain into the soldiers' faces.

> Lights out! Knives out!
> Three men to stir the blood!

A few revolutionary types want to vent their wrath on the officers, but the others won't go for that—can't have the new era beginning with chaos—and in view of the good organization of the retreat, and the prospect of being home again soon, all opposition soon fades away.

Up, down, schnapps.

The story goes that Dauntless wept. That he is said to have wept. But he's nowhere in sight now; he must be somewhere else.

> See, the conquering hero comes! . . .

It's a painful business, slogging back through the countryside that has been wrenched from the enemy with sweat and blood, a sense of bitterness rises: all for nothing, all for nothing . . . that's what rings in the soldiers' ears as they tramp wordlessly along, stupefied and dejected at the same time.

> Germanski kaputt!

They march past discarded equipment, past overthrown cannons and plundered depots. Through ruined villages, lonely chimneys in the rubble, and once they are almost blown up by an exploding heap of dynamite.

They also march through Liège, familiar to them from their advance, and the Belgians can hardly contain themselves. Every street is decked out with the Belgian national colors, black, yellow, and red. And the children run alongside the marching columns carrying flags on sticks and singing patriotic songs, in a single voice or in two voices, songs the soldiers don't know and don't want to know: and they have to march through all that.

Then in Cologne they march across the Rhine Bridge with baggage carts and steaming field kitchens, in good order but mute. Outside the black, silent cathedral stands General von Larisch acknowledging the march-past, beside him a few revolutionary types who first keep their hands in their pockets and smoke but then refrain. Beside him also the band, but the instruments remain in their cases. Crunch-crunch-crunch, that is the only music.

The populace lines the streets and silently watches the soldiers, women, oh well, who have lost their sons, and fathers in black suits, tears caught in their still-waxed moustaches.

And there are the young girls, whose eyes keep overflowing, and: crunch-crunch-crunch, the soldiers with desperate faces: what hurts is not that they are dead, all their comrades, but that they will be forgotten. Despite all the monuments.

A NOTE ABOUT THE AUTHOR

Walter Kempowski was born in Rostock in 1929. Shortly after graduating from high school, at the end of World War II, he worked for the American occupation forces in Wiesbaden. On his return to what had become the Eastern Zone, he was arrested and sentenced to twenty-five years hard labor "for political reasons." Set free after eight years, he resumed his studies in Göttingen, and became a schoolteacher. His first book, *Im Block*, was awarded the prestigious Lessing Prize in 1969. Since 1971, he has been at work on his acclaimed cycle of novels about Germany from 1900 to the 1960s, of which this is the first to appear in English. He is married, with two children, and lives in a small village near Hamburg.

A NOTE ON THE TYPE

The text of this book was set in Weiss, a typeface designed in Germany by Emil Rudolf Weiss (1875–1942). The design of the roman was completed in 1928 and that of the italic in 1931. Both are well balanced and even in color, and both reflect the subtle skill of a fine calligrapher.

Composition by American–Stratford Graphic Services, Inc., Brattleboro, Vermont. Printing and binding by American Book–Stratford Press, Saddle Brook, New Jersey

Typography and binding design by
Dorothy Schmiderer